STACK COMPUTERS
The New Wave

ELLIS HORWOOD SERIES IN COMPUTERS AND THEIR APPLICATIONS

Series Editor: IAN CHIVERS, Consultant to the Monitoring and Assessment Research Centre, London and formerly Senior Programmer and Analyst, Imperial College of Science and Technology, University of London

Series continued at back of book

STACK
COMPUTERS
The New Wave

PHILIP KOOPMAN, Jr.
Vice President, WISC Technologies
Pittsburgh, USA

ELLIS HORWOOD LIMITED
Publishers · Chichester

Halsted Press: a division of
JOHN WILEY & SONS
New York · Chichester · Brisbane · Toronto

First published in 1989 by
ELLIS HORWOOD LIMITED
Market Cross House, Cooper Street,
Chichester, West Sussex, PO19 1EB, England
*The publisher's colophon is reproduced from James Gillison's drawing of the ancient
Market Cross, Chichester.*

Distributors:
Australia and New Zealand:
JACARANDA WILEY LIMITED
GPO Box 859, Brisbane, Queensland 4001, Australia
Canada:
JOHN WILEY & SONS CANADA LIMITED
22 Worcester Road, Rexdale, Ontario, Canada
Europe and Africa:
JOHN WILEY & SONS LIMITED
Baffins Lane, Chichester, West Sussex, England
North and South America and the rest of the world:
Halsted Press: a division of
JOHN WILEY & SONS
605 Third Avenue, New York, NY 10158, USA
South-East Asia
JOHN WILEY & SONS (SEA) PTE LIMITED
37 Jalan Pemimpin # 05–04
Block B, Union Industrial Building, Singapore 2057
Indian Subcontinent
WILEY EASTERN LIMITED
4835/24 Ansari Road
Daryaganj, New Delhi 110002, India

© **1989 P. Koopman/Ellis Horwood Limited**

British Library Cataloguing in Publication Data
Koopman, Philip
Stack computers: the new wave. —
(Ellis Horwood books in computing science. Series in computers and their applications)
1. Computer systems
I. Title
004

Library of Congress Card No. 89–1812

ISBN 0–7458–0418–7 (Ellis Horwood Limited)
ISBN 0–470–21467–8 (Halsted Press)

Typeset in Times by Ellis Horwood Limited
Printed in Great Britain by The Camelot Press, Southampton

Table of contents

To Mary

Foreword

During the past 8 years of chairing the Rochester Forth Conference, I have had a chance to focus on a variety of computer applications and implementations. Although the 1985 Conference covered Software Productivity, the greater interest was in real-time AI and the Novix Forth chip. The following conference was on Real Time Artificial Intelligence, which seemed to offer up almost intractable computing problems in everything from speech recognition to Strategic Defense. My invited speakers covered this ground well, though I noted again that an underlying theme of the Conference was Forth Machines. In particular, I listened to papers by Glen Haydon and Phil Koopman on their WISC CPU/16 (then called the MVP CPU/16 processor).

These Forth Machines offered performance gains of an order of magnitude or more over conventional computers, as well as important tradeoffs in reduced resource usage; resources including the commonly observed, but rarely conserved, transistor counts. But the CPU/16 processor also offered)another gain: an integrated learning environment from computer architecture through programming languages, and operating systems through real applications. In two or three semesters, a student could reasonably expect to build a computer, use microcode, develop a high level language, add an operating system, and do something with it. Immediately, I saw answer to the continuing fragmentation of computer science and electrical engineering curricula, and a practical way of rejoining hardware and software.

The following year I asked Phil to be an invited speaker at my Conference on Comparative Computer Architectures. By then his ideas on writable instruction set, stack computers were full-fledged, not just in theory, but in fact. During successive nights of the Conference, his 32-bit MSI-based processor amazed a growing group of followers as it cranked out fractal landscapes and performed Conway's Game of Life via an expert system.

After the Conference I knew Phil was beginning intensive studies at Carnegie Mellon University, and starting what would become this book. What I didn't know was that he was also reducing his processor to a chip set. He began hinting at great things to come during the Spring of 1988, and he presented the operational Harris RTX 32P that June. The speed with which the WISC CPU/32 was reduced to the RTX 32P speaks well of Phil's capabilities, the soundness of his architecture, and the support Harris Semiconductor has put behind this technology. Now I can't wait to hear in detail what he's been hinting at doing *with* the processor, and getting my hands on one too!

As for this book, it presents another view of the RISC versus CISC controversy, and if only for its commentary on that debate it would be worthwhile. Yet, it does considerably more. It provides key insights into how stack machines work, and what their strengths and weaknesses are. It presents a taxonomy of existing serial processors and shows that for over 25 years the stack architecture has been subtly influencing both hardware and software, but that major computational gains have begun in only the past few years. Although stack processors are unlikely to dominate the much-publicized enginering workstation market, they may very well fill enormously larger niches in everything from consumer electronics to high-performance military avionics.

After you read this book, find yourself a stack machine and take it for a spin.

Lawrence P. Forsley
Publisher, *The Journal of Forth Application and Research*
Rochester, New York

Preface

This book is about the new breed of stack computers sparked by the introduction of the Novix NC4016 microprocessor. Some readers may incorrectly associate any reference to stack computers with the Burroughs or HP stack machine families. The focus of this book is quite different. These new stack computers encompass an entirely different set of technology and application area tradeoffs, resulting in machines that are quite unlike the older generations of stack computers.

This book covers a wide variety of topics so that these new stack machines may be understood not only for their technical merits, but also within the context of how they can be used to solve problems, and where they fit in the overall computer architecture picture.

Chapter 1 is a review of stacks and their usage, as well as an introduction to the rest of the book.

Chapter 2 presents a taxonomy of hardware support for stacks, categorized in terms of the number of stacks, size of stack buffers, and the number of operands in the instruction format. This taxonomy points out the tradeoffs that are made by different classes of machines, and shows where the stack machines discussed in the remainder of the book fit in.

Chapter 3 focuses on the part of the stack computer design space that employs multiple stacks with 0-operand addressing. This set of design tradeoffs characterizes the new generation of stack machines described in the following chapters. This chapter also presents a detailed description of a generic stack machine as a point of departure for discussing the designs in subsequent chapters.

Chapter 4 describes four 16-bit stack machines in detail. The WISC CPU/16, MISC M17, Novix NC4016, and Harris RTX 2000 cover a wide spectrum of design decisions, exploring many of the options possible in stack machine design. Each of the four designs is described in terms of its block diagram, instruction set, architectural features, implementation technology, and intended application areas.

Chapter 5 continues the format of Chapter 4 with a discussion of three 32-bit stack machines. The machines included are the JHU/APL FRISC 3 (also known as the Silicon Composers SC32), Harris RTX 32P, and the Wright State University SF1.

Chapter 6 is a detailed discussion of the issues of stack machine design from a computer architect's point of view. Stack machines differ from other machines in many important respects, including program size, processor complexity, system complexity, and processor performance on different kinds of programs. They can require different ways of thinking about program execution characteristics and resource management. Much of the 'conventional wisdom' about stack machines is incorrect. This chapter presents detailed discussions as well as experimental data to reveal how stack machines really work.

Chapter 7 discusses the software issues that arise when using stack computers. The concept of a fast subroutine call is central to using a stack machine effectively, as is the concept of uniformity of interface between all levels of hardware and software. This chapter also discusses the issue of choosing a programming language, and how stack machines can efficiently support many different languages.

Chapter 8 shows how stack machines can be used in a variety of application areas, especially real-time embedded control. Important decisions must be made when selecting a stack computer to use in a commercial product. The alternatives include whether to use a 16-bit or 32-bit processor, and selecting an appropriate balance between system cost and performance.

Chapter 9 is filled with predictions and speculation on the future of stack machines and their place in the world of computers. Stack machine designers are beginning to address issues such as dedicated hardware support for conventional languages, memory management, and dealing with the limits of memory bandwidth.

Appendix A is a survey of the stack machines included in the taxonomy of Chapter 2. With entries for 70 machines, it is a single reference summary of most published designs having special support for stacks.

Appendix B provides a glossary of Forth primitives.

Appendix C gives an unabridged listing of some experimental results from Chapter 6.

Appendix D gives addresses for more information about the stack machines discussed in Chapters 4 and 5.

The chapters are intended to be read more or less in order, but readers with varying interests may find that they want to concentrate only on certain sections of the book. In general the book progresses from a theoretical basis for understanding stack machines at the beginning to practical applications at the end.

Chapters 2, 3, 6, and 9 concentrate on understanding the mechanisms of stack machine operation and the engineering tradeoffs associated with the stack model of computation. Chapters 4 and 5 describe stack machines at two levels: one for the potential user of a stack machine, and one for those who wish to see how design decisions affect the computer architecture and performance. Chapters 7 and 8 are geared more for potential users of stack machines who need answers to practical questions of software selection and application areas. Appendix A will be especially interesting for those readers who wish to gain a perspective on the history of stack machines.

ACKNOWLEDGEMENTS

My venture into the world of stack computers was started and encouraged by Glen Haydon, whose support, enthusiasm, and advice are deeply appreciated. Brian Meek and Rick Van Norman helped me refine the manuscript. Marty Fraeman, John Hayes, Charles Johnsen, Charles Longway, and the staff at Novix provided valuable advice and ensured the accuracy of various portions of Chapters 4, 5, and 6. Larry Forsley and Jerry Lilly also helped along the way.

pjk

1

Introduction and review

1.1 OVERVIEW

Hardware supported Last In First Out (LIFO) stacks have been used on
computers since the late 1950's. Originally, these stacks were added to
increase the execution efficiency of high level languages such as ALGOL.
Since then they have fallen in and out of favor with hardware designers,
eventually becoming incorporated as a secondary data handling structure in
most computers. To many a stack advocate's dismay, computers that use
hardware stacks as their primary data handling mechanism never really
found the wide acceptance enjoyed by register-based machines.

With the introduction of Very Large Scale Integration (VLSI) processors, conventional methods of computer design are being questioned
once again. Complex Instruction Set Computers (CISCs) have evolved into
complicated processors with comprehensive instruction sets. Reduced
Instruction Set Computers (RISCs) have challenged this approach by using
simplified processing cores to achieve higher raw processing speeds for some
applications.

Once more the time has come to consider stack machines as an alternative to other design styles. New stack machine designs based on VLSI design
technology provide additional benefits not found on previous stack
machines. These new stack computers use the synergy of their features to
attain an impressive combination of speed, flexibility, and simplicity.

Stack machines offer processor complexity that is much lower than that
of CISC machines, and overall system complexity that is lower than that of
either RISC or CISC machines. They do this without requiring complicated
compilers or cache control hardware for good performance. They also attain
competitive raw performance, and superior performance for a given price in
most programming environments. Their first successful application area has
been in real-time embedded control environments, where they outperform
other system design approaches by a wide margin. Stack machines also show
great promise in executing logic programming languages such as Prolog,
functional programming languages such as Miranda and Scheme, and
artificial intelligence research languages such as OPS-5 and Lisp.

The major difference between this new breed of stack machine and the
older stack machines is that large, high speed dedicated stack memories are
now cost effective. Where previously the stacks were kept mostly in program

memory, newer stack machines maintain separate memory chips or even an area of on-chip memory for the stacks. These stack machines provide extremely fast subroutine calling capability and superior performance for interrupt handling and task switching. When put together, these traits create computer systems that are fast, nimble, and compact.

We shall start out in this chapter with a discussion of the role of stacks in computing. This will be followed in subsequent chapters by a taxonomy of hardware stack support in computer design, a discussion of an abstract stack machine and several commercially implemented stack machines, results of research into stack machine performance characteristics, hardware and software considerations, and some predictions about future directions that may be taken in stack machine design.

1.2   WHAT IS A STACK?

LIFO stacks, also known as 'push down' stacks, are the conceptually simplest way of saving information in a temporary storage location for such common computer operations as mathematical expression evaluation and recursive subroutine calling.

1.2.1   Cafeteria tray example

As an example of how a stack works, consider a spring-loaded tray dispenser of the type often found in cafeterias. Let us say that each tray has a number engraved upon it. One tray at a time is loaded in from the top, each resting on the already loaded trays with the spring compressing to make room for more trays as necessary. For example, in Fig. 1.1, the trays numbered 42, 23, 2, and 9 are loaded onto the stack of trays with 42 loaded first and 9 loaded last.

The 'Last In' tray is number 9. Thus, the 'First Out' tray is also number 9. As customers remove trays from the top of the stack, the first tray removed is tray number 9, and the second is tray number 2. Let us say that at this point more trays were added. These trays would then have to come off the stack before the very first tray we loaded. After any sequence of pushes and pops of the stack of trays, tray 42 would still be on the bottom. The stack would be empty once again only after tray 42 had been popped from the top of the stack.

1.2.2   Example software implementations

LIFO stacks may be programmed into conventional computers in a number of ways. The most straightforward way is to allocate an array in memory, and keep a variable with the array index number of the topmost active element. Those programmers who value execution efficiency will refine this technique by allocating a block of memory locations and maintaining a pointer with the actual address of the top stack element. In either case, 'pushing' a stack element refers to the act of allocating a new word on the stack and placing data into it. 'Popping' the stack refers to the action of

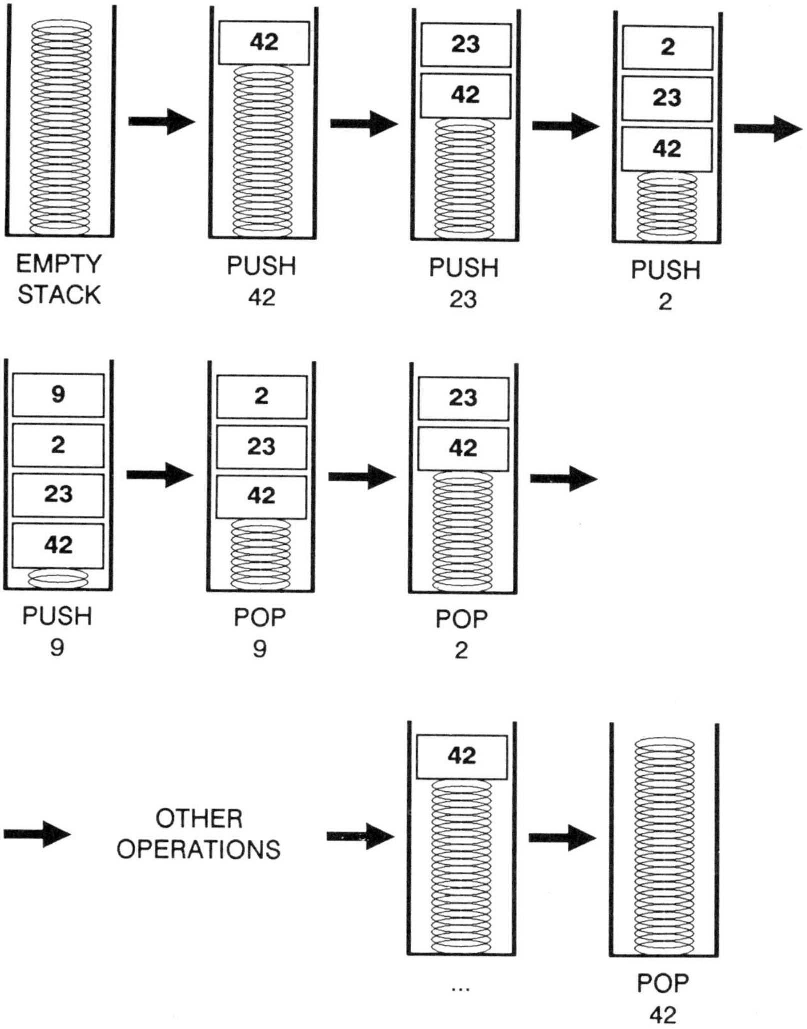

Fig. 1.1 — An example of stack operation.

removing the top element from the stack and then returning the data value removed to the routine requesting the pop.

Stacks often are placed in the uppermost address regions of the machine. They usually grow from the highest memory location towards lower memory locations, allowing the maximum flexibility in the use of the memory between the end of program memory and the 'top' of the stack. In our discussions, whether the stack grows 'up' in memory or 'down' in memory is largely irrelevant. The 'top' element of the stack is the element that was last pushed and will be the first to be popped. The 'bottom' element of the stack is the one that, when removed, will leave the stack empty.

A very important property of stacks is that, in their purest form, they only allow access to the top element in the data structure. We shall see later that this property has profound implications in the areas of program compactness, hardware simplicity and execution speed.

Stacks make excellent mechanisms for temporary storage of information within procedures. A primary reason for this is that they allow recursive invocations of procedures without risk of destroying data from previous invocations of the routine. They also support reentrant code. As an added advantage, stacks may be used to pass the parameters between these same procedures. Finally, they can conserve memory space by allowing different procedures to use the same memory space over and over again for temporary variable allocation, instead of reserving room within each procedure's memory for temporary variables.

There are other ways of creating stacks in software besides the array approach. Linked lists of elements may be used to allocate stack words, with elements of the stack not necessarily in any order with respect to actual memory addresses. Also, a software heap may be used to allocate stack space, although this is really begging the question since heap management is really a superset of stack management.

1.2.3 Example hardware implementations

Hardware implementation of stacks has the obvious advantage that it can be much faster than software management. In machines that refer to the stack with a large percentage of instructions, this increased efficiency is vital to maintaining high system performance.

While any software method of handling stacks can be implemented in hardware, the generally practiced hardware implementation is to reserve contiguous locations of memory with a stack pointer into that memory. Usually the pointer is a dedicated hardware register that can be incremented or decremented as required to push and pop elements. Sometimes a capability is provided to add an offset to the stack pointer to nondestructively access the first few elements of the stack without requiring successive pop operations. Often times the stack is resident in the same memory devices as the program. Sometimes, in the interest of increased efficiency, the stacks reside in their own memory devices.

Another approach that may be taken to building stacks in hardware is to use large shift registers. Each shift register is a long chain of registers with one end of the chain being visible as a single bit at the top of the stack. Thirty-two such shift registers of N bits each may be placed side-by-side to form a 32-bit-wide by N element stack. While this approach has not been practical in the past, VLSI stack machines may find this a viable alternative to the conventional register pointing into memory implementation.

1.3 WHY ARE STACK MACHINES IMPORTANT?

From a theoretical viewpoint, stacks themselves are important, since stacks are the most basic and natural tool that can be used in processing well structured code (Wirth 1968). Machines with LIFO stacks are also required to compile computer languages, and may be a requirement for the translation of natural languages (Evey 1963). Any computer with hardware support for stack structures will probably execute applications requiring stacks more efficiently than other machines.

Some say that programming stack machines is easier than programming conventional machines, and that stack machine programs run more reliably than other programs (McKeeman 1975). Stack machines are easier to write compilers for, since they have fewer exceptional cases to complicate a compiler (Lipovski 1975). Since running compilers can take up a significant percentage of machine resources in some installations, building a machine that can have an efficient compiler is important (Earnest 1980).

As we shall see in this book, stack machines are also much more efficient at running certain types of programs than register-based machines, particularly programs which are well modularized. Stack machines also are simpler than other machines, and provide very good computational power using little hardware. A particularly favorable application area for stack machines is in real-time embedded control applications, which require a combination of small size, high processing speed, and excellent support for interrupt handling that only stack machines can provide.

1.4   WHY ARE STACKS USED IN COMPUTERS?

Both hardware and software stacks have been used to support four major computing requirements: expression evaluation, subroutine return address storage, dynamically allocated local variable storage, and subroutine parameter passing.

1.4.1   Expression evaluation stack

Expression evaluation stacks were the first kind of stacks to be widely supported by special hardware. As a compiler interprets an arithmetic expression, it must keep track of intermediate stages and precedence of operations using an evaluation stack. In the case of an interpreted language, two stacks are kept. One stack contains the pending operations that await completion of higher precedence operations. The other stack contains the intermediate inputs that are associated with the pending operations. In a compiled language, the compiler keeps track of the pending operations during its instruction generation, and the hardware uses a single expression evaluation stack to hold intermediate results.

To see why stacks are well suited to expression evaluation, consider how the following arithmetic expression would be computed:

$$X = (A + B) * (C + D)$$

First, A and B would be added together. Then, this intermediate result must be saved somewhere. Let us say that it is pushed onto the expression evaluation stack. Next, C and D are added and the result is also pushed onto the expression evaluation stack. Finally, the top two stack elements ($A+B$ and $C+D$) are multiplied and the result is stored in X. The expression evaluation stack provides automatic management of intermediate results of expressions, and allows as many levels of precedence in the expression as there are available stack elements. Those readers who have used Hewlett Packard calculators, which use Reverse Polish Notation, have direct experience with an expression evaluation stack.

The use of an expression evaluation stack is so basic to the evaluation of expressions that even register-based machine compilers often allocate registers as if they formed an expression evaluation stack.

1.4.2   The return address stack

With the introduction of recursion as a desirable language feature in the late 1950s, a means of storing the return address of a subroutine in dynamically allocated storage was required. The problem was that a common method for storing subroutine return addresses in nonrecursive languages like FORTRAN was to allocate a space within the body of the subroutine for saving the return address. This, of course, prevented a subroutine from directly or indirectly calling itself, since the previously saved return address would be lost.

The solution to the recursion problem is to use a stack for storing the subroutine return address. As each subroutine is called, the machine saves the return address of the calling program on a stack. This ensures that subroutine returns are processed in the reverse order of subroutine calls, which is the desired operation. Since new elements are allocated on the stack automatically at each subroutine call, recursive routines may call themselves without any problems.

Modern machines usually have some sort of hardware support for a return address stack. In conventional machines, this support is often a stack pointer register and instructions for performing subroutine calls and subroutine returns. This return address stack is usually kept in an otherwise unused portion of program memory.

1.4.3   The local variable stack

Another problem that arises when using recursion, and especially when also allowing reentrancy (the possibility of multiple uses of the same code by different threads of control), is the management of local variables. Once again, in older languages like FORTRAN, management of information for a subroutine was handled simply by allocating storage assigned permanently to the subroutine code. This kind of statically allocated storage is fine for programs which are neither reentrant nor recursive.

However, as soon as it is possible for a subroutine to be used by multiple threads of control simultaneously or to be recursively called, statically defined local variables within the procedure become almost impossible to maintain properly. The values of the variables for one thread of execution can be easily corrupted by another competing thread. The solution that is most frequently used is to allocate the space on a local variable stack. New blocks of memory are allocated on the local variable stack with each subroutine call, creating working storage for the subroutine. Even if only registers are used to hold temporary values within the subroutine, a local variable stack of some sort is required to save register values of the calling routine before they are destroyed.

The local variable stack not only allows reentrancy and recursion — it can also save memory. In subroutines with statically allocated local variables, the variables take up space whether the subroutine is active or not. With a local variable stack, space on the stack is reused as subroutines are called and the stack depth increases and decreases.

1.4.4   The parameter stack

The final common use for a stack in computing is as a subroutine parameter stack. Whenever a subroutine is called it must usually be given a set of parameters upon which to act. Those parameters may be passed by placing values in registers, which has the disadvantage of limiting the possible number of parameters. The parameters may also be passed by copying them or pointers to them into a list in the calling routine's memory. In this case, reentrancy and recursion may not be possible. The most flexible method is to simply copy the elements onto a parameter stack before performing a procedure call. The parameter stack allows both recursion and reentrancy in programs.

1.4.5   Combination stacks

Real machines combine the various stack types. It is common in register-based machines to see the local variable stack, parameter stack, and return address stack combined into a single stack of activation records, or 'frames'. In these machines, expression evaluation stacks are eliminated by the compiler, and instead registers are allocated to perform expression evaluation.

The approach taken by the stack machines described later in this book is to have separate hardware expression evaluation and return stacks. The expression evaluation stacks are also used for parameter passing and local variable storage. Sometimes, especially when conventional languages such as C or Pascal are being executed, a frame pointer register is used to store local variables in an area of program memory.

1.5   THE NEW GENERATION OF STACK COMPUTERS

The new breed of stack computer that forms the focus of this book draws upon the rich history of stack machine design and the new opportunities offered by VLSI fabrication technology. This combination produces a unique blend of simplicity and efficiency that has in the past been lacking in computers of all kinds. The reasons for the advantages of stack machines for many applications will be explored in great detail in the following chapters. The features that produce these results and distinguish these machines from conventional designs are: multiple stacks with hardware stack buffers, zero-operand stack-oriented instruction sets, and the capability for fast procedure calls.

These design characteristics lead to a number of features in the resulting machines. Among these features are high performance without pipelining, very simple processor logic, very low system complexity, small program size, fast program execution, low interrupt response overhead, consistent program execution speeds across all time scales, and a low cost for context switching. Some of these results are obvious, some are only clear when thought about, and some results are completely contrary to the conventional wisdom of the computer architecture community.

Many of the designs for these stack computers have their roots in the Forth programming language. This is because Forth forms both a high level language and an assembly language for a stack machine that has two hardware stacks: one for expression evaluation/parameter passing, and one for return addresses. In a sense, the Forth language actually defines a stack-based computer architecture which is emulated by the host processor while executing Forth programs. The similarities between this language and the hardware designs are not an accident. Members of the current generation of stack machines have without exception been designed and promoted by people with Forth programming backgrounds.

An interesting point to note is that, although some of these machines are designed primarily to run Forth, they are also good at running conventional languages. Thus, while they may not take over as the processors of choice inside personal computers and workstations anytime soon, they are quite practical to use in many applications programmed in conventional languages. Of special interest are those applications that require stack machines' special advantages: small system size, good response to external events, and efficient use of limited hardware resources.

1.6 HIGHLIGHTS FROM THE REST OF THE BOOK

Many different facets of stack machines are explored in the following chapters. For the curious, here is a preview of some of the important points which will be discussed:

- Stack machines of all kinds may be classified by a taxonomy based upon the number of stacks, the size of the dedicated stack buffer memory, and the number of operands in the instruction format. The stack machines featured in this book are those with multiple stacks and 0-operand addressing. The size of the stack buffer memory is a design tradeoff between system cost and operating speed. For the bulk of this volume, 'stack machines' refers to these particular machines.
- Stack machines have small program size, low system complexity, high system performance, and good performance consistency under varying conditions.
- Stack machines run conventional languages reasonably well, and do so

using less hardware for a given level of performance than register-based machines.

- Stack machines are very good at running the Forth language, which is known for rapid program development because of its interactivity and flexibility. Forth is also known for producing compact code that is very well suited to real-time control problems.

- Four 16-bit stack machine designs span the range of design tradeoffs with respect to level of integration and speed. The designs presented in detail are the WISC CPU/16, the MISC M17, the Novix NC4016, and the Harris RTX 2000.

- Three 32-bit stack machine designs span a wide range of design tradeoffs. The designs presented in detail are: the Johns Hopkins/APL FRISC 3 (also known as the Silicon Composers SC32), the Harris RTX 32P, and Wright State University's SF1.

- Understanding stack machines requires the gathering and analysis of extensive metrics and comparison with the operation of register-based machines. Some of the measurements presented are: dynamic and static Forth instruction frequencies for approximately 10 million executed instructions, the effects of combining opcodes with subroutine calls in the same instruction on the RTX 32P, stack buffer size requirements, stack buffer overflow management strategies, and performance degradations in the face of frequent interrupts and context switching.

- Software selection for stack machines must encompass a large number of factors. Applications written largely in conventional languages can be quite efficient on stack machines, especially if a small effort is made to optimize frequently used sections of the code.

- A very good application area for stack machines is embedded real-time control. This application area encompasses a large portion of possible uses for computers. Other interesting applications are also discussed.

- The future hardware and software trends for stack machines will probably include increasingly efficient support for conventional programming languages as well as hardware that does not suffer from the ill effects of limits to memory bandwidth as much as other processors.

2

A taxonomy of hardware stack support

Historically, computer designs that promise a great deal of support for high level language processing have offered the most hardware stack support. This support ranges from a stack pointer register to multiple hardware stack memories within the central processing unit. Two recent classes of processors have provided renewed interest in hardware stack support: RISC processors, which frequently feature a large register file arranged as a stack, and stack oriented real-time control processors, which use stack instructions to reduce program size and processor complexity.

A taxonomy is an important step in understanding the nature of stack oriented computers. A good taxonomy allows making observations about global design tradeoff issues without delving into the implementation details of a particular machine. A taxonomy also helps in understanding where a proposed architecture stands with respect to existing designs. The purpose of beginning our discussion of stack machines with a taxonomy is to geta glimpse of the bigger picture before we focus in on multiple-stack, 0-operand machines in the following chapters.

In section 2.1 we shall describe a taxonomy for stack machines based on three attributes: the number of stacks, the size of stack buffer memories, and the number of operands in the instruction format. We shall also discuss the strengths and weaknesses inherent in the design tradeoffs that result in a particular machine belonging to one of the taxonomy categories.

In section 2.2 we shall categorize most published stack machine designs according to the taxonomy; then in section 2.3 we shall be looking for similarities and differences within the taxonomy groupings. The similarities within each grouping and differences between groupings show that the taxonomy helps us to think about the tradeoffs made in designing stack machines.

2.1 THE THREE-AXIS STACK DESIGN SPACE

The stack computer design space may be categorized by coordinates along a three-axis system as shown in Fig. 2.1. The three dimensions of the design space are: number of stacks supported by the hardware, the size of any

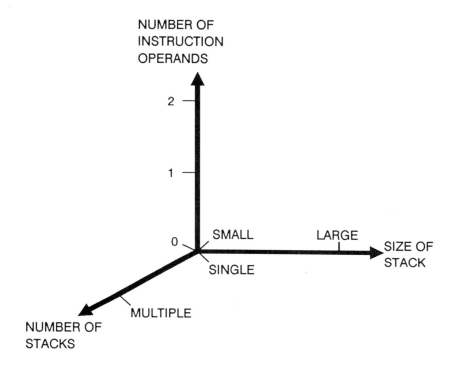

Fig. 2.1 — The three-axis stack machine design space.

dedicated buffer for stack elements, and how many operands are permitted by the instruction format.

In some respects these three dimensions can present a continuum, but for the purposes of this taxonomy we shall break the design space into 12 categories, with the three dimensions having the possible values of:

Number of stacks = Single or Multiple
Size of stack buffers = Small or Large
Number of operands = 0 or 1 or 2

2.1.1 Single vs. multiple stacks

The most obvious example of a stack supported function is a single stack used to support subroutine return addresses. Often times this stack also is used to pass parameters to subroutines. Sometimes one or more additional stacks are added to allow processing subroutine calls without affecting parameter lists, or to allow processing values on an expression stack separately from subroutine information.

Single-stack computers are those computers with exactly one stack supported by the instruction set. This stack is often intended for state saving for subroutine calls and interrupts. It may also be used for expression evaluation. In either case, it is probably used for subroutine parameter passing by compilers for some languages. In general, a single stack leads to simple hardware, but at the expense of intermingling data parameters with return address information.

An advantage of having a single stack is that it is easier for an operating system to manage only one block of variable-sized memory per process. Machines built for structured programming languages often employ a single stack that combines subroutine parameters and the subroutine return address, often using some sort of frame pointer mechanism.

A disadvantage of a single stack is that parameter and return address information are forced to become mutually well nested. This imposes an overhead if modular software design techniques force elements of a parameter list to be propagated through multiple layers of software interfaces, repeatedly being copied into new activation records.

Multiple-stack computers have two or more stacks supported by the instruction set. One stack is usually intended to store return addresses; the other stack is for expression evaluation and subroutine parameter passing. Multiple stacks allow separating control flow information from data operands.

In the case where the parameter stack is separate from the return address stack, software may pass a set of parameters through several layers of subroutines with no overhead for recopying the data into new parameter lists.

An important advantage of having multiple stacks is one of speed. Multiple stacks allow access to multiple values within a clock cycle. As an example, a machine that has simultaneous access to both a data stack and a return address stack can perform subroutine calls and returns in parallel with data operations.

2.1.2   Size of stack buffers

The amount of dedicated memory used to buffer stack elements is a crucial performance issue. Implementation strategies range from using only program memory to store stack elements, to having a few top-of-stack registers in the processor, to having a completely separate stack memory unit. The taxonomy divides the design space into those designs that have stacks residing mostly in program memory (with perhaps a few buffering elements in the CPU) and those designs that provide significant stack buffering.

An architecture with a **Small Stack Buffer** typically views the stack as a reserved portion of the general-purpose program memory address space. Stacks use the same memory subsystem as instructions and variables, allowing the regular memory reference instructions to access stack operands if desired. Stack elements may also be addressed by an offset from a stack pointer or frame pointer into memory.

To be competitive in speed, a stack machine must have at least one or two stack elements buffered inside the processor. To see the reason for this, consider an addition operation on a machine with unbuffered stacks. A single instruction fetch for the addition would generate three more memory cycles to fetch both operands and store the result. With two elements in a stack buffer, only one additional memory cycle is generated by an addition. This memory cycle is used to fetch the new second-from-top stack element, filling the hole created by the addition's consumption of a stack argument.

A small stack buffer with primary stacks residing in program memory allows quick switching between stacks for different tasks since the stack elements are predominately memory resident at all times.

The fact that a small dedicated stack buffer is simple to implement and easy to manage makes it very popular. In particular, the fact that most stack elements reside in main memory makes managing pointers, strings, and other data structures quite easy. The disadvantage of this approach is that significant main memory bandwidth is consumed to read and write stack elements.

If an architecture has a large enough stack buffer that main memory bandwidth is usually not consumed to access stack elements, then the architecture has a **Large Stack Buffer**. This large buffer may take one of several forms. It may be a large set of registers accessed using a register window scheme such as that used by the RISC I processor (Sequin & Patterson 1982), a separate memory unit that is isolated from program memory, or a dedicated stack memory cache in the processor (Ditzel & McLellan 1982). In any event, the stack buffer is considered 'large' if several levels of subroutines (say, 5 or more) may be processed without exhausting the capacity of the stack memory. In the case of a stack that is only used as an expression evaluation stack, 'large' may only be approximately 16 elements, since single expressions seldom nest very deeply (Haley 1962). In Chapter 6, we shall examine some program execution statistics that will give more insight into how large is large enough.

An advantage of a large stack buffer is that program memory cycles are not consumed while accessing data elements and subroutine return addresses. This can lead to significant speedups, particularly in subroutine-intensive environments.

A disadvantage of a separate stack memory unit is that it may not be large enough for all applications. In this case a spilling of data into program memory to make room for new stack entries may be required. Also, saving the entire stack buffer when switching between tasks in a multitasking environment may impose an unacceptably large context switching over-head, although it should be noted that this can be solved by dividing the stack memory into separate areas for separate tasks. At a lower level, separate data buses for off-chip stack memories and program memory will add pins and expense to a microprocessor.

Clearly, the delineation between 'large' and 'small' stack buffers can get hazy, but in practice it is usually clear which of these two alternatives the designer had in mind.

2.1.3 0-, 1-, and 2-operand addressing

The number of operands in the machine instruction format might at first not seem to have much to do with hardware support for stacks. In practice, however, the number of addressing modes has a tremendous effect on how the stacks are constructed and how the stacks can be used by programs.

0-operand instructions do not allow any operands to be associated with the opcode. All operations are implicitly specified to be performed on the top stack element(s). This kind of addressing is often called 'pure' stack addressing. A 0-operand stack architecture must, of course, use one of its stacks for expression evaluation.

Even in a pure stack machine, there must be a few instructions that specify addresses for loading and storing variables in program memory, loading literal (constant) values, subroutine calls, and conditional branching instructions. These instructions tend to have extremely simple formats, often just using the memory word after the opcode to hold the operand.

There are several advantages to the simplicity of 0-operand instructions. One is that only the top one or two stack locations can be referenced by an instruction. This can simplify construction of the stack memory by allowing the use of a single ported memory with one or two top-of-stack registers. A speed advantage may also be gained by loading the operand registers in parallel with instruction decoding, since the operands for each instruction are known in advance to be the top stack elements. This can completely eliminate the need for pipelining to fetch and store operands.

Another advantage is that individual instructions can be extremely compact, with an 8-bit instruction format sufficing for 256 different opcodes. Furthermore, instruction decoding is simplified, since no operand addressing modes need be interpreted by the decoding hardware.

A disadvantage to the 0-operand addressing mode is that complex addressing modes for data structure accessing may take several instructions to synthesize. Also, data elements that are deeply buried on the stack can be difficult to access if provisions are not made for copying the Nth-deep data stack element to the top of the stack.

A machine with a **1-operand** instruction format usually performs operations on the specified operand and uses the top stack element as the implicit second operand. 1-operand addressing, also called stack/accumulator addressing, offers more flexibility than 0-operand addressing, since it combines the fetching of an operand with the operation on the stack.

Keedy (1978a,b) has argued that a stack/accumulator architecture uses fewer instructions than a pure stack architecture for expression evaluation. His argument suggests that overall program size for 1-operand designs may be smaller than for 0-operand design. Of course, there is a tradeoff involved. Since the operand is specified by the instruction, an efficient implementation must either incorporate an operand-fetching pipeline or have a longer clock cycle to allow for operand access time. In the case when an operand is resident on a subroutine parameter stack or evaluation stack, the stack memory must be addressed with the offset of the operand to fetch the element. This requires more execution time or more pipelining hardware than having the top elements prefetched and waiting for an operation.

A 1-operand stack architecture almost always has an evaluation stack.

Most 1-operand architectures also support a 0-operand addressing mode to save instruction bits when the operand field would be unused.

2-operand instruction formats, which for the purposes of this taxonomy include 3-operand instruction formats as a special case, allow each instruction to specify both a source and a destination. In the case where stacks are only used to store return addresses, a 2-operand machine is simply a general-purpose register machine. If subroutine parameters are passed on the stack, then the 2 operands either specify an offset from a stack or frame pointer, or specify a pair of registers in the current register window for the operation. 2-operand machines do not need an expression evaluation stack, but place the burden of tracking intermediate results for evaluated expressions on the compiler.

2-operand machines offer a maximum of flexibility, but require more complicated hardware to perform efficiently. Since no operands are known before an instruction is decoded, a data pipeline and dual ported register file must be used to supply operands to the execution unit.

2.2 TAXONOMY NOTATION AND CATEGORIES

2.2.1 Notation
In order to convey the category for a particular architecture, we shall use a three-character shorthand notation based on the three axes of classification. The first letter of the abbreviation specifies the number of stacks (**Single** or **Multiple**). The second letter of the abbreviation specifies the size of dedicated stack memory (**Small** or **Large**). The third letter of the abbreviation specifies the number of operands in the instruction format (**0, 1,** or **2**). Thus, the abbreviation **SS0** would signify an architecture with a single stack, small dedicated stack memory, and 0-operand addressing, and the abbreviation **ML2** would signify an architecture with multiple stacks, large dedicated stack memory, and 2-operand addressing.

2.2.2 List of the categories in the design space
Table 2.1 shows the categorization of existing and historical stack oriented architectures by taxonomy category. Appendix A briefly discusses each of these architectures and how they implement features related to the taxonomy.

2.3 INTERESTING POINTS IN THE TAXONOMY

Perhaps the most surprising feature of the taxonomy space is that all twelve categories are populated by designs. This indicates that a significant amount of research on diverse stack architectures has been performed. Another observation is that different machine types tend to group along the operand axis as the major design parameter, with the number and size of stack buffers creating distinctions within each grouping.

Table 2.1 — Population of the stack machine taxonomy

Category	Machines
SS0	Aerospace Computer, Burroughs family, Caltech Chip, EULER, GLOSS, HITAC-10, ITS, LAX2, Mesa, Microdata 32/S, Transputer, WD9000
SS1	AAMP, Buffalo Stack Machine, EM-1, HP300/HP3000, ICL2900, IPL-VI, MCODE, MU5, POMP Pascal
SS2	Intel 80x86
SL0	G Machine, NORMA
SL1	AADC, μ3L
SL2	AM29000, CRISP, Dragon, Pyramid 90x, RISC I, SOAR
MS0	Action Processor, APL Language Machine, FORTRAN Machine, HUT, Internal Machine, MISC M17, Rockwell Microcontrollers, Symbol, Tree Machine
MS1	PDP-11
MS2	Motorola 680x0
ML0	ALCOR, An ALGOL Machine, FRISC 3, KDF-9, Kobe University Machine, MF1600, NC4016, OPA, PASCAL Machine, QFORTH, Reduction Language Machine, Rekursive, RTX 2000, RTX 32P, RUFOR, The Forth Engine, TM, Vaughan & Smith's Machine, WISC CPU/16, WISC CPU/32
ML1	Lilith, LISP machines, SF1, Soviet Machine
ML2	PSP, SF1, Socrates

The taxonomy categories with 0-operand addressing are 'pure' stack machines. Unsurprisingly, these categories have the most academic and conceptual design entries, since they include the canonical stack machine forms. Because of its inherent simplicity, the SS0 machine category is populated by designs constrained by scarce hardware resources, limited design budget, or both. Designs in the SS0 category may have efficiency problems if return addresses and data elements are intermingled on the stack and an efficient deep stack element copy operation is not provided.

The SL0 category seems to only be applicable to special-purpose machines used for combinator graph reduction (a technique used to execute functional programming languages (Jones 1987)). Graph reduction requires performing a tree traversal to evaluate the program, using a stack to store node addresses while doing the traversal. No expression evaluation stack is required, since the results are stored in the tree memory itself.

The MS0 and ML0 categories have similarly designed machines, distinguished mainly by the amount of chip or board area spent for buffering stack elements. All the Forth language machines and many of the other high level language machines fall into these categories. Machines in these categories are finding increasing use as real-time embedded control processors because of their simplicity, high processing speed, and small program sizes (Danile & Malinowski 1987, Fraeman *et al.* 1986). Many MS0 and ML0 designs allow for very fast or even zero-cycle subroutine calls and returns.

The entries with 1-operand addressing are designs that attempt to break bottlenecks that may arise in 0-operand designs by altering the pure stack model into a stack/accumulator design. The SS1 designs can use an address to access local variables and frame pointers more easily than SS0 designs. In general, the perceived advantage of a 1-operand design is that a push operation can be combined with an arithmetic operation, saving instructions in some circumstances. Additionally, the Pascal and Modula-2 machines use 1-operand addressing because of the nature of P-code and M-code.

The entries with 2-operand addressing tend to be more mainstream designs. Conventional microprocessors fall into the SS2 category. The RISC designs fall into the SL2 category because of their register windows, and no other designs fall into this category. The MS2 categorization for the 680x0 family reflects the flexibility of that machine, which can use any one of its eight address registers as a stack pointer. The ML2 entry for the PSP machine reflects an attempt in a conceptual design to carry the register window to an extreme for speeding up subroutine calls. The SF1 machine also uses multiple stacks, but dedicates a hardware stack to each active process in a real-time control environment.

From the preceding discussion, we see that designs can be found that fall into all twelve categories of the taxonomy. Designs within each group of the taxonomy display strong similarities, while designs in different groups can be shown to have differences that affect implementation and system operation. Thus, the taxonomy is a useful tool for gaining insight into the nature of stack oriented computers.

In the next chapter, we shall focus on a certain sector of the stack machine design space: MS0 and ML0 machines. In all future references, we shall mean either an MS0 or an ML0 machine when we use the term 'stack machine'.

3

Multiple stack, 0-operand machines

This chapter focuses attention on multiple-stack, 0-operand machines comprising the MS0 and ML0 categories of the taxonomy described in Chapter 2. In section 3.1, we shall compare stack machines to conventional complex instruction set computer (CISC) and reduced instruction set computer (RISC) architectures.

In section 3.2, we shall describe a generic stack machine architecture called the Canonical Stack Machine. We shall cover the hardware at a block diagram level, as well as implementation of the instruction set. This two-stack machine will serve as a point of departure for discussions of real stack machines in subsequent chapters.

In section 3.3, we shall briefly discuss the Forth programming language. Forth is an unconventional programming language which uses a two-stack model of computation and strongly encourages frequent calls to many small procedures. Many ML0 and MS0 designs have their roots in the Forth language, and are well suited to execution of Forth programs.

3.1   WHY THESE MACHINES ARE INTERESTING

Multiple-stack, 0-operand machines have two inherent advantages over other machines: 0-operand addressing leads to a small instruction size, and multiple stacks allow concurrent subroutine calls and data manipulations. These features and others lead to small programs, low system complexity, and high system performance. The main difference between MS0 and ML0 machines is that MS0 machines give up some performance in order to reduce the CPU cost by minimizing the resources used for the stack buffers.

We shall examine the details behind how stack machines achieve their advantages in Chapter 6. For now, let us just summarize their benefits.

Stack machines support small program sizes by encouraging frequent use of subroutines to reduce code size, and by the fact that stack machines can have short instructions. Small program sizes reduce memory costs, component count, and power requirements, and can improve system speed by allowing the cost effective use of smaller, higher speed memory chips. Additional benefits include better performance in a virtual memory environment, and a requirement for less cache memory to achieve a given hit ratio. 0-operand stack machines tend to have smaller code size than other machines.

Decreased system complexity decreases system development time and chip size. This decreased chip size leaves more room on-chip for semicustom features and program memory.

System performance includes not only raw execution speed, but also total system cost and system adaptability when used in real-world applications. The execution speed component of system performance includes not only how many instructions can be performed per second on straight line code, but also speed in handling interrupts, context switches, and performance degradation due to factors such as conditional branches and procedure calls. In stack machines, the very same 0-operand addressing mode and frequent subroutine calls that reduce code size and system complexity actually result in improved system performance for application programs.

An additional benefit of the fact that stack processors support efficient procedure calls is that well structured code with many small procedures is encouraged by the architecture. This increases maintainability by encouraging better coding practices, and increases code reuse by allowing the use of small subroutines as building blocks.

3.2   A GENERIC STACK MACHINE

Before embarking on a detailed review of real MS0 and ML0 designs, a baseline for comparison needs to be established. Therefore, we shall explore the design for a canonical ML0 machine. The design presented is as simple as possible to present a common point of departure for comparing other designs.

3.2.1   Block diagram

Fig. 3.1 is a block diagram of the Canonical Stack Machine. Each box on the diagram represents a logical resource for the machine corresponding to the essential minimum components for an ML0 design. These components are: the data bus, the data stack (DS), the return stack (RS), the arithmetic/logic unit (ALU) with its top-of-stack (TOS) register, the program counter (PC), program memory with a memory address register (MAR), control logic with an instruction register (IR), and an input/output section (I/O).

3.2.1.1   *Data bus*

For simplicity, the Canonical Stack Machine has a single bus connecting the system resources. Real processors may have more than one data path to allow for parallel operation of instruction fetching and calculations. In the Canonical Stack Machine, the data bus allows a single transmitting functional block and a single receiving functional block during any single operation cycle.

3.2.1.2   *Data stack*

The data stack is a memory with an internal mechanism to implement a LIFO stack. A common implementation for this might be a conventional

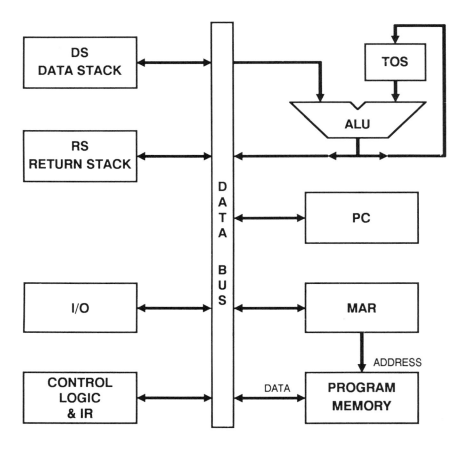

Fig. 3.1 — The Canonical Stack Machine.

memory with an up/down counter used for address generation. The data stack allows two operations: **push** and **pop**. The **push** operation allocates a new cell on the top of the stack and writes the value on the data bus into that cell. The **pop** operation places the value on the top cell of the stack onto the data bus, then deletes the cell, exposing the next cell on the stack for the next processor operation.

3.2.1.3   Return stack
The return stack is a LIFO stack implemented in an identical manner to the data stack. The only difference is that the return stack is used to store subroutine return addresses instead of instruction operands.

3.2.1.4   ALU and top-of-stack register
The ALU functional block performs arithmetic and logical computations on pairs of data elements. One of the data element pairs is the top-of-stack (TOS) register, which holds the topmost element of the data stack as used by

the programmer. Thus, the top element of the data stack block is actually the second item on the data stack as perceived by the programmer, while the top perceived data stack element is kept in the one-register TOS buffer at the ALU. This scheme allows using a single ported data stack memory while allowing operations, such as addition, on the top two stack elements.

The ALU supports the standard primitive operations needed by any computer. For the purposes of our illustration, this includes addition, subtraction, logical functions (AND, OR, XOR), and test for zero. For the purposes of this conceptual design, all arithmetic will be integer. There is no reason why floating point arithmetic could not be added to the ALU as a generalization of the concept.

3.2.1.5   Program counter
The program counter holds the address of the next instruction to be executed. The PC may be loaded from the bus to implement branches, or may be incremented to fetch the next sequential instruction from program memory.

3.2.1.6   Program memory
The program memory block has both a Memory Address Register (MAR) and a reasonable amount of random access memory. To access the memory, first the MAR is written with the address to be read or written. Then, on the next system cycle, the program memory is either read onto or written from the system data bus.

3.2.1.7   I/O
As with most conceptual designs, the issue of input/output from and to the outside world will be swept under the rug. Suffice it to say that there is some system resource, the I/O box, that handles this task.

3.2.2   Data operation
Table 3.1 shows the minimum set of operators for the Canonical Stack Machine. This set of operators was chosen in order to illustrate the use of the machine — it is obviously not adequate for efficient program execution. In particular, multiply, divide and shift operations have been omitted in the interest of simplicity. Notation derived from the Forth language (see section 3.3) has been used to maintain consistency with discussions of instruction sets in later chapters. An important point to note is that Forth notation often makes extensive use of special characters, such as ! (which is pronounced 'store' in Forth) and @ (which is pronounced 'fetch' in Forth).

3.2.2.1   Reverse Polish Notation
Stack machines execute data manipulation operations using postfix operations. These operations are usually called 'Reverse Polish' after the Reverse Polish Notation (RPN) that is often used to describe postfix operations. Postfix operations are distinguished by the fact that the oper-

Table 3.1 — Canonical Stack Machine instruction set

Instruction	input	Data Stack → output	Function
!	N1 ADDR	→	Store N1 at location ADDR in program memory
+	N1 N2	→ N3	Add N1 and N2, giving sum N3
−	N1 N2	→ N3	Subtract N2 from N1, giving difference N3
>R	N1	→	Push N1 onto the return stack
@	ADDR	→ N1	Fetch the value at location ADDR in program memory, returning N1
AND	N1 N2	→ N3	Perform a bitwise AND on N1 and N2, giving result N3
DROP	N1	→	Drop N1 from the stack
DUP	N1	→ N1 N1	Duplicate N1, returning a second copy of it on the stack
OR	N1 N2	→ N3	Perform a bitwise OR on N1 and N2, giving result N3
OVER	N1 N2	→ N1 N2 N1	Push a copy of the second element on the stack, N1, onto the top of the stack
R>		→ N1	Pop the top element of the return stack, and push it onto the data stack as N1
SWAP	N1 N2	→ N2 N1	Swap the order of the top two stack elements
XOR	N1 N2	→ N3	Perform a bitwise eXclusive OR on N1 and N2, giving result N3
[IF]	N1	→	If N1 is false (value is 0) perform a branch to the address in the next program cell, otherwise continue
[CALL]		→	Perform a subroutine call to the address in the next program cell
[EXIT]		→	Perform a subroutine return
[LIT]		→ N1	Treat the value in the next program cell as an integer constant, and push it onte stack as N1

ands come before the operation. For example, an expression in conventional (infix) notation might be represented as:

$$(12+45) * 98$$

In this expression, parentheses are used to force the addition to occur before the multiplication. Even in expressions without parentheses, an implied operator precedence is in force. For example, without parentheses the multiplication would be done before the addition. The equivalent to the above parenthesized expression would be written in postfix notation as:

$$98 \quad 12 \quad 45 \quad + \quad *$$

In postfix notation, the operator acts upon the most recently seen operands, and uses an implied stack for evaluation. In this postfix example, the numbers 98, 12, and 45 would be pushed onto a stack as shown in Fig. 3.2. Then the + operator would act upon the top two stack elements (namely

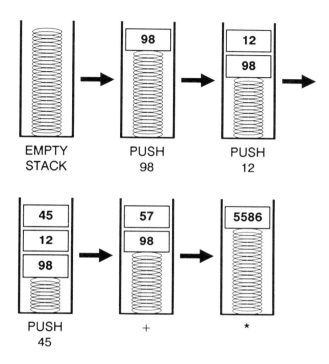

Fig. 3.2 — An example stack computation.

45 and 12) leaving the result 57. Then the * operator would work upon the new two top stack elements 57 and 98 leaving 5586.

Postfix notation has an economy of expression when compared to infix notation in that neither operator precedence nor parentheses are necessary. It is much better suited to the needs of computers. In fact, compilers as a matter of course translate infix expressions in languages such as C and FORTRAN into postfix machine code, sometimes using explicit register allocation instead of an expression stack.

The Canonical Stack Machine described in the preceding section is designed to execute postfix operations directly without burdening the compiler with register allocation bookkeeping.

3.2.2.2   *Arithmetic and logical operators*
In order to accomplish basic arithmetic, the Canonical Stack Machine needs both arithmetic and logical operators. In this and the following sections each instruction will be discussed and described in terms of a register transfer level pseudocode, which should be self explanatory. For example, the first operation is addition.

Operation:	$+$
Stack:	N1 N2 $\rightarrow$ N3
Description:	Add N1 and N2, giving sum N
Pseudocode:	$TOSREG \Leftarrow TOSREG + POP(DS)$

For the $+$ operation, the top two elements of the user's perceived data stack N1 and N2 are popped and added, with the result N3 pushed back onto the stack. From an implementation point of view, this would mean popping the DS (which gives N1) and adding it to the TOSREG value which contains N2. The result is placed back into TOSREG, leaving N3 in at the top of the user's perceived data stack. The DS element which is accessed by *POP(DS)* is actually the second-to-top element of the stack as seen by the programmer, but is the top element on the actual hardware stack. This operation of *POP(DS)* is consistent with the notion of TOSREG as a top-of-stack register as seen by the user. Note that by keeping the TOSREG as a 1-element stack buffer, a *POP* of element N2 and a subsequent *PUSH* of element N3 were eliminated.

Operation:	$-$
Stack:	N1 N2 $\rightarrow$ N3
Description:	Subtract N2 from N1, giving difference N3
Pseudocode:	$TOSREG \Leftarrow POP(DS) - TOSREG$

Operation:	AND
Stack:	N1 N2 $\rightarrow$ N3
Description:	Perform a logical AND on N1 and N2, giving result N3
Pseudocode:	$TOSREG \Leftarrow TOSREG \text{ and } POP(DS)$

Operation:	OR
Stack:	N1 N2 $\rightarrow$ N3
Description:	Perform a logical OR on N1 and N2, giving result N3
Pseudocode:	$TOSREG \Leftarrow TOSREG \text{ or } POP(DS)$

Operation:	XOR
Stack:	N1 N2 $\rightarrow$ N3
Description:	Perform a logical exclusive OR on N1 and N2, giving result N3
Pseudocode:	$TOSREG \Leftarrow TOSREG \text{ xor } POP(DS)$

It is obvious that the top-of-stack buffer register saves a considerable amount of work when performing these operations.

3.2.2.3 Stack manipulation operators

One of the problems associated with pure stack machines is that they are able to access only the top two stack elements for arithmetic operations. Therefore, some overhead instructions must be spent on preparing operands to be consumed by other operations. Of course, it should be said that some register-based machines also spend a large number of instructions doing register-to-register moves to prepare for operations, so the question of which approach is better becomes complicated.

The following instructions all deal with manipulating stack elements.

Operation:	DROP
Stack:	N1 →
Description:	Drop N1 from the stack
Pseudocode:	*TOSREG ⇐ POP(DS)*

In this and many subsequent instruction definitions, notation similar to *TOSREG ⇐ POP(DS)* is used. In order to accomplish this operation, the data stack information is placed onto the data bus, then brought through the ALU by performing a dummy operation (such as adding 0) to be placed in the top-of-stack register.

Operation:	DUP
Stack:	N1 → N1 N1
Description:	Duplicate N1, returning a second copy of it on the stack
Pseudocode:	*PUSH(DS) ⇐ TOSREG*

Operation:	OVER
Stack:	N1 N2 → N1 N2 N1
Description:	Push a copy of the second element on the stack, N1, onto the top of the stack
Pseudocode:	*PUSH(RS) ⇐ TOSREG* (Place N2 on RS)
	TOSREG ⇐ POP(DS) (Place N1 into TOSREG)
	PUSH(DS) ⇐ TOSREG (Push N1 onto DS)
	PUSH(DS) ⇐ POP(RS) (Push N2 onto DS)

OVER seems conceptually simple when looking at the description. However, the operation is complicated by the need to store N2 temporarily to get it out of the way. In actual machines, one or more temporary storage registers are added to the system to reduce this thrashing for **OVER, SWAP**, and other stack manipulation instructions.

Operation:	SWAP	
Stack:	N1 N2 → N2 N1	
Description:	Swap the order of the top two stack elements	
Pseudocode:	*PUSH(RS) ⇐ TOSREG*	(Save N2 on the RS)
	TOSREG ⇐ POP(DS)	(Place N1 into TOSREG)
	PUSH(DS) ⇐ POP(RS)	(Push N2 onto DS)

Operation:	>R	(Pronounced 'to R')
Stack:	N1 →	
Description:	Push N1 onto the return stack	
Pseudocode:	*PUSH(RS) ⇐ TOSREG*	
	TOSREG ⇐ POP(DS)	

The instruction **>R** and its complement **R>** allow shuffling data elements between the data and return stacks. This technique is used to access stack elements buried more than two elements deep on the stacks by temporarily placing the topmost data stack elements on the return stack.

Operation:	R>	(Pronounced 'R from')
Stack:	→ N1	
Description:	Pop the top element of the return stack, and push it onto the data stack as N1	
Pseudocode:	*PUSH(DS) ⇐ TOSREG*	
	TOSREG ⇐ POP(RS)	

3.2.2.4 *Memory fetching and storing*
Even though all arithmetic and logical operations are performed on data elements on the stack, there must be some way of loading information onto the stack before operations are performed, and storing information from the stack into memory. The Canonical Stack Machine uses a simple load/store architecture, so has only a single load instruction '@' and a single store instruction '!'.

Since instructions do not have an operand field, the memory address is taken from the stack. This eases access to data structures, since the stack may be used to hold a pointer that indexes through array elements. Since memory must be accessed once for the instruction and once for the data, these instructions take two memory cycles to execute.

Operation:	! (Pronounced 'store')
Stack:	N1 ADDR →
Description:	Store N1 at location ADDR in program memory
Pseudocode:	*MAR ⇐ TOSREG*
	MEMORY ⇐ POP(DS)
	TOSREG ⇐ POP(DS)

Operation:	@ (Pronounced 'fetch')
Stack:	ADDR → N1
Description:	Fetch the value at location ADDR in program memory, returning N1
Pseudocode:	*MAR ⇐ TOSREG*
	TOSREG ⇐ MEMORY

3.2.2.5   Literals

Somehow there must be a way to get a constant value onto the stack. The instruction to do this is called the literal instruction, which is often called a load-immediate instruction in register-based architectures. The literal instruction uses two consecutive instruction words: one for the actual instruction, and one to hold a literal value to be pushed onto the stack. Literal requires two memory cycles, one for the instruction, one for the data element.

Operation:	[LIT]
Stack:	→ N1
Description:	Treat the value in the next program cell as an integer constant, and push it onto the stack as N1
Pseudocode:	*MAR ⇐ PC* (Address of literal)
	PC ⇐ PC + 1
	PUSH(DS) ⇐ TOSREG
	TOSREG ⇐ MEMORY

This implementation assumes that the PC is pointing to the location of the next instruction word after the current opcode.

3.2.3   Instruction execution

Thus far we have ignored the mechanics of how an instruction actually gets fetched from program memory and is executed. This execution sequence involves a typical sequence of instruction fetch, instruction decode, and instruction execute.

3.2.3.1   Program Counter

The Program Counter is the register that holds a pointer to the next instruction to be executed. After fetching an instruction, the program counter is automatically incremented to point to the next word in memory. In the case of a branch or subroutine call instruction, the program counter is loaded with a new value to accomplish the branch.

An implied instruction fetching sequence which is performed before every instruction is:

Operation: Fetch next instruction
Pseudocode: $MAR \Leftarrow PC$
                  $INSTRUCTION\ REGISTER \Leftarrow MEMORY$
                  $PC \Leftarrow PC + 1$

3.2.3.2   Conditional branching
In order to be able to make decisions, the machine must have available some method for conditional branching. The Canonical Stack Machine uses the simplest method possible. A conditional branch may be performed based on whether the top stack element is equal to 0. This approach eliminates the need for condition codes, yet allows implementation of all control flow structures.

Operation: [IF]
Stack: $N1 \rightarrow$
Description: If N1 is false (value is 0) perform a branch to the address contained in the next program cell, otherwise continue
Pseudocode: $if\ TOSREG\ is\ 0$
                  $\qquad MAR \Leftarrow PC$
                  $\qquad PC \Leftarrow MEMORY$
                  $else$
                  $\qquad PC \Leftarrow PC + 1$
                  $endif$
                  $TOSREG \Leftarrow POP(DS)$

3.2.3.3   Subroutine calls
Finally, the Canonical Stack Machine must have a method of efficiently implementing subroutine calls. Since there is a dedicated return address stack, subroutine calls simply require pushing the current program counter value onto the stack, then loading the program counter with a new value. We will assume that the instruction format for subroutine calls allows specifying a full address for the subroutine call within a single instruction word, and will ignore the mechanics of actually extracting the address field from the instruction. Real machines in later chapters will offer a variety of methods for accomplishing this with extremely low hardware overhead.

Subroutine returns are accomplished by simply popping the return address from the top of the return address stack and placing the address in the program counter. Since data parameters are maintained on the data stack, no pointers or memory locations need be manipulated by the subroutine call instruction.

Operation:	[CALL]
Stack:	→
Description:	Perform a subroutine call
Pseudocode:	$PUSH(RS) \Leftarrow PC$ (Save return address)
	$PC \Leftarrow INSTRUCTION\ REGISTER\ ADDRESS\ FIELD$

Operation:	[EXIT]
Stack:	→
Description:	Perform a subroutine return
Pseudocode:	$PC \Leftarrow POP(RS)$

3.2.3.4   *Hardwired vs. microcoded instructions*

While the Canonical Stack Machine description has been kept free from implementation considerations for conceptual simplicity, a discussion of one major design tradeoff that is seen in real implementations is in order. The tradeoff is one between hardwired control and microcoded control. An introduction to the concepts of hardwired versus microcoded implementation techniques may be found in Koopman (1987a).

Hardwired designs traditionally allow faster and more space efficient implementations to be made. The cost for this performance increase is usually increased complexity in designing decoding circuitry, and a major risk of requiring a complete control logic redesign if the instruction set specification is changed near the end of the product design cycle.

With a stack machine, the instruction format is extremely simple (just an opcode) and the usual combinatorial explosion of operand/type combinations is completely absent. For this reason hardwired design of a stack machine is relatively straightforward.

As an additional benefit, if a stack machine has a 16-bit or larger word length, the word size is very large compared to the few bits needed to specify the possible operations. Hardwired stack machines usually exploit this situation by using pre-decoded instruction formats to further simplify control hardware and increase flexibility. Pre-decoded (also called unencoded) instructions have a microcode-like format in that specific bit fields of the instruction perform specific tasks. This allows for the possibility of combining several independent operations (such as **DUP** and **[EXIT]**) in the same instruction.

While 16-bit instructions may seem wastefully large, the selection of a fixed length instruction simplifies hardware for decoding, and allows a subroutine call to be encoded in the same length word as other instructions. A simple strategy for encoding a subroutine call is to simply set the highest bit to 0 for a subroutine call (giving a 15-bit address field) or 1 for an opcode (giving a 15-bit unencoded instruction field). In general, the speed advantage of a fixed length instruction when combined with the possibility of compressing multiple operations into the same instruction makes the selection of a fixed length instruction justifiable. The technique of unencoded hardwired design on stack machines was pioneered by the Novix NC4016 and has since been used by other machines.

With all the benefits of hardwired instruction decoding for stack machines, it might seem at first glance that microcoded instruction execution would never be used. However, there are several advantages to using a microcoded implementation scheme.

The major advantage to a microcoded approach is flexibility. Since most combinations of bits in an unencoded hardwired instruction format are not useful, a microcoded machine can use fewer bits to specify the same possible instructions, including optimized instructions that perform a sequence of stack functions. This leaves room for user-specified opcodes in the architecture. A microcoded machine can have several complex, multicycle user-specific instructions that would be unfeasible to implement using hardwired design techniques. If some or all of the microcode memory is constructed of RAM instead ROM, then the instruction set can be customized for each user or even each application program.

One potential drawback is that using a microcoded design often establishes a microinstruction fetching pipeline to avoid a speed penalty for accessing microcode program memory. This can result in a requirement that instructions take more than one clock cycle, whereas hardwired designs are optimized for single-clock-cycle execution.

As it turns out, this is not really a penalty. Using a realistic match of processor speed and affordable memory speed, most processors can perform two internal stack operations in the time it takes for a single memory access. Thus, both a hardwired design and a microcoded design can execute instructions in a single *memory* cycle. Furthermore, since a microcoded design can slip in twice as many operations per memory cycle period, opportunities for code optimization and user-specified instructions are that much greater.

As a practical matter, microcoded implementations are more convenient to implement in discrete component designs, so they predominate in board-level implementations. Most single-chip implementations are hardwired.

3.2.4   State changing

An important consideration in real-time control applications is how the processor can handle interrupts and task switches. The specified instruction set for the Canonical Stack Machine sidesteps these issues to a certain extent, so we will talk about the standard ways of handling these events to build a base upon which to contrast designs in the next sections.

A potential liability for stack machines with independent stack memories is the large state that must be saved if the stacks are swapped into program memory to change tasks. We will see how this state change can be avoided much of the time. Chapter 6 speaks about advanced design techniques that can further reduce the penalties of a task switch.

3.2.4.1   Stack overflow/underflow interrupts
Interrupts are caused either by exceptional events, such as stack overflow, or by requests for I/O service. Both events require quick resolution without disturbing the flow of the current task.

Stack Overflow/Underflow is by far the most frequent exceptional condition on a stack machine, so it will be used as an example for how 'large grain' interrupts are handled.

Stack Overflow/Underflow occurs when the hardware stack memory capacity is exceeded by the application program. Several possible responses to this situation include: ignore the overflow and let the software crash (an easy to implement but rather messy solution), halt the program with a fatal execution error, or copy a portion of the stack memory to program memory to allow continued program execution. Clearly, the last alternative gives the most flexibility, but a fatal execution error may be acceptable and simpler to implement in some environments. Other exceptional conditions such as a memory parity may be handled by the system as well.

Exceptional conditions can take a long time to resolve, but all have the property of requiring the state of the current task to remain intact during resolution so that the task may be restarted if possible. Thus, these conditions require no action from the processor except to force a hardware generated subroutine call to a condition handling code.

3.2.4.2   I/O service interrupts
I/O servicing is a potentially frequent event that must be handled quickly for real-time control tasks. Fortunately, interrupts usually require very little processing and almost no temporary storage. For this reason, stack machines treat interrupts as hardware generated subroutine calls.

These subroutine calls push parameters onto the stack, perform their calculations, then perform a subroutine exit to restart the program that was interrupted. The only constraint is that the interrupt service routine must leave no 'garbage' behind on the stack.

Interrupts are much less expensive on stack machines than on conventional machines for several reasons: registers need not be saved since the stack allocates working storage automatically, there are no condition code flags to be saved since the only branch conditions are kept as flags on the data stack, and most stack processors have a short or nonexistent data pipeline, so there is no penalty for saving the pipeline state when an interrupt is received.

3.2.4.3   Task switching
Task switching occurs when a processor switches between programs to give the appearance of multiple simultaneously executing programs. The state of the program which is stopped at a task switch must be preserved so that it

may be resumed at a later time. The state of the program which is started must be properly placed into the machine before execution is resumed.

The traditional way of accomplishing this is to use a timer and swap tasks on every timer tick, sometimes subject to prioritization and scheduling algorithms. In a simple processor, this can lead to a large overhead for saving both stacks to memory and reloading them on every context swap. A technique that can be used to combat this problem is programming 'light weight' tasks which use little stack space. These tasks can push their own parameters on top of existing stack elements, then remove their stack elements when terminating, thus eliminating the potentially more expensive saving and restoring of stacks for a 'heavy weight' process.

Another solution is to use multiple sets of stack pointers for multiple tasks within the same stack memory hardware.

3.3   OVERVIEW OF THE FORTH PROGRAMMING LANGUAGE

3.3.1 Forth as a common thread

Since the majority of modern stack machines have their roots in the Forth programming language, an introduction to the terms of this language is in order.

The Forth programming language was invented by Charles Moore for control of telescopes in observatories using small computers (Moore 1980). Because of its roots, Forth stresses efficiency, compactness, flexible and efficient hardware/software interaction. At the same time, Forth is sufficiently powerful that it can and has been used for a large variety of general-purpose programming tasks including: database management, accounting software, word processors, graphics, expert systems, and scientific computations. Appendix B contains a glossary of the primitive operations in the Forth language.

Some of the advantages of programming in the Forth language include ease of program modification and debugging, extreme flexibility, a very quick compile/edit/test cycle, high portability across a wide variety of machines, and compact source and object code (Jonak 1986). Kogge (1982) describes threaded code software environments, with an emphasis on the underlying mechanisms of the Forth language.

3.3.2   The Forth virtual machine

In order to solve the original telescope control problem, Forth needed several important qualities. It had to be suitable for real-time control, highly interactive for easy use by nonprogrammers, and had to fit within severe memory space constraints.

From these origins, the language took on two major features: the use of threaded code, and 0-operand stack instructions. In order to conceptualize the operation of the language, the Forth virtual machine is used as a model for computation. The Forth virtual machine has two stacks: a data stack and a return stack. Forth programs are actually an emulation of MS0 machine code running on the host hardware. Forth programs consist of very small subroutines that execute only calls to other subroutines and primitive stack operation instructions. Programs are built in a tree-like fashion, with each subroutine calling upon a small collection of underlying subroutines.

It is easy to see that Forth is a natural machine language for 0-operand stack hardware as exemplified by the Canonical Stack Machine.

It should be noted that even if a processor is designed as a Forth processor, it is still capable of executing any other high level language. This is because the primitives of the Forth language are defined at a very low level, and correspond to the machine code operations that would have to be present in any stack machine. Thus, a machine that is advertised as a 'Forth machine' is usually suitable for running other languages as well.

3.3.2.1   Stack architecture/RPN
The primitives of the Forth language include all the operations of the Canonical Stack Machine listed in Table 3.1. All the operations' names not enclosed by '[...]' correspond exactly to Forth function names.

The bracketed names **[IF]**, **[CALL]**, **[EXIT]** and **[LIT]** correspond to internal Forth functions that are automatically compiled to support programs. For example, **[IF]** would be compiled to perform a conditional branch when the Forth construct **IF ... THEN** is encountered. **[CALL]** would be compiled any time a reference to a Forth word that is not a machine primitive operation is encountered. **[EXIT]** is compiled by the **;** at the end of a Forth definition and by the word **EXIT**. Finally, **[LIT]** would be compiled every time a literal value such as **1234** is encountered in a program.

Several Forth constructions such as **LOOP**, variables, and constants are not directly supported by the Canonical Stack Machine, but can be synthesized from simpler operations. Obviously, an efficient Forth language computer will have direct support for all frequently used Forth structures.

3.3.2.2   Short, frequent procedure calls
The main characteristic of Forth programs that separates Forth from most other languages is the high frequency of subroutine calls. Good Forth programming style encourages incremental program development and testing with small subroutines. Subroutines often only consist of 5 or 10 instructions. A static frequency of approximately 50% of the instructions being subroutine calls is considered normal.

This kind of software environment allows extraordinarily rapid and accurate program construction, and is especially effective in environments with limited memory capacity. It also encourages the use of machines with fast subroutine calls.

3.3.3   Emphasis on interactivity, flexibility
A major advantage of the Forth programming language is that it provides an unprecedented level of interactivity in its development environment. The development tools include an integrated incremental compiler and editor which allow interactive testing and modification of individual procedures.

The encouragement for writing small procedures and modular code allows easy and fast testing during development, with a greatly reduced need for fixing words after they are first written. The consensus among Forth programmers is that use of the Forth language reduces development time by a factor of 10 compared to other languages over a wide range of applications.

Forth programs tend to emphasize flexibility for problem solving. Since Forth is an extensible language, new data and control structures may be added to the language to support specific application areas. This flexibility allows one or two programmers to solve a problem that might require a larger team effort in other languages, reducing project management overhead and thus magnifying the productivity increase. Forth has not been used extensively in extremely large programming efforts, so its effectiveness in very large applications is as yet unknown.

4

Architecture of 16-bit systems

In this chapter we shall discuss a representative selection of 16-bit stack computer designs. The designs have been chosen to span a wide range of implementation philosophies and tradeoffs. Section 4.1 discusses the characteristics of 16-bit systems. An important consideration is that 16-bit hardware is compact enough to allow for complete systems on a single chip for embedded control applications.

The remaining sections discuss four different 16-bit stack computers. The sections are arranged in order of increasing integration level, from a system made with off-the-shelf discrete components to a highly integrated processor-on-a-chip.

In section 4.2 we discuss the WISC CPU/16, a discrete component implementation of a generalized stack processor with a writable control store. The CPU/16 is a technology development platform designed for simplicity and flexibility.

In section 4.3 we discuss the MISC M17 processor. The M17 is targeted at 'low end', price-sensitive applications. Consequently, it keeps its stacks in program memory to eliminate the cost of separate stack memory hardware.

In section 4.4 we discuss the Novix NC4016, which was the first Forth chip to enter the marketplace. The NC4016 provides an intermediate range of price and performance, with dedicated off-chip stack memories.

In section 4.5, we discuss the Harris RTX 2000, which is a high performance microcontroller based on the Novix NC4016 design. The RTX 2000 uses a standard cell design approach, which enables it to include on-chip stack memory for speed and compactness. The standard cell approach also allows the addition of a hardware multiplier and counter/timers to the processor chip.

The CPU/16, NC4016, and RTX 2000 are ML0 stack machines. The M17, in keeping with its emphasis on low cost, is an MS0 stack machine.

4.1 CHARACTERISTICS OF 16-BIT DESIGNS

The systems discussed here are 16 bits wide because that is the smallest configuration that makes sense for most commercial stack processor applications.

4.1.1 Good fit with the traditional Forth model

The primary motivating factor for making Forth machines 16 bits wide is that the Forth programming model has traditionally been 16 bits. This is consistent with average Forth program sizes of less than 32K bytes and the implementation of most of the first Forth compilers on microprocessors with 64K byte address ranges.

4.1.2 Smallest interesting width

A major reason that Forth has historically been a 16-bit language is that 8 bits is too small for general-purpose computations and addressing data structures. While 12 bits was tried in some of the earliest minicomputers, 16 bits seems to be the smallest integer size that is truly useful. Forth traditionally has not used more than a 16-bit computing model because it was developed before 32-bit microprocessors were available.

16-bit machines are capable of addressing 64K of memory, which for a stack machine is a rather large program memory. 16-Bit machines have single precision integers in the range of $-32\,768$ to $+32\,767$ which is large enough for most computations. Using double precision (32-bit integers), a 16-bit machine can represent integers in the range of $-2\,147\,483\,648$ to $+2\,147\,483\,647$, which is large enough for all but the most demanding applications.

Of course, a machine with a 4-bit or 8-bit data path can be made to emulate a 16-bit machine. The result is generally unsatisfactory performance, because an 8-bit machine can be expected to be about half as fast as a 16-bit machine when manipulating 16-bit data. Since the machines discussed in this chapter are all designed for high speed processing, all have 16-bit internal data paths.

4.1.3 Small size allows integrated embedded system

The three Forth chips discussed in this chapter (the M17, NC4016, and RTX 2000) are all targeted at the embedded applications market. Embedded applications require a small processor with a small amount of program memory to satisfy demanding power, weight, size, and cost considerations. A 16-bit processor is often a good compromise that provides higher levels of performance than an 8-bit processor, which probably would need to spend a lot of time synthesizing 16-bit arithmetic operations, and a 32-bit processor, which is overkill for many applications.

4.2 ARCHITECTURE OF THE WISC CPU/16

4.2.1 Introduction

The WISC Technologies CPU/16 was designed by this author as a very simple (in terms of TTL component count) stack machine with a good mixture of flexibility and speed. The WISC CPU/16 uses discrete MSI components throughout. It is a 16-bit machine that features a completely RAM-based microcode memory (writable control store) to allow full user programmability. The CPU/16 is implemented as a pair of printed circuit boards that plug into an IBM PC compatible computer as a coprocessor.

The name WISC comes from 'Writable Instruction Set Computer', although a more complete term for the technology used would be 'WISC/ Stack', since hardware stacks are an integral part of the design.

The primary purpose for developing the CPU/16 was to investigate technology and design alternatives before designing the RTX 32P described in Chapter 5. The resulting product is a reasonably fast processor in its own right, and has a very simple and uncluttered design. The original wire-wrapped prototype for the CPU/16 fitted onto a single IBM PC expansion card (13 inches by 4 inches) with 16K bytes of program memory. The use of RAM for microcode memory and the simple microinstruction format makes the processor useful as a teaching tool for computer design courses.

4.2.2 Block diagram

Fig. 4.1 is an architectural block diagram of the CPU/16.

The Data Stack and Return Stack are implemented as identical hardware stacks consisting of an 8-bit up/down counter (the Stack Pointer) feeding an address to a 256 by 16-bit memory. The stack pointers are readable and writable by the system to provide an efficient capability to access deeply buried stack elements.

The ALU section includes a standard multifunction ALU built from 74LS181 chips with a DHI register for holding intermediate results. By convention, the DHI register acts as a buffer for the top stack element. This means that the Data Stack Pointer actually addresses the element perceived by the programmer to be the second-to-top stack element. The result is that an operation on the top two stack elements, such as addition, can be performed in a single cycle, with the A side of the ALU reading the second stack element from the Data Stack and the B side of the ALU reading the top stack element from the Data Hi register.

There are no condition codes visible to machine language programs. Add-with-carry and other multiple precision operations are supported by microcoded instructions that push the carry flag onto the data stack as a logical value (0 for carry clear, -1 for carry set).

The DLO register acts as a temporary holding register for intermediate results within a single instruction. Both the DHI and the DLO registers are shift registers, connected to allow 32-bit shifting for multiplication and division.

The Program Counter is connected directly to the memory address bus. This allows fetching the next instruction in parallel with data operations in the rest of the system. Thus, the system can overlap data operations involving the ALU and the Data Stack with instruction-fetching operations. In order to save the program counter for subroutine call operations, the Program Counter Save register captures the program counter value before it is loaded with the subroutine starting address. The Program Counter Save register is then pushed onto the Return Stack during the subroutine calling process. During subroutine returns, the saved Program Counter value is

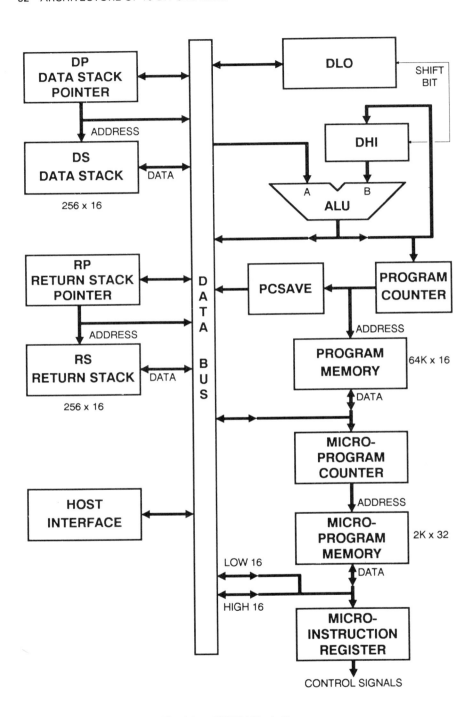

Fig. 4.1 — CPU/16 block diagram.

routed from the Return Stack through the ALU to add 1 before storing as
the new Program Counter value. This saves a Program Counter increment
that would otherwise cost a clock cycle.

Program memory is organized as 64K words of 16 bits. It is accessed on
word boundaries only, but a microcoded byte-swapping operation is supported to allow for manipulation of single-byte quantities.

Microprogram Memory is a read/write memory containing 2K elements
by 32 bits. The memory is addressed as 256 pages of 8 words each. The
Microprogram Counter supplies an 8-bit page address, and microprograms
execute within the 8-word page. This scheme allows supplying only 3 bits of
the next microprogram instruction from the microinstruction, one bit of
which is the result of a 1-in-8 conditional microbranch selection. This allows
conditional branching and looping during the execution of a single opcode.

Instruction decoding is accomplished simply by loading an 8-bit opcode
into the Microprogram Counter and using that as the page address to
Microprogram Memory. Since the Microprogram Counter is built with
counter hardware, operations can span more than one 8-microinstruction
page if required.

The Microinstruction Register holds the output of the Microprogram
Memory, forming a 1-stage pipeline. This pipeline allows the next microinstruction to be accessed from Microprogram Memory in parallel with
execution of the current microinstruction. This completely removes the
delay of Microprogram Memory access time from the system's critical path.
It also enforces a lower limit of two clock cycles on instructions. If an
instruction only requires a single clock cycle, a second no-op microinstruction must be added to allow the next instruction to flow through the pipeline
properly.

The Host interface block allows the CPU/16 to operate in two possible
modes: Master Mode and Slave Mode. In Slave Mode, the CPU/16 is
controlled by the personal computer host to allow program loading, microprogram loading, and alteration of any register or memory location on the
system for initialization or debugging. In Master Mode, the CPU/16 runs its
program freely, while the host computer monitors a status register for a
request for service. While the CPU/16 is in master mode, the host computer
may enter a dedicated service loop. Alternatively, the host computer may
perform other tasks, such as prefetching the next block of a disk input stream
or displaying an image, and only periodically poll the status register. The
CPU/16 will wait for service from the host for as long as is necessary.

4.2.3   Instruction set summary

The CPU/16 has two instruction formats: one for invoking microcoded
opcodes and one for subroutine calls.

Fig. 4.2(a) shows the operation instruction format used to invoke
microcoded instructions. Since 256 possible opcodes are supported by the
256 pages of Microcode Memory, only 8 bits of each instruction are needed
to specify the opcode. This results in an instruction format for a microcoded
opcode which has the highest 8 bits set to ones. This allows the subroutine

(a)

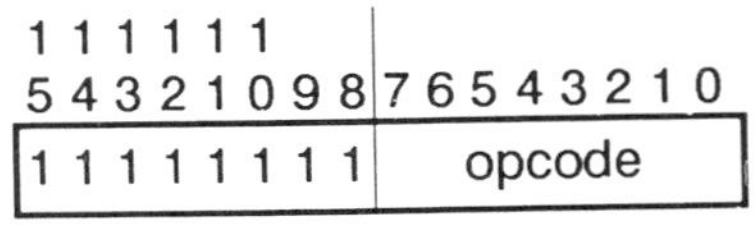

```
1 1 1 1 1 1
5 4 3 2 1 0 9 8 7 6 5 4 3 2 1 0
┌─────────────────┬──────────────┐
│ 1 1 1 1 1 1 1 1 │    opcode     │
└─────────────────┴──────────────┘
```

Bits   Function
8-15   All 1, specifying an operation instruction
0-7   Opcode

(b)

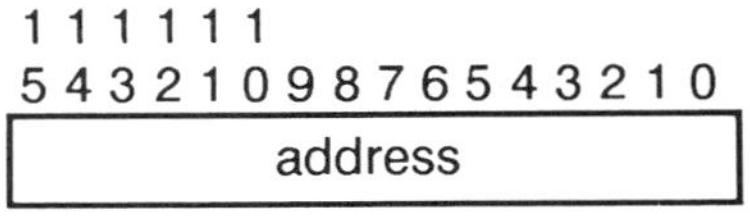

```
1 1 1 1 1 1
5 4 3 2 1 0 9 8 7 6 5 4 3 2 1 0
┌──────────────────────────────┐
│            address            │
└──────────────────────────────┘
```

Bits   Function
0-15   Subroutine address
       Note that bits 8-15 of the address must not all be 1

Fig. 4.2 — CPU/16 instruction formats. (a) Operation. (b) Subroutine call.

call format, shown in Fig. 4.2(b), to be any address that does not have all 8 highest bits set to 1. The strategy eliminates the constraint of 15-bit subroutine addresses found on the other designs in this chapter. A disadvantage of this strategy is that parameters for instructions cannot be contained in the instruction word. As a consequence, targets for conditional branches are stored in the memory word after the instruction, as opposed to a small offset within the instruction. This design tradeoff was made in the interest of minimizing the amount of instruction decoding logic used.

Since the CPU/16 uses RAM chips for the microcode memory, the microcode may be completely changed by the user if desired. The standard software environment for the CPU/16 is MVP-FORTH, a FORTH-79 dialect (Haydon 1983). Some of the Forth instructions included in the standard microcoded instruction set are shown in Table 4.1. Of course, other software environments are possible, but none except Forth has been implemented.

One thing that is noticeable in this instruction set is the diversity of instructions supported. The instructions in Table 4.1(a) are a very large set of Forth primitive operations. Table 4.1(b) shows some common Forth word combinations that are available as single instructions. Table 4.1(c) shows some words that are used to support underlying Forth operations such as subroutine call and exit. Table 4.1(d) lists some high level Forth words that use specialized microcode to speed up their execution. Table 4.1(e) shows words which were added to support extended precision integer operations and 32-bit floating point calculations.

Execution time of instructions varies according to the considerable range in complexity of the instructions. Simple instructions that manipulate data on the stack such as + and **SWAP** take 2 or 3 microcycles each. Complex instructions take more clock cycles (e.g. **Q+**, which is 64-bit addition, takes 18 cycles) but are still much faster than comparable high level code. If desired, microcoded loops can be written that can potentially last thousands of clock cycles for block memory moves and other repetitive operations.

As mentioned earlier, each instruction invokes a sequence of microinstructions on a Microprogram Memory page corresponding to the 8-bit opcode for the instruction. Fig. 4.3 shows the microcode format for a microinstruction. The microcode used is horizontal, which means that there is only one format for microcode which is broken into separate fields to control different portions of the machine.

Because of the simplicity of the stack machine approach and the CPU/16 hardware, only 32 bits are needed in each microinstruction. This 32-bit format can be contrasted with the microinstruction formats of 48 bits and wider found in other horizontally microcoded machines, such as any machine using the AMD 2900 series bit-slice components. This simplicity makes microprogramming not much harder than assembly language programming on a conventional machine.

As an example, the pseudocode description for the addition operation on the Canonical Stack Machine was:

$$TOSREG \Leftarrow TOSREG + POP(DS)$$

The same operation in CPU/16 microcode would be written as the microinstruction:

$$SOURCE=DS \quad ALU=A+B \quad DEST=DHI \quad INC[DP]$$

Where the microoperation $SOURCE=DS$ routes the current top element of the hardware Data Stack onto the Data Bus, $ALU=A+B$ directs to ALU to add the A input (from the Data Bus) and the B input (the top-of-stack element buffered in DHI), and $DEST=DHI$ deposits the result back into the Data Hi register. Meanwhile, the $INC[DP]$ microoperation increments the Data Stack Pointer after the Data Stack has been read, thus popping the stack.

4.2.4 Architectural features

The CPU/16 is very similar to the Canonical Stack Machine. This probably has a lot to do with the fact that both were designed by this author, and the major goal for both the Canonical Stack Machine and the CPU/16 is simplicity.

The major efficiency improvement of the CPU/16 over the Canonical Stack Machine is the replacement of the Memory Address Register with the Program Counter. This has the advantage of allowing the next instruction to be fetched without tying up the data bus, so that stack computations can be overlapped with instruction fetches. A disadvantage of this technique is that the @ and ! operations require overwriting the Program Counter with the

Table 4.1 —CPU/16 instruction set summary

4.1(a) Forth primitives:(see Appendix B for descriptions)

!	DDROP
+	DDUP
+!	DNEGATE
−	DROP
0	DSWAP
0>	DUP
0=	I
0BRANCH	I'
1+	J
1−	LEAVE
2*	LIT
2/	NEGATE
>	NOP
PICK	NOT
ROLL	OR
=	OVER
>R	R>
?DUP	R@
@	ROT
ABS	S−>D
AND	SWAP
BRANCH	U*
D!	U/MOD
D+	XOR
D@	

4.1(b) Compound Forth primitives

@+	
@−	
DROP ;	
DROP DUP	
I +	
I + @	
OVER +	
OVER −	
R> DROP	
R> SWAP >R	
SWAP −	
SWAP DROP	
DUP @ SWAP 1+	(fetch & increment address)
DUP ROT ROT ! 1−	(store & decrement address)
@ @	(indirect fetch)
@ !	(indirect store)
DUP @ @ 1 ROT +!	(auto-postincrement indirect fetch for software stack)
−1 OVER +! @ !	(auto-predecrement indirect store for software stack)

Table 4.1 – Continued.

4.1(c) Special words

Opcode	Data stack	Return stack
DOCOL	→	→ADDR
Performs a subroutine call		
SEMIS	→	ADDR→
Performs a subroutine return		
HALT	→	→
Returns control to host processor		
SYSCALL	N→	→
Requests I/O service number N from host		
DOVAR	→ADDR	→
Used to implement Forth variables		
DOCON	→N	→
Used to implement Forth constants		

4.1(d) Support words for high level operations

The following Forth operations have microcoded support words for inner loops or the run-time action:

SP@	(fetch contents of data stack pointer)
SP!	(initialize data stack pointer)
RP@	(fetch contents of return stack pointer)
RP!	(initialize return stack pointer)
MATCH	(string compare primitive)
ABORT″	(error checking & reporting word)
+LOOP	(variable increment loop)
/LOOP	(variable unsigned increment loop)
CMOVE	(string move)
<CMOVE	(reverse order string move)
DO	(loop initialization)
ENCLOSE	(text parsing primitive)
LOOP	(increment by 1 loop)
FILL	(block memory initialization word)
TOGGLE	(bit mask/set primitive)

4.1(e) Extended math & floating point support words

Opcode	Data stack	Return stack
<UDNORM>	EXP1 UD2 → EXP2 UD4	→
Floating point normalize of unsigned 32-bit mantissa		
ADC	N1 N2 CIN → N3 COUT	→
Add with carry. CIN and COUT are logical flags on the stack.		
ASR	N1 → N2	→
Arithmetic shift right.		

Table 4.1 – Continued.

Opcode	Data stack	Return stack
BYTESWAP	N1 → N2	→
Swap high and low bytes within N1.		
D+!	D ADDR →	→
Sum D into 32-bit number at ADDR.		
D>R	D →	→D
Move D to return stack.		
DLSLN	D1 N2 → D3	→
Logical shift left of D1 by N2 bits.		
DLSR	D1 → 2 D2	→
Logical shift right of D1 by 1 bit.		
DLSRN	D1 N2 → D3	→
Logical shift right of D1 by N2 bits.		
DR>	→ D	D→
Move D from return stack to data stack.		
DROT	D1 D2 D3 → D2 D3 D1	→
Perform double precision ROT.		
LSLN	N1 N2 → N3	→
Logical shift left of N1 by N2 bits.		
LSR	N1 → N2	→
Logical shift right of N1 by 1 bit.		
LSRN	N1 N2 → N3	→
Logical shift right of N1 by N2 bits.		
Q+	Q1 Q2 → Q3	→
64-bit addition.		
QLSL	Q1 → Q2	→
Logical shift left of Q1 by 1 bit.		
RLC	N1 CIN → N2 COUT	→
Rotate left through carry N1 by 1 bit. CIN is carry-in; COUT is carry-out.		
RRC	N1 CIN → N2 COUT	→
Rotate right through carry N1 by 1 bit. CIN is carry-in; COUT is carry-out.		
TDUP	D1 N2 → D1 N2 D1 N2	→
Duplicate a temporary floating point number (32-bit mantissa, 16-bit integer).		

Note: The CPU/16 uses RAM microcode memory, so the user may add or modify any instructions desired. The above list merely indicates the instructions supplied with the standard development software package.

memory address, then restoring the Program Counter with the contents of the Program Counter Save register. Obviously the program counter and a memory address register (or the DHI register) could be multiplexed onto the RAM Address bus, but this would introduce added complexity and components.

The DLO register was added to the design primarily to provide for efficient 32-bit shifting to support multiplication and division. However, the presence of an intermediate storage register measurably improves performance, because four intermediate results are available at any one time (DHI, DLO, Data Stack, and a temporary result pushed onto the Return Stack). For example, the DLO register is used as the intermediate storage location for the **SWAP** operation, which is conceptually cleaner than using the Return Stack for this purpose.

An important implementation feature of the CPU/16 is that all resources on the machine can be directly controlled by the host computer. This can be done because the host interface supports Microinstruction Register load and single-step clock features. With these features, any microinstruction desired can be executed by first loading values into any or all registers in the system, loading a microinstruction, cycling the clock, then reading data values back to examine the results. This design technique makes writing microcode extremely straightforward and avoids the need for expensive microcode development support hardware. It also makes diagnostic programs very simple to write.

The CPU/16 is not designed to handle interrupts.

4.2.5 Implementation and featured application areas

The CPU/16 is constructed using conservative (some might even say obsolete) 74LS00 series chips and relatively slow 150 ns static RAMs for stack and program memories. The design priorities for the CPU/16 are, in decreasing order of importance: simplicity, minimum design & development costs, compactness, flexibility, and speed. The CPU/16 clock cycle time is 280 ns, with an average of three clock cycles per instruction.

Discrete components were chosen because they are inexpensive and require little initial development investment when compared to a single-chip gate array. Discrete component designs are also much easier and cheaper to change for bug extermination and design upgrades. This is in keeping with the philosophy of a design exploration project. It also results in a much slower processor than could be produced using a single-chip design. Even so, at the time of its introduction, the CPU/16 was speed competitive with the slower versions of the Novix NC4016 (the leading stack machine of the time) when running many application programs.

In order to allow increased flexibility and to limit the required microinstruction width, the CPU/16 uses discrete ALU chips (74LS181) instead of bit-sliced components. The primary application area is general-purpose stack processing as a coprocessor for IBM PC family of personal computers. While the redefinable instruction set makes the machine suitable for most languages, the primary application language is Forth.

An additional application area that is attractive is that of a teaching aid in computer architecture courses. Since the machine is constructed using less than 100 simple TTL chips including memory, a student can readily understand the design. An additional result of using discrete component technology is that all signals in the system are accessible with external

```
3 3 2 2 2 2 2 2 2 2 2 2 1 1 1 1 1 1 1 1 1 1
1 0 9 8 7 6 5 4 3 2 1 0 9 8 7 6 5 4 3 2 1 0 9 8 7 6 5 4 3 2 1 0
e c s cond nxt m d p dhi dlo rp  dp    alu      dest  source
```

Bits Function

31   Execute next macroinstruction when 0

30   ALU carry in

29   Shift input for ALU/DLO shifters

26-28   Condition code select for bit 0 of next microaddress
   000 Always 0   011 DLO lowest bit   110 ALU equal to 0 bit
   001 ALU carry out   100 DHI lowest bit   111 Always 1
   010 DHI highest bit   101 ALU sign bit

24-25   Bits 1 and 2 of next microaddress

23   Increment MPC when 0

22   Fetch and start decode of next macroinstruction when 0

21   Increment the PC when 0

19-20   DHI shift control
   00 Load DHI from ALU   10 DHI shift right   11 nop
   01 DHI shift left

17-18   DLO shift control
   00 Load DLO from bus   10 DLO shift right   11 nop
   01 DLO shift left

15-16   RP increment/decrement
   00 Decrement RP   01 Increment RP   11 nop

13-14   DP increment/decrement
   00 Decrement DP   01 Increment DP   11 nop

8-12   ALU function select (not all functions are useful)
   00000 A + CIN   10001 A nor B   11010 B
   00110 A - B - not(CIN) 10011 0   11011 A and B
   01001 A + B + CIN   10100 A nand B   11100 -1
   01100 A + A + CIN   10101 not B   11110 A or B
   01111 A - not(CIN)   10110 A xor B   11111 A
   10000 not A   11001 A xnor B

4-7   Bus destination select
   0000 none   0101 PC   1010 MPC
   0001 DP   0110 RAM   1011 MRAM low 16 bits
   0010 DS   0111 DLO   1100 MRAM high 16 bits
   0011 RP   1000 DHI
   0100 RS   1001 Status register

0-3   Bus source select
   0000 none   0100 RS   1011 MRAM low 16 bits
   0001 DP   0101 PCSAVE   1100 MRAM high 16 bits
   0010 DS   0110 RAM   1111 ALU output
   0011 RP   0111 DLO

Fig. 4.3 — CPU/16 microinstruction format.

probes, making the system suitable for experimentation by students learning how hardware, software, and microcode interact.

The information in this section is derived from the CPU/16 Technical Reference Manual (Koopman 1986). Additional information about the CPU/16 may be found in Haydon & Koopman (1986) and Koopman & Haydon (1986). Also, Koopman (1987b) describes a conceptual WISC architecture that is extremely similar to the CPU/16.

4.3   ARCHITECTURE OF THE MISC M17

4.3.1   Introduction

The MISC M17 microprocessor was designed by Minimum Instruction Set Computer, Inc., as a low cost, embedded microprocessor. In order to achieve low system cost, the M17 keeps its two stacks in program memory with a few top-of-stack buffer registers on the chip. Other design tradeoffs have been made to keep both chip production costs and total system costs low, while maintaining reasonably high system performance.

The MISC M17 is aimed at high volume embedded control applications where a low cost processor chip with reasonably high performance (compared to other stack machines — very high performance when compared to standard microcontrollers) is required.

4.3.2   Block diagram

Fig. 4.4 shows the block diagram of the M17.

Both the Data Stack and the Return Stack reside in program memory, with the top elements of each held in on-chip registers for speed. The X, Y, and Z registers hold the top three elements of the data stack, with X being the top element. These registers are connected with multiplexers so that values can be transferred between registers in a single clock cycle. Simultaneously, the Z register can be read from or written to the portion of the stack resident in program memory. Thus, a Data Stack popping operation (Forth **DROP** operation) is accomplished by simultaneously reading Z from memory, copying Z to Y, and copying Y to X. Similarly, a Data Stack pushing operation (such as the Forth **DUP** operation) is accomplished by copying X to Y while retaining the old value of X, copying Y to Z, and writing Z to program memory.

The LASTX register can be updated with the contents of the X register on each instruction cycle. It therefore contains the top-of-stack value that was overwritten by the previous instruction, which is useful for many instruction sequences.

The ALU on the M17 is designed to generate all possible ALU functions simultaneously, only at the last moment selecting the correct function output for writing back to the X and/or Y registers. This technique allows the ALU delay to overlap the instruction decoding time, since once the instruction is decoded its only task is to select the correct ALU output from the functions already computed.

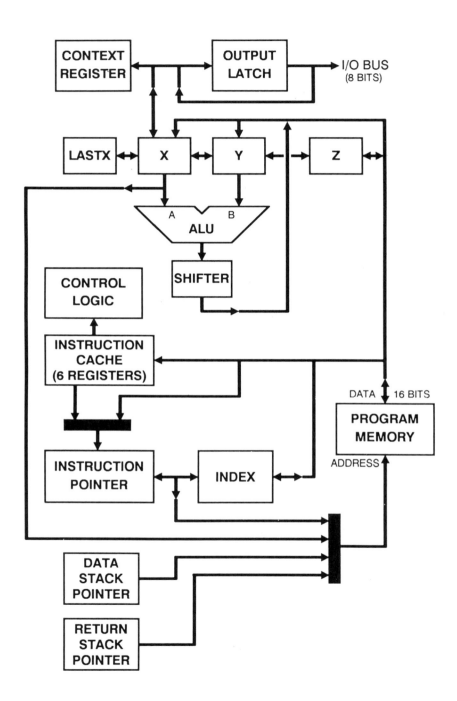

Fig. 4.4 — M17 block diagram.

The M17 has an 8-bit I/O bus that allows concurrent operations in the ALU while performing data transfers. This feature, found on all the 16-bit single-chip Forth machines discussed here, allows high speed I/O without tying up the memory data bus.

The Return Stack is kept in program memory, just as the Data Stack is. The top element of the Return Stack is buffered in the INDEX register. The INDEX register doubles as a count-down counter for use in program loops and the instruction repeat feature.

The Instruction Pointer is a conventional program counter that can be loaded from the Instruction Register for subroutine calls, from the memory data bus for branches, or from the INDEX register for subroutine returns. The INDEX register can also be loaded from the Instruction Pointer to save the return address for subroutine calls.

The Return Stack Pointer is an up/down counter that contains the memory address of the top element of the return stack resident in program memory (which is actually the second-from-top element visible to the programmer, since the INDEX register contains the top element). Similarly, the Data Stack Pointer points to the top data stack element resident in program memory, which is actually the fourth element on the stack since the top three elements are buffered in X, Y, and Z. The data stack grows from high memory locations to low memory locations. The return stack grows up from low memory locations to high memory. With this arrangement, the free space between the top of the data stack and top of return stack can be shared for more efficient use of memory space.

The M17 directly addresses five segments of up to 64K words of 16-bit-wide memory. Byte swapping, byte packing, and byte unpacking instructions are available to allow access to 8-bit quantities. The M17 provides five signal pins to indicate which memory space is active: data stack, return stack, code space, A buffer, and B buffer. The activated pin indicates which address space is being used by the address bus. In simple systems, these pins can be ignored. For somewhat larger systems, each pin can control its own memory chips, providing five independent banks of 64K words of memory. Using a companion memory controller chip, up to 16M words of memory can be addressed.

The M17 takes two clock cycles for each instruction: one clock cycle to load the instruction from program memory, and another clock cycle to perform the operation while doing a read from or write to one of the stacks in program memory. By performing two-cycle instruction execution, the memory bus is kept continuously busy, and simple systems can operate with only two 8-bit memory packages.

The M17 also has six instruction cache registers. These registers form a short history buffer that retains sequences of consecutive instructions as they are executed. If a repeat sequence is triggered with a special instruction, from one to six of these retained instructions are formed into a loop and repeated until an exit condition is true. The loop executes at one clock cycle per instruction instead of two on the second and subsequent iterations, since instructions do not need to be fetched from memory. In order to simplify the interrupt and control logic, these loops are required to be properly aligned within an address range evenly divisible by 8. The sequence is interruptible, but the interrupt service routine is responsible for saving a special flag if it intends to use a repeat sequence itself.

A final feature of the M17 is that it can support variable length clock cycles by using an asynchronous memory interface. In the asynchronous mode of operation, the M17 provides a memory request signal for each memory cycle. The responding memory device is responsible for asserting a device-ready signal when its data is valid. This handshaking process actually eliminates the need for an oscillator, and results in asynchronous operation of the system. One advantage of this scheme is that different speed memory devices may be used with different device-ready delays to avoid wasting memory bandwidth. Another advantage is that a very short delay can be provided for clock cycles that do not address memory, allowing internal operation cycles to proceed faster than memory reference cycles. In extremely cost sensitive applications, an ordinary clock oscillator can be used to run the entire system.

4.3.3   Instruction set summary

Fig. 4.5 shows the instruction formats for the M17. Instructions are accomplished in two clock cycles: one for the instruction fetch, and one for the operation and stack memory access. All of the Canonical Stack Machine's primitive operations listed in Table 3.1 can be executed in a single instruction cycle (two clock cycles). The details of operation of some instructions are slightly different on the M17 to accomplish single-instruction-cycle execution. For example, a memory store operation does not pop the data and address from the stack because this would require two additional memory transactions.

Fig. 4.5(a) shows the subroutine call instruction. A subroutine call is made by using the address of the subroutine (which must be an even address) as the instruction. The zero in bit 0 of the instruction designates a subroutine call. This forces subroutines to start on even memory locations, but allows code to span the entire 64K words of address space.

The M17 has three conditional instructions: SET, RETURN, and JUMP. Fig. 4.5(b) shows the format of a generic conditional instruction. Bits 6–15 indicate which conditions are selected as inputs into a logical OR condition evaluation function. For example, if bits 15 and 13 are set, a 'less than or equal to zero' condition is selected. When bit 5 is set, it causes a logical inversion of the condition value. For example, if bits 15, 13, and 5 are set, a 'greater than zero' condition is selected. Bit 4 controls the INDEX register and its function. For RETURN, it allows programmer control of the return stack drop. For SET and JUMP it selects a test for zero and decrement INDEX step. In this way many useful conditions based on the data in X, Y, Z, or INDEX can be created in one instruction step.

It is important to note that conditional instructions in the M17 do not

(a)

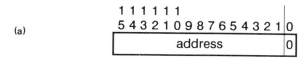

Bits Function

1-15 Subroutine address, aligned on an even byte

   0 Constant value of 0

(b)

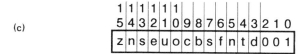

Bits Function

 15 Condition select: X = 0

 14 Condition select: X = -1

 13 Condition select: sign bit of X

 12 Condition select: X = Y

 11 Condition select: X - Y underflows

 10 Condition select: X + Y overflows

  9 Condition select: carry out of X + Y

  8 Condition select: borrow in of X - Y

  7 Condition select: sign bit of Z

  6 Condition select: user flag value

  5 Invert value of ORed condition result

  4 Test INDEX for 0 with decrement

2-3 Conditional instruction select
     00 Set instruction   11 Conditional jump
     01 Conditional return

0-1 Constant 01 specifies conditional instruction

(c)

1 1 1 1 1 1
5 4 3 2 1 0 9 8 7 6 5 4 3 2 1 0

| z | n | s | e | u | o | c | b | s | f | n | t | d | 0 | 0 | 1 |

Bits Function

5-15 Condition selection as shown in Figure 4.5b

  4 Test INDEX for 0 with decrement

  3 Pop data stack

0-2 Constant 001 specifies set user flag instruction

Fig. 4.5 — M17 instruction formats. (a) Subroutine call. (b) Conditional instruction
template. (c) Set user flag.

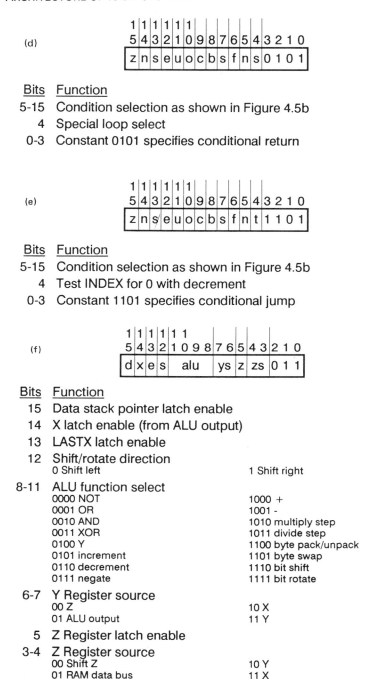

(d)

1	1	1	1	1	1										
5	4	3	2	1	0	9	8	7	6	5	4	3	2	1	0
z	n	s	e	u	o	c	b	s	f	n	s	0	1	0	1

Bits Function

5-15 Condition selection as shown in Figure 4.5b

4 Special loop select

0-3 Constant 0101 specifies conditional return

(e)

1	1	1	1	1	1										
5	4	3	2	1	0	9	8	7	6	5	4	3	2	1	0
z	n	s	e	u	o	c	b	s	f	n	t	1	1	0	1

Bits Function

5-15 Condition selection as shown in Figure 4.5b

4 Test INDEX for 0 with decrement

0-3 Constant 1101 specifies conditional jump

(f)

1	1	1	1	1	1										
5	4	3	2	1	0	9	8	7	6	5	4	3	2	1	0
d	x	e	s		alu			ys		z	zs		0	1	1

Bits Function

15 Data stack pointer latch enable

14 X latch enable (from ALU output)

13 LASTX latch enable

12 Shift/rotate direction
    0 Shift left   1 Shift right

8-11 ALU function select
      0000 NOT   1000 +
      0001 OR   1001 -
      0010 AND   1010 multiply step
      0011 XOR   1011 divide step
      0100 Y   1100 byte pack/unpack
      0101 increment   1101 byte swap
      0110 decrement   1110 bit shift
      0111 negate   1111 bit rotate

6-7 Y Register source
     00 Z   10 X
     01 ALU output   11 Y

5 Z Register latch enable

3-4 Z Register source
     00 Shift Z   10 Y
     01 RAM data bus   11 X

0-2 Constant 011 specifies process instruction

Fig. 4.5 — M17 instruction formats. (d) Conditional return. (e) Conditional jump.
(f) Process.

(g)

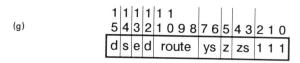

Bits Function
  15 Data stack address
  14 Source latch enable
  13 LASTX latch enable
  12 Destination latch control
      0 Read   1 Write
8-11 Routing function select
      0000 Read = 0/Write = intr enable   1000 Bias [(RSP) < -- > X]
      0001 I/O data (lower byte)   1001 INDEX < -- > X
      0010 Return Stack Pointer   1010 Literal
      0011 Read = remndr/Write = intr disable 1011 Reserved
      0100 Z   1100 X addr, Y data, RS seg
      0101 Data stack pointer   1101 X addr, Y data, DS seg
      0110 Context register   1110 X addr, Y data, A seg
      0111 LASTX   1111 X addr, Y data, B seg
 6-7 Y Register source
      00 Z   10 X
      01 ALU output   11 Y
   5 Z Register latch enable
 3-4 Z Register source
      00 Shift Z   10 Y
      01 RAM data bus   11 X
 0-2 Constant 111 specifies access instruction

Fig. 4.5 — M17 instruction formats. (g) Access.

change the data on the stack. They simply extract a condition code value from the data in the system and perform a conditional operation. For example, selecting the carry out condition (bit 9) will give a carry bit as if X and Y were added, but does not actually modify the contents of either X or Y. The results of the conditional evaluation are not retained unless the SET instruction is used.

Fig. 4.5(c) shows the format of the SET conditional instruction. This instruction sets the User Flag, which may be thought of as a conventional condition code register, with the value of the condition code selected by bits 4–15. The User Flag can be tested by other instructions in the program for later branching. Bit 3 specifies whether the top stack element is to be popped (equivalent to a Forth **DROP** operation) after the evaluation is performed.

Fig. 4.5(d) shows the format of the conditional subroutine RETURN instruction. When bit 4 is 0, the instruction performs as a conditional subroutine return, performing the return and popping the return address from the Return Stack (resident in the INDEX register) only if the condition evaluates as true. When bit 4 is set to 1, the branch to the address at the top of the Return Stack is still made, but the return stack is only popped if the condition is false. This is a convenient way of implementing a BEGIN... UNTIL_FALSE conditional control structure that stores the start address of the loop in INDEX and uses data stack conditions for determining when to terminate.

A conditional JUMP instruction is shown in Fig. 4.5(e). This instruction evaluates the specified condition and jumps if it is true. The destination address is stored at the memory location after the JUMP instruction. If the jump condition is false, the M17 skips the jump destination value and executes the instruction in the next memory location (the second word after the JUMP instruction). The JUMP instruction can be used to implement a countdown loop using the INDEX register by setting bit 4 to 1.

Fig. 4.5(f) shows the PROCESS instruction format. This instruction has several independent control fields, reminiscent of the horizontal microcode format seen in the CPU/16. Bits 3–5 specify control for the Z register, bits 6–7 for the Y register, bit 13 for the LASTX register, and bit 14 for the X register. Additionally, bits 8–12 select the ALU/shifter function to be performed, with the results loaded into the X or Y register. Finally, bit 15 can cause the Data Stack Pointer to be updated by the instruction.

Fig. 4.5(g) shows the ACCESS instruction format. This instruction has a very similar format to the PROCESS instruction. The major difference is that bits 8–11 specify a source or a source/destination pair for routing data around the processor. Bits 12 and 14 control the updating of the source and destination registers, allowing exchanges between internal registers.

The M17 handles interrupts as a hardware-forced subroutine call to memory address 0. Another address can be supplied by the interrupting device. It also has a context register which allows saving the state of the processor when receiving an interrupt.

4.3.4 Architectural features

The biggest difference between the M17 and the Canonical Stack Machine described in Chapter 3 is that the M17's stack memory and program memory accesses use the same bus, and may reside in the same memory chips. In order to maintain a reasonably high level of performance, the M17 buffers the top three Data Stack elements and the top Return Stack element in internal registers.

In contrast to the single internal bus used by the Canonical Stack Machine, the M17 provides a rich interconnect structure between registers. These interconnects not only allow moving data along the LASTX/X/Y/Z register chain to perform pushes and pops, but also allow routing to perform fairly complex stack manipulations within a single decode/execute clock cycle pair.

Since stacks are kept in program memory, a multiplexer is used to select the address to be fed to program memory. An advantage of placing stacks in program memory is that the amount of information that must be saved from the chip on a context swap is quite low. Instead of copying the elements of an on-chip stack into a holding area of main memory, the top-of-stack registers can be flushed to memory and the stack pointers redirected to point to a different memory block to activate a new task.

4.3.5   Implementation and featured application areas

The M17 is implemented using 6600 gates on 2.0 micron HCMOS gate array technology, packaged in a 68-pin Plastic Leadless Chip Carrier (PLCC). This technology choice is meant to keep development and production costs low while providing reasonably high performance. The main off-chip components required for operation are a 16-bit-wide bank of memory to hold the program and stacks.

The maximum clock speed on the M17 is approximately 15 MHz using 30 ns static RAMs, and 6 MHz using 120 ns static RAMs. Each instruction takes two clock cycles. Sequences stored in the six-element instruction cache execute at the rate of one clock cycle per instruction.

Several features of the MISC M17 are directed to the designer of small volume, high performance products. Example applications include remote sensing for smoke stacks, mines, hazardous areas, and remote equipment installations. The decision to place stacks in program memory results in lower system cost and complexity. The asynchronous memory bus protocol allows coupling high speed processing and data transmission operations without complicating the interface to low speed data acquisition devices.

The information in this section is derived from the MISC M17 Technical Reference Manual (MISC 1988).

4.4   ARCHITECTURE OF THE NOVIX NC4016

4.4.1   Introduction

The Novix NC4016, formerly called the NC4000, is a 16-bit stack-based microprocessor designed to execute primitives of the Forth programming language. It was the first single-chip Forth computer to be built, and originated many of the features found on subsequent designs. Intended applications are real-time control and high speed execution of the Forth language for general-purpose programming.

The NC4016 uses dedicated off-chip stack memories for the Data Stack and the Return Stack. Since three separate groups of pins connect the two stacks and the RAM data bus to the NC4016, it can execute most instructions in a single clock cycle.

4.4.2   Block diagram

Fig. 4.6 shows the block diagram of the NC4016.

The ALU section contains a 2-element buffer for the top elements of the data stack (T for Top data stack element, and N (Next) for the second-from-top data stack element). It also contains a special MD register for support of multiplication and division as well as an SR register for fast integer square roots. The ALU may perform operations on the T register and any one of the N, MD, or SR registers.

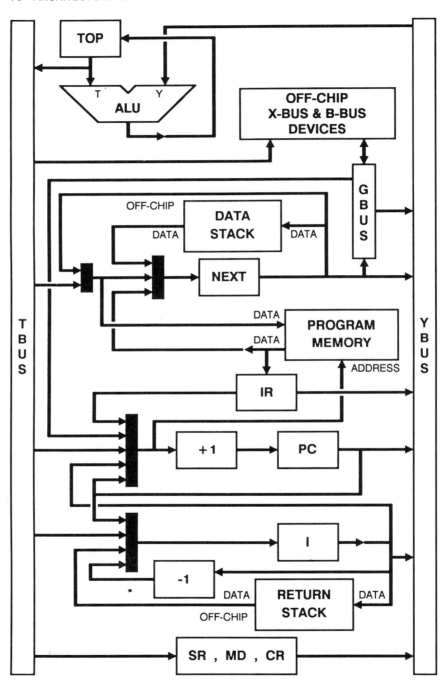

Fig. 4.6 — NC4016 block diagram.

The Data Stack is an off-chip memory holding 256 elements. The data stack pointer is on-chip and provides a stack address to the off-chip memory. A separate 16-bit stack data bus allows the Data Stack to be read or written in parallel with other operations. As noted previously, the top two Data Stack elements are buffered by the T and N registers in the ALU.

The Return Stack is a separate memory that is very similar to the Data Stack, with the exception that only the top return stack element is buffered on-chip, in the Index register. Since Forth keeps loop counters as well as subroutine return addresses on the return stack, the Index register can be decremented to implement countdown loops efficiently.

The stacks do not have on-chip underflow or overflow protection. In a multitasking environment, an off-chip stack page register can be controlled using the I/O ports to give each task a separate piece of a larger than 256-word stack memory. This gives hardware protection to avoid one task overwriting another task's stack, and reduces context swapping overhead to a minimum.

The Program Counter points to the location of the next instruction to be fetched from external program memory. It is automatically altered by the jump, loop, and subroutine call instructions. Program memory is arranged in 16-bit words. Byte addressing is not directly supported.

The NC4016 also has two I/O busses leading off-chip on dedicated pins. The B-port is a 16-bit I/O bus, and the X-port is a 5-bit I/O bus. The I/O ports allow direct access to I/O devices for control applications without stealing bandwidth from the memory bus. Some bits of the I/O ports can also be used to extend the program memory address space by providing high order memory address bits.

The NC4016 can use four separate 16-bit busses for data transfers on every clock cycle for high performance (program memory, Data Stack, Return Stack, and I/O busses).

4.4.3   Instruction set summary

The NC4016 pioneered the use of unencoded instruction formats for stack machines. In the NC4016 the ALU instruction is formatted in independent fields of bits that simultaneously control different parts of the machines, much like horizontal microcode. The NC4016, and many of its Forth processor successors, are the only 16-bit computers that use this technique. Using an unencoded instruction format allows simple hardware decoding of instructions. Fig. 4.7 shows the instruction formats for the NC4016.

Fig. 4.7(a) shows the instruction format for subroutine calls. In this format, the highest bit of the instruction is set to 0, and the remainder of the instruction is used to hold a 15-bit subroutine address. This limits programs to 32K words of memory.

Fig. 4.7(b) shows the conditional branch instruction format. Bits 12 and 13 select either a branch if T is zero, an unconditional branch, or a decrement and branch-if-zero using the index register for implementing loops. Bits 0–11 specify the lowest 12 bits of the target address, restricting

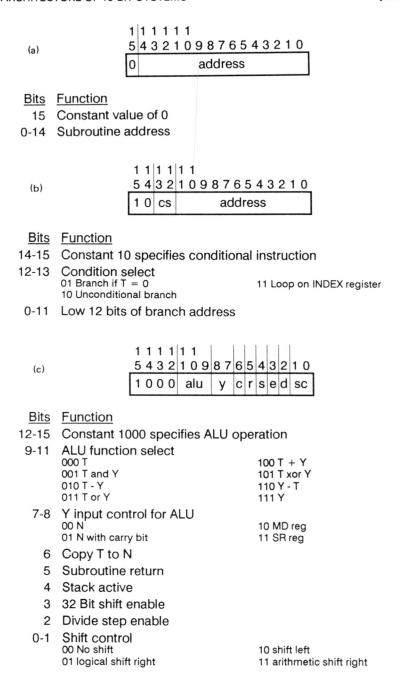

(a)

|1|1 1 1 1|
|5|4 3 2 1 0 9 8 7 6 5 4 3 2 1 0|

| 0 | address |

Bits Function
  15 Constant value of 0
0-14 Subroutine address

(b)

|1 1|1 1|1 1|
|5 4|3 2|1 0 9 8 7 6 5 4 3 2 1 0|

| 1 0 | cs | address |

Bits Function
14-15 Constant 10 specifies conditional instruction
12-13 Condition select
       01 Branch if T = 0   11 Loop on INDEX register
       10 Unconditional branch
 0-11 Low 12 bits of branch address

(c)

|1 1 1 1|1 1|
|5 4 3 2|1 0 9 8 7 6 5 4 3 2 1 0|

| 1 0 0 0 | alu | y | c | r | s | e | d | sc |

Bits Function
12-15 Constant 1000 specifies ALU operation
 9-11 ALU function select
       000 T   100 T + Y
       001 T and Y   101 T xor Y
       010 T - Y   110 Y - T
       011 T or Y   111 Y
  7-8 Y input control for ALU
       00 N   10 MD reg
       01 N with carry bit   11 SR reg
    6 Copy T to N
    5 Subroutine return
    4 Stack active
    3 32 Bit shift enable
    2 Divide step enable
  0-1 Shift control
       00 No shift   10 shift left
       01 logical shift right   11 arithmetic shift right

Fig. 4.7 — NC4016 instruction formats. (a) Subroutine call. (b) Conditional branch.
(c) ALU operation.

```
              1 1 1 1 1 1
(d)           5 4 3 2 1 0 9 8 7 6 5 4 3 2 1 0
              ┌─────────────────────────────────┐
              │ 1 1 1│w│ alu │ y │c│r│  const    │
              └─────────────────────────────────┘
```

Bits Function
13-15 Constant 111 specifies memory reference
12   Read/write control
      0 Read   1 Write
9-11 ALU function select
      000 T   100 T + Y
      001 T and Y   101 T xor Y
      010 T - Y   110 Y - T
      011 T or Y   111 Y
7-8   Y input control for ALU
      00 N   10 MD reg
      01 N with carry bit   11 SR reg
6   Copy T to N
5   Subroutine return
0-4   Auto-increment/decrement constant


```
              1 1 1 1 1 1
(e)           5 4 3 2 1 0 9 8 7 6 5 4 3 2 1 0
              ┌─────────────────────────────────┐
              │ 1 1 0│w│ alu │ y │c│r│  offset   │
              └─────────────────────────────────┘
```

Bits Function
13-15 Constant 110 specifies instruction format
12   Read/write control
      0 Read   1 Write
9-11 ALU function select
      000 T   100 T + Y
      001 T and Y   101 T xor Y
      010 T - Y   110 Y - T
      011 T or Y   111 Y
7-8   Y input control for ALU
      00 N   10 MD reg
      01 N with carry bit   11 SR reg
6   Copy T to N
5   Subroutine return
0-4   Offset within user space/short literal

Fig. 4.7 — NC4016 instruction formats. (d) Memory reference. (e) User space/register tranfer/literal.

the branch target to be in the same 4K byte block of memory as the branch instruction.

Fig. 4.7(c) shows the format of the ALU instruction. This instruction has several bit fields that control various resources on the chip. Bits 0 and 1 control the operation of the shifter at the ALU output. Bit 2 specifies a nonrestoring division cycle. Bit 3 enables shifting of the T and N registers connected as a 32-bit shift register.

Bit 5 of the ALU instruction indicates a subroutine return operation. This allows subroutine returns to be combined with preceding arithmetic operations to obtain 'free' subroutine returns in many cases.

Bit 6 specifies whether a stack push is to be accomplished. It, combined with bit 4, controls pushing and popping stack elements.

Bits 7 and 8 control the input select for the ALU as well as allow specify a step for iterative multiply or square root functions. Bits 9-11 specify the ALU function to be performed.

Fig. 4.7(d) shows the format of a memory reference instruction. These instructions take two clock cycles: one cycle for the instruction fetch, and one cycle for the actual reading or writing of the operand. The address for the memory access is always taken from the T register. Bit 12 indicates whether the operation is a memory read or write. Bits 0–4 specify a small constant that can be added or subtracted to the T value to perform autoincrement or autodecrement addressing functions. Bits 5–11 of this instruction specify ALU and control functions almost identical to those used in the ALU instruction format.

Fig. 4.7(e) shows the miscellaneous instruction format. This instruction can be used to read or write a 32-word 'user space' residing in the first 32 words of program memory, saving the time taken to push a memory address on the stack before performing the fetch or store. It can also be used to transfer values between registers within the chip, or push either a 5-bit literal (in a single clock cycle) or a 16-bit literal (in two clock cycles) onto the stack. Bits 5–11 of this instruction specify ALU and control functions very similar to those in the ALU instruction format.

The NC4016 is specifically designed to execute the Forth language. Because of the unencoded format of many of the instructions, machine operations that correspond to a sequence of Forth operations can be encoded in a single instruction. Table 4.2 shows the Forth primitives and instruction sequences supported by the NC4016.

4.4.4   Architectural features

The internal structure of the NC4016 is designed for single-clock-cycle instruction execution. All primitive operations except memory fetch, memory store, and long literal fetch execute in a single clock cycle. This requires many more on-chip interconnection paths than are present on the Canonical Stack Machine, but provides much better performance.

The NC4016 allows combining nonconflicting sequential operations into the same instruction. For example, a value can be fetched from memory and added to the top stack element using the sequence @+ in a Forth program. These operations can be combined into a single instruction on the NC4016.

The NC4016 subroutine return bit allows combining a subroutine return with other instructions in a similar manner. This results in most subroutine exit instructions executing 'for free' in combination with other instructions. An optimization that is performed by NC4016 compilers is tail-end recursion elimination. Tail-end recursion elimination involves replacing a subroutine call/subroutine exit instruction pair by an unconditional branch to the subroutine that would have been called.

Another innovation of the NC4016 is the mechanism to access the first 32 locations of program memory as global 'user' variables. This mechanism can ease problems associated with implementing high level languages by allowing key information for a task, such as the pointer to an auxiliary stack in main memory, to be kept in a rapidly accessible variable. It also allows reasonable performance using high level language compilers, which may have originally been developed for register machines, by allowing the 32 fast-access variables to be used to simulate a register set.

4.4.5 Implementation and featured application areas

The NC4016 is implemented using fewer than 4000 gates on a 3.0 micron HCMOS gate array technology, packaged in a 121-pin Pin Grid Array (PGA). The NC4016 runs at up to 8 MHz.

When the NC4016 was designed, gate array technology did not permit placing the stack memories on-chip. Therefore a minimum NC4016 system consists of three 16-bit memories: one for programs and data, one for the data stack, and one for the return stack.

Because the NC4016 executes most instructions, including conditional branches and subroutine calls, in a single cycle, there is a significant amount of time between the beginning of the clock cycle and the time that the memory address is valid for fetching the next instruction. This time is approximately half the clock cycle, meaning that program memory access time must be approximately twice as fast as the clock rate.

The NC4016 was originally designed as a proof-of-concept and prototype machine. It therefore has some inconveniences that can be largely overcome by software and external hardware. For example, the NC4016 was intended to handle interrupts, but a bug in the gate array design causes improper interrupt response. Novix has since published an application note showing how to use a 20-pin PAL to overcome this problem. A successor product will eliminate these implementation difficulties and add additional capabilities.

The NC4016 is aimed at the embedded control market. It delivers very high performance with a reasonably small system. Among the appropriate applications for the NC4016 are: laser printer control, graphics CRT display control, telecommunications control (T1 switches, facsimile controllers, etc.), local area network controllers, and optical character recognition.

The information in this section is derived from Golden *et al.* (1985), Miller (1987), Stephens & Watson (1985), and Novix's *Programmers' Introduction to the NC4016 Microprocessor* (Novix 1985).

Table 4.2 — NC4016 instruction set summary

4.2(a) Forth primitives (see Appendix B for descriptions)

: (subroutine call)	AND
; (subtroutine exit)	BRANCH
!	DROP
+	DUP
−	I
0	LIT
0<	NOP
0BRANCH	OR
1+	OVER
1−	R>
2*	R@
>R	SWAP
@	XOR

4.2(b) Compound Forth primitives

---

nn	@+
nn !	@ +c
nn +	@ −
nn +c	@ −c
nn −	@ SWAP −
nn −c	@ SWAP −c
nn @	@ OR
nn @ +	@ XOR
nn @ +c	@ AND
nn @ −	DROP DUP
nn @ −c	DUP nn !
nn @ AND	DUP nn ! +
nn @ SWAP −	DUP nn ! −
nn @ SWAP −c	DUP nn ! AND
nn @ OR	DUP nn ! OR
nn @ XOR	DUP nn ! SWAP −
nn AND	DUP nn ! XOR
nn I@	DUP nn I!
nn I@ +	DUP nn I! +
nn I@ −	DUP nn I! −
nn I@ AND	DUP nn I! AND
nn I@ OR	DUP nn I! OR
nn I@ SWAP −	DUP nn I! SWAP −
nn I@ XOR	DUP nn I! XOR
nn I@!	DUP @ SWAP nn +
nn I!	DUP @ SWAP nn −
nn OR	OVER +
nn SWAP −	OVER +c
nn SWAP −c	OVER −
nn XOR	OVER −c
lit +	OVER SWAP−
lit +c	OVER SWAP −c

Table 4.2 – Continued.

lit −	R> DROP
lit −c	R> SWAP >R
lit AND	SWAP −
lit OR	SWAP −c
lit SWAP −	SWAP DROP
lit SWAP −c	SWAP OVER !
lit XOR	SWAP OVER ! nn +
	SWAP OVER ! nn−

Notes: 'nn' represents a 5-bit literal or user offset value. 'lit' represents a 16-bit literal stored in the memory location after the instruction.

4.2(c) Special-purpose word

Instruction	Data stack	Return stack
nn I@	→ N	→
Fetch the value from internal register nn (stored as a 5-bit literal in the instruction).		
nn I!	N→	→
Store N into the internal register nn (stored as a 5-bit literal in the instruction)		
+c	N1 N2→ N3	→
Add with carry (using internal carry bit)		
−c	N1 N2→ N3	→
Subtract with borrow (using internal carry bit)		
*'	D1→ D2	→
Unsigned Multiply step (takes two 16-bit numbers and produces a 32 bit product).		
*−	D1→ D2	→
Signed Multiply step (takes two 16-bit numbers and produces a 32-bit product).		
*F	D1→ D2	→
Fractional Multiply step (takes two 16-bit fractions and produces a 32-bit product).		
*/'	D1→ D2	→
Divide step (takes a 16-bit dividend and divisor and produces 16-bit remainder and quotients).		
*/"	D1→ D2	→
Last Divide step (to perform nonrestoring division fixup).		
2/	N1→ N2	→
Arithmetic shift right (same as division by two for nonnegative integers.		
D2/	D1→ D2	→
32-bit arithmetic shift right (same as division by two for nonnegative integers.		
S'	D1→ D2	→
Square Root step.		
TIMES	→	N1 → N2
Count-down loop using top of return stack as a counter.		

4.5   ARCHITECTURE OF THE HARRIS RTX 2000

4.5.1   Introduction

The Harris Semiconductor RTX 2000 is a 16-bit stack processor that is a descendent of the Novix NC4016. The RTX 2000 has a very high level of integration. It includes not only the core processor, but also stack memories, a hardware multiplier, and counter/timers on a single chip.

4.5.2   Block diagram

Fig. 4.8 shows the block diagram of the RTX 2000. The major difference between the RTX 2000 and the NC4016 are the on-chip resources in addition to the CPU core. These resources include: a 256-element return stack, 256-element data stack, 16×16-bit single-cycle hardware multiplier, three counter/timers, and a prioritized vectored interrupt controller. Apart from the on-chip stacks, all the RTX 2000's extra features are accessed via the I/O bus (called the G bus in the NC4016 and the ASIC Bus in the RTX 2000).

Other enhancements to the original Novix design available in the RTX 2000 include: a byte swapping capability for manipulation of 8-bit data, the ability to jump between adjacent memory blocks when performing conditional branches, and interrupt on stack overflow/underflow.

Another feature of the RTX 2000 is the on-chip memory page controller logic. This allows extending the 32K word program memory limit by specifying separate page registers for the code segment, the data segment (for fetches and stores), the user memory base address and page registers (for relocating the user variable area), and the index page register (for extending the value of the Return Stack address). Since the Return Stack holds a full 21 bits, subroutine calls can be made anywhere in memory with a special far call instruction sequence that saves the full return address in a single Return Stack location.

4.5.3   Instruction set summary

The instructions of the RTX 2000 are quite similar in function to those of the NC4016, but are sufficiently different in format to merit a separate description. Fig. 4.9 shows the instruction formats for the RTX 2000.

Fig. 4.9(a) shows the instruction format for subroutine calls. In this format, the highest bit of the instruction is set to 0, and the remainder of the instruction is used to hold a 15-bit subroutine address. This limits programs to 32K words of memory.

Fig. 4.9(b) shows the conditional branch instruction format. Bits 11 and 12 select either a branch if T is zero (with either a conditional or an unconditional popping of the data stack), an unconditional branch, or a decrement and branch-if-zero using the index register for implementing loops. Bits 0–8 specify the lowest 9 bits of the target address, while bits 9 and 10 control an incrementer/decrementer for the upper 6 bits of the branch address to allow branching within the same 512-byte-memory page, to adjacent pages, or to page 0.

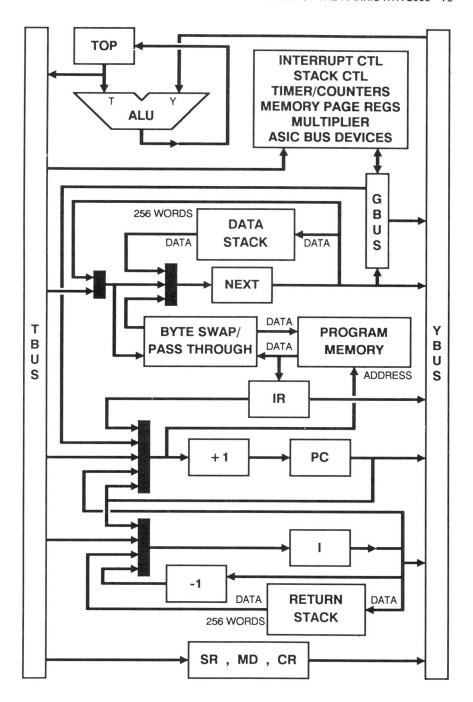

Fig. 4.8 — RTX 2000 block diagram.

(a)

```
1 1 1 1 1 1
5 4 3 2 1 0 9 8 7 6 5 4 3 2 1 0
┌─┬─────────────────────────────┐
│0│          address            │
└─┴─────────────────────────────┘
```

Bits Function
  15 Constant value of 0
0-14 Subroutine address

(b)

```
  1 1 1 1 1 1
  5 4 3 2 1 0 9 8 7 6 5 4 3 2 1 0
┌─────┬───┬───┬─────────────────┐
│1 0 0│cs │pg │     address     │
└─────┴───┴───┴─────────────────┘
```

Bits   Function
13-15 Constant 100 specifies conditional instruction
11-12 Condition select
       00 Branch / DROP T if T = 0   10 Unconditional branch
       01 Branch if T = 0 / DROP T   11 Decrement INDEX & branch if not 0

 9-10 Page control for high address bits
       00 Same page   10 Page 0
       01 Next page   11 Previous page

  0-8 Low 9 bits of branch address

(c)

```
  1 1 1 1 1 1
  5 4 3 2 1 0 9 8 7 6 5 4 3 2 1 0
┌───────┬───────┬─┬─┬─┬─┬───────┐
│1 0 1 0│  alu  │i│-│r│0│  sc   │
└───────┴───────┴─┴─┴─┴─┴───────┘
```

Bits   Function
12-15,4   Constant 1010,0 specifies normal ALU operation
   8-11   ALU function select
          0000 T   1000 T + Y
          0001   1001 T + Y + carry
          0010 T and Y   1010 T xor Y
          0011 T nor Y   1011 T xnor Y
          0100 Y - T   1100 T - Y
          0101 Y - T - borrow   1101 T - Y - borrow
          0110 T or Y   1110
          0111 T nand Y   1111 Y

      7   Logical inverse bit (1's complement)

      5   Subroutine return

    0-3   Shift control
          0000 none   1000 Shift N left
          0001 0   1001 Shift N left/carry
          0010 Shift left   1010 32 bit shift left
          0011 Shift left with carry   1011 32 bit shift left/carry
          0100 Logical shift right/carry   1100 32 bit logical shift right/cy
          0101 Arithmetic shift right/carry 1101 32 bit arithmetic shift right/cy
          0110 Logical shift right   1110 32 bit logical shift right
          0111 Arithmetic shift right   1111 32 bit arithmetic shift right
```

Fig. 4.9 — RTX 2000 instruction formats. (a) Subroutine call. (b) Conditional branch. (c) ALU operation.
```

(d)

```
 1 1 1 1 1 1
 5 4 3 2 1 0 9 8 7 6 5 4 3 2 1 0
┌───────┬───┬─┬───┬─┬─┬─────────┐
│1 0 1 0│alu│a│ctl│r│1│   sc    │
└───────┴───┴─┴───┴─┴─┴─────────┘
```

Bits   Function

12-15,4 Constant 1010,1 specifies multi-step ALU operation

9-11   ALU function select

000 T   100 T + Y
001 T and Y   101 T xor Y
010 T - Y   110 Y - T
011 T or Y   111 Y

8   Register access

0 MD   1 MD*2 or SR

6-7   Multi-step special control field

5   Subroutine return

0-3   Shift control

0000 none   1000 Shift N left
0001 0   1001 Shift N left/carry
0010 Shift left   1010 32 bit shift left
0011 Shift left with carry   1011 32 bit shift left/carry
0100 Logical shift right/carry 1100 32 bit logical shift right/cy
0101 Arithmetic shift right/carry 1101 32 bit arithmetic shift right/cy
0110 Logical shift right   1110 32 bit logical shift right
0111 Arithmetic shift right   1111 32 bit arithmetic shift right

(e)

```
 1 1 1 1 1 1
 5 4 3 2 1 0 9 8 7 6 5 4 3 2 1 0
┌─────┬─┬───┬───┬─┬───────────┐
│1 1 1│b│alu│r/w│r│   const   │
└─────┴─┴───┴───┴─┴───────────┘
```

Bits   Function

13-15   Constant 111 specifies memory reference

12   Byte access control

0 Word access   1 Byte access

8-11   ALU function select

0000 T   1000 T + Y
0001   1001 T + Y + carry
0010 T and Y   1010 T xor Y
0011 T nor Y   1011 T xnor Y
0100 Y - T   1100 T - Y
0101 Y - T - borrow   1101 T - Y - borrow
0110 T or Y   1110
0111 T nand Y   1111 Y

6-7   Read/write and routing control

5   Subroutine return

0-4   Auto-increment/decrement constant

Fig. 4.9 — RTX 2000 instruction formats. (d) ALU operation (multistep mode). (e)
Memory reference.

(f)

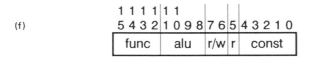

Bits   Function

12-15   Function selection
        1011 I/O, Register, Short literal
        1100 User memory access
        1101 Long literal access

8-11   ALU function select

0000 T	1000 T + Y
0001	1001 T + Y + carry
0010 T and Y	1010 T xor Y
0011 T nor Y	1011 T xnor Y
0100 Y - T	1100 T - Y
0101 Y - T - borrow	1101 T - Y - borrow
0110 T or Y	1110
0111 T nand Y	1111 Y

6-7   Read/write and routing control

5   Subroutine return

0-4   Literal/ASIC address/user memory offset

Fig. 4.9 — RTX 2000 instruction formats. (f) Miscellaneous instructions.

Fig. 4.9(c) shows the format of the ALU instruction. Bits 0–3 control the operation of the shifter that shifts the output of the ALU.

Bit 5 of the ALU instruction indicates a subroutine return operation. This allows subroutine returns to be combined with preceding arithmetic operations to obtain 'free' subroutine returns in many cases.

Bits 8–11 select an ALU function, with bit 7 controlling whether the output of the ALU is inverted.

Fig. 4.9(d) shows the format of the ALU instruction in multi-step mode. This format is quite similar to the ALU instruction format. Bits 0–3 select a shift control function, bit 5 controls the subroutine return function, and bits 9–11 selects the ALU operation.

In multi-step mode, bit 8 selects either the Multiply/Divide register or the Square Root register for special operations, while bits 6–7 select special multi-step control functions. A primary use of the multi-step mode is for repeated multiplication and division step operations.

Fig. 4.9(e) shows the format of a memory reference instruction. These instructions take two clock cycles: one for the instruction fetch, and one for the actual reading or writing of the operand. The address for the memory access is always taken from the T register. Bit 12 selects either a byte or a word memory access. Since the RTX 2000 uses word memory addresses, this bit selects a 'low half/high half' or 'full word' operation at the selected memory word.

Bits 6 and 7 indicate whether the operation is a memory read or write as well as other control information. Bits 0–4 specify a small constant that can be added or subtracted to the T value to perform an autoincrement or autodecrement addressing function. Bits 8–11 of this instruction specify the same ALU functions as the ALU instruction format.

Fig. 4.9(f) shows the miscellaneous instruction format. This instruction can be used to read or write a word in the 32-word relocatable user space, saving the time taken to push a memory address on the stack before performing the fetch or store. It can also be used to transfer registers within the chip, or push either a 5-bit literal (in a single clock cycle) or a 16-bit literal (in two clock cycles) onto the stack. Bits 8–11 of this instruction specify the same ALU functions as the ALU instruction format.

The RTX 2000 is specifically designed to execute the Forth language. Because of the unencoded format of many of the instructions, machine operations that correspond to a sequence of Forth operations can be encoded in a single instruction. Table 4.3 shows the Forth primitives and instruction sequences that can be executed by the RTX 2000.

4.5.4 Architectural features

Like the NC4016, the internal structure of the RTX 2000 is optimized to provide single-clock-cycle instruction execution. All primitive operations except memory fetch, memory store, and long literal execute in a single clock cycle.

The RTX 2000 also allows some sequences of Forth instructions to be combined into a single instruction. A key capability is provided by the return bit in some formats that allows combining subroutine returns with ALU operations.

4.5.5 Implementation and featured application areas

The RTX 2000 is implemented on 2.0 micron CMOS standard cell techno-logy, packaged in an 84-pin Pin Grid Array (PGA). The RTX 2000 runs at up to 10 MHz. A large advantage of standard cell technology is that RAM and logic may be mixed on the same chip, allowing both the return stacks and the data stacks to be placed on-chip.

Because the RTX 2000 executes most instructions, including conditional branches and subroutine calls, in a single cycle, there is a significant amount of time between the beginning of the clock cycle and the time that the memory address is valid for fetching the next instruction. This time is approximately half the clock cycle, meaning that program memory must be approximately twice as fast as the clock rate.

While the RTX 2000 was originally based on the NC4016 design, it has been substantially improved and does not have the hardware anomalies found on the NC4016.

The RTX 2000 is aimed at the high end 16-bit microcontroller market. Because it is implemented with semicustom technology, specialized versions of the processor can be made for specific design applications. Some possible applications include laser printer control, Graphics CRT display control,

Table 4.3 — RTX 2000 instruction set summary

4.3(a) Forth primitives (see Appendix B)

: (subroutine call)	AND
; (subroutine exit)	BRANCH
!	DROP
+	DUP
−	I
0	LIT
0<	NOP
0BRANCH	OR
1+	OVER
1−	R>
2*	R@
>R	SWAP
@	XOR

4.3(b) Compound Forth primitives

inv shift	DUP @ SWAP
lit inv	DUP nn G! inv
lit SWAP inv	DUP U! inv
lit SWAP op	DUP U@ op
nn inv (short literal)	nn G! inv
nn OVER op	nn G@ inv
nn SWAP op	nn G@ DROP inv
op shift	nn G@ OVER op
! inv	nn G@ SWAP op
! nn	OVER inv shift
@ inv	OVER SWAP op shift
@ nn	OVER SWAP ! inv
@ SWAP inv	OVER SWAP ! nn
@ SWAP op	OVER SWAP @ op
?DUP ?BRANCH	SWAP inv shift
DDUP inv shift	SWAP DROP inv shift
DDUP nn SWAP op	SWAP DROP @ nn
DDUP !	SWAP DROP DUP inv shift
DROP inv shift	SWAP DROP DUP @ nn ROT op
DROP lit inv	SWAP DROP DUP @ SWAP
DROP nn inv	SWAP OVER op shift
DROP DUP inv shift	SWAP OVER !
DUP inv shift	U! inv
DUP lit op	U@ op
DUP @ nn ROT op	U@ SWAP inv

Notation: inv — 1's complement or no-op
        lit — long literal value
        nn — short literal value
        op — ALU operation
        shift — shift select or no-op

Table 4.3 — Continued.

4.3(c) Special purpose word

Instruction	Data stack	Return stack
nn G@	→ N	→
Fetch the value from internal register or ASIC bus device nn (stored as a 5-bit literal in the instruction).		
nn G!	N→	→
Store N into the internal register or ASIC bus device nn (stored as a 5-bit literal in the instruction)		
*	N1 N2→ D3	→
Single-clock-cycle hardware multiply.		
*'	D1→ D2	→
Unsigned Multiply step (takes two 16-bit numbers and produces a 32-bit product).		
*−	D1→ D2	→
Signed Multiply step (takes two 16-bit numbers and produces a 32-bit product).		
*F	D1→ D2	→
Fractional Multiply step (takes two 16-bit fractions and produces a 32-bit product).		
*/'	D1→ D2	→
Divide step (takes a 16-bit dividend and divisor and produces 16-bit remainder and quotients).		
*/"	D1→ D2	→
Last Divide step (to perform nonrestoring division fixup step).		
2/	N1→ N2	→
Arithmetic shift right (same as division by two for nonnegative integers.		
D2/	D1→ D2	→
32-bit arithmetic shift right (same as division by two for nonnegative integers.		
S'	D1→ D2	→
Square Root step.		
NEXT	→	N1 → N2
Count-down loop using top of return stack as a counter.		

telecommunications control, optical character recognition, signal processing, and military control applications.

The information in this section is derived from the *RTX 2000 Data Sheet* (Harris semiconductor 1988a) and the *RTX 2000 Instruction Set Manual* (Harris semiconductor 1988b).

4.5.6 Standard cell designs

The Harris RTX 2000 derives many of its benefits from the fact that it is built using standard cell technology instead of a gate array. The difference is that in a gate array, the designer is customizing a regular pattern of preplaced logic gates on the silicon. In standard cell design, the designer is working with a library of logic functions that can be arbitrarily arranged on the silicon, as no predetermined gate arrangement scheme is used. While gate arrays with predefined memory areas are coming into use, the flexibility afforded by standard cell design techniques is not equalled by a gate array approach.

Thus, the major differences between the NC4016 and the RTX 2000 become apparent: the RTX 2000 is able to take advantage of the flexibility of standard cells to include stack RAM cells on-chip. Because of this flexibility, a family of RTX 2000 processors with differing capabilities is planned using the same core processor as a large standard cell in the design process.

In addition to standard product versions of the RTX family, users can benefit from application-specific hardware. Examples of special-purpose hardware include serial communication ports, FFT address generators, data compression circuitry, or any other hardware that might otherwise have to be built off-chip. With standard cell technology, users can have tailored versions of the chip made for their own use. This tailoring can include, as the process technology gets denser than 2.0 microns, a significant amount of program RAM and ROM on-chip.

5

Architecture of 32-bit systems

32-bit stack computers are only beginning to come into production in 1989, but will soon play a central role in the future of stack machines. In section 5.1 we shall discuss some of the strengths and problems associated with 32-bit stack processors.

In section 5.2, we shall discuss the Johns Hopkins University/Applied Physics Laboratory FRISC 3 design, which is also known as the Silicon Composers SC32. The FRISC 3 is a hardwired stack processor designed in the spirit of the NC4016 and its successors, but with more flexibility. It uses fairly small on-chip stack buffers that are managed by automatic buffer control circuitry.

In section 5.3, we shall discuss the Harris RTX 32P design. The RTX 32P is a microcoded processor that is a descendent of the WISC CPU/16. It is a two-chip implementation of the WISC CPU/32 processor. The RTX 32P uses RAM-based microprogram memory to achieve flexibility. It also has rather large on-chip stack buffers. The RTX 32P is a prototype processor for a commercial 32-bit stack processor under development.

In section 5.4, we shall discuss the Wright State University SF1 design. The SF1 is actually an ML1 stack machine which uses stack frames in multiple hardware stacks for support of C and other conventional languages. However, the SF1 has strong ML0 roots, so it forms an interesting example of how an ML1 design 'stacks up' against ML0 designs.

While the implementation strategies of these three processors are quite different, all accomplish the goal of very high speed execution of stack programs.

5.1 WHY 32-BIT SYSTEMS?

The 16-bit processors described in Chapter 4 are sufficiently powerful for a wide variety of applications, especially in an embedded control environment. But, there are some applications that require the added power of a 32-bit processor. These applications involve extensive use of 32-bit integer arithmetic, large memory address spaces, or floating point arithmetic.

One of the difficult technical challenges that arises when designing a 32-bit stack processor is the management of the stacks. A brute force approach is to have separate off-chip stack memories in the manner of the NC4016.

Unfortunately, on a 32-bit design this requires having 64 extra pins for just the data bits, making the approach unpractical for cost-sensitive applications. The FRISC 3 solves this problem by maintaining two automatically managed top-of-stack buffers on-chip, and using the normal RAM data pins to spill individual stack elements to and from program memory. The RTX 32P simply allocates a large amount of chip space to on-chip stacks and performs block moves of stack elements to and from memory for stack spilling. Chapter 6 goes into more detail about the tradeoffs involved with these approaches.

5.2   ARCHITECTURE OF THE FRISC 3 (SC32)

5.2.1   Introduction
The Johns Hopkins University/Applied Physics Laboratory (JHU/APL) FRISC 3 is a hardwired 32-bit processor optimized for executing the Forth programming language. The name 'FRISC' stands for 'Forth Reduced Instruction Set Computer'. The '3' acknowledges two previous prototype stack processors. The focus of the FRISC 3 is on single-cycle execution of Forth primitives in a real-time control environment.

JHU/APL developed the FRISC 3 in response to their need for a fast Forth language processor for spaceborne control processing applications in satellites and Space Shuttle experiments. The roots of the FRISC 3 project may be traced back to the JHU/APL HUT project (see Appendix A), which was a bit-slice processor optimized for the Forth language.

After the completion of the HUT processor, the design team at Johns Hopkins designed a prototype 4.0 micron silicon-on-sapphire 32-bit Forth processor (FRISC 1) and a 3 micron bulk CMOS version (FRISC 2), both of which were full-custom designs. The latest version, FRISC 3, is the commercial quality processor that is an outgrowth of their earlier work.

Silicon Composers has purchased commercial production rights to the FRISC 3, and has renamed the design the SC32. The description in this section applies to both the FRISC 3 and the SC32, although we shall call the design the FRISC 3 throughout the remainder of the book.

The primary use of the FRISC 3 is for embedded real-time control, especially in spacecraft (which is the focus of the JHU/APL group), but also for other industrial and commercial applications.

5.2.2   Block diagram
Fig. 5.1 is an architectural block diagram of the FRISC 3.

The Data Stack and Return Stack are implemented as identical hardware stacks. They each consist of a stack pointer with special control logic feeding an address to a 16-element by 32-bit stack memory arranged as a circular buffer. The top four elements of both stacks are directly readable onto the Bbus. In addition, the topmost element of the Data Stack may be read onto the Tbus (Top-of-stack bus) and the topmost element of the Return Stack may be read onto the Abus (return Address bus). Both stack buffers are

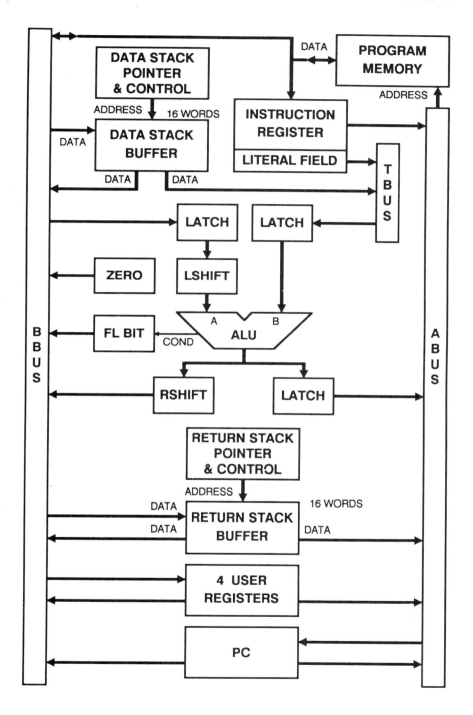

Fig. 5.1 — FRISC 3 block diagram.

dual-ported, which allows two potentially different elements of the stacks to be read simultaneously. Only one stack element may be written at a time.

One of the innovative features of the FRISC 3 is the use of stack management logic associated with the stack pointers. This logic automatically moves stack items between the 16-word on-chip stacks and a program memory stack spilling area to guarantee that the on-chip stack buffers never experience an overflow or underflow. This logic steals program memory cycles from the processor to accomplish this, avoiding the extra stack data pins on the chip in exchange for a small performance degradation spread throughout program execution. The designers of the FRISC 3 call this feature a stack cache, because it caches the top few stack elements for quick access on-chip. This cache is not like normal data or instruction caches in that it does not employ an associative memory lookup structure to allow access to data residing in scattered areas of memory.

The ALU section of the FRISC 3 includes a standard ALU that is fed by latches on the Bbus and the Tbus. These two ALU sources on separate busses allow the topmost Data Stack element (via the Tbus) and any of the top four Data Stack elements (via the Bbus) to be operated on by an instruction since the Data Stack is dual-ported. The Bbus can feed any nonstack bus source through the B side of the ALU as well.

The latches from the Bbus and Tbus that feed the ALU inputs are used to capture data during the first half of a clock cycle. This allows the Bbus to be used to write data from the ALU to other registers within the chip on the second half of the clock cycle. The shift block on the B input of the ALU is used to shift the B input left one bit for division, but can also pass data through unshifted. Similarly, the shift unit on the ALU output can shift data right one bit for multiplication, if desired, while feeding the Bbus.

The latch on the ALU output allows pointer-plus-offset addressing to access memory. On the first clock cycle of a memory fetch or store, the ALU adds the literal field value via the Tbus to the selected data stack word from the Bbus. On the second cycle, the Bbus is used to transfer the selected 'bus destination' to or from memory.

The flag register (FL) is used to store one of 16 selectable condition codes generated by the ALU for use in conditional branches and multiple precision arithmetic. The ZERO register is used to supply the constant value 0 to the Bbus.

Four User Registers are provided to store pointers into memory or other values. Two of these registers are reserved for use by the stack control logic to store the location of the top element of the program memory resident portions of the Data Stack and Return Stack.

A Program Counter (PC) is used to supply the Abus with program memory addresses for fetching instructions. The PC may also be routed via the ALU to the Return Stack for subroutine calls. The Return Stack may be used to drive the Abus instead of the PC for subroutine returns. The Instruction Register may be used to drive the Abus for instruction fetching, subroutine calls, and for branching.

5.2.3 Instruction set summary

Fig. 5.2 shows FRISC 3's four instruction formats: one for control flow, one for memory loads and stores, one for ALU operations, and one for shift operations. The FRISC 3 uses unencoded instruction formats similar in spirit to those found on the NC4016, RTX 2000, and M17. All instruction formats use the highest 3 bits of the instruction to specify the instruction type.

Fig. 5.2(a) shows the control flow instruction format. The three control flow instructions are subroutine call, unconditional branch, and conditional branch. The conditional branch instruction is taken if the FL register was set to zero by the most recent instruction to set the FL register. The address field contains a 29-bit absolute address. Unconditional branches may be used by the compiler to accomplish tail-end recursion elimination.

Fig. 5.2(b) shows the memory access instruction format. Bits 0–15 contain an unsigned offset to be added to the address supplied by the bus source operand. This is accomplished by latching the bus source and the offset field from the instruction at the ALU inputs, performing an addition, and routing the resultant ALU output to the Abus for memory addressing.

Bits 16–19 specify control information for incrementing and decrementing the Return Stack Pointer and/or Data Stack Pointer. Bits 20–23 specify the Bbus Destination. In this notation, 'TOS' means Top of Data Stack, 'SOS' means Second on Data Stack, '3OS' means 3rd element of Data Stack, 'TOR' means Top of Return Stack, etc. Bits 24–27 specify the Bus Source for the Bbus in a similar manner.

Bit 28 specifies whether the next instruction fetched will be addressed by the top element of the Return Stack or the Program Counter. Using bit 28 to specify the Return Stack as the instruction address is combined with a Return Stack pop operation to accomplish a subroutine return in parallel with other operations.

Bits 29–31 specify the instruction type. For the memory access format instructions, the four possible instructions are: load from memory, store to memory, load address (low), and load address (high). The load and store from/to memory instructions use the bus source to supply an address, and the bus destination field to specify the data register destination or source. The load and store instructions are the only instructions that take two clock cycles, since they must access memory twice to accomplish both data movement and the next instruction fetch.

The two load address instructions simply load the computed memory address into the destination register without accessing memory at all. This may also be thought of as an add-immediate instruction. The load address high instruction shifts the offset left 16 bits before performing the addition. The load address instructions are also the means for loading literal values, since the address register can be selected to the ZERO register. In this manner a load address high followed by a load address low instruction can be used to synthesize a full 32-bit literal.

Fig. 5.2(c) shows the ALU instruction format. Bits 0–6 of this instruction

```
      3 3 2 2 2 2 2 2 2 2 2 2 1 1 1 1 1 1 1 1 1 1
(a)   1 0 9 8 7 6 5 4 3 2 1 0 9 8 7 6 5 4 3 2 1 0 9 8 7 6 5 4 3 2 1 0
```

type	address

Bits Function

29-31 Instruction type
    000 Call   010 Conditional branch
    001 Branch

  0-28 Branch target address

```
      3 3 2 2 2 2 2 2 2 2 2 2 1 1 1 1 1 1 1 1 1 1
(b)   1 0 9 8 7 6 5 4 3 2 1 0 9 8 7 6 5 4 3 2 1 0 9 8 7 6 5 4 3 2 1 0
```

type	r	source	dest	stacks	offset

Bits Function

29-31 Instruction type
    100 Load   110 Load address low
    101 Store   111 Load address high

   28 Subroutine return

24-27 Bus source
    0000 TOS   1000 UDR0
    0001 SOS   1001 UDR1
    0010 3OS   1010 UDR2
    0011 4OS   1011 UDR3
    0100 TOR   1100 PC
    0101 SOR   1101 PSW
    0110 3OR   1110 ZERO
    0111 4OR   1111 none

20-23 Bus destination
    0000 TOS   1000 UDR0
    0001 SOS   1001 UDR1
    0010 3OS   1010 UDR2
    0011 4OS   1011 UDR3
    0100 TOR   1100 PC
    0101 SOR   1101 PSW
    0110 3OR   1110 ZERO
    0111 4OR   1111 none

16-19 Stack pointer control
    0000 Push DS   1000 nop
    0001 Pop DS   1001 nop
    0010 Push RS   1010 nop
    0011 Pop RS   1011 nop
    0100 Pop DS and RS   1100 nop
    0101 Push DS and RS   1101 nop
    0110 Push DS, Pop RS   1110 nop
    0111 Pop DS, Push RS   1111 nop

  0-15 Offset value added to address

Fig. 5.2 — FRISC 3 instruction formats. (a) Control flow. (b) Memory access.

(c)

3 3 2	2 2 2 2	2 2 2 2	1 1 1 1	1	1	1 1 1 1			
1 0 9	8 7 6 5	4 3 2 1	0 9 8 7	6	5	4 3 2 1	0 9 8 7	6 5 4 3 2 1 0
type	r source	dest	stacks	0	b	cond	cin e	alu

Bits   Function

29-31,15 Constant value of 011,0 specifies ALU instruction

28 Subroutine return

24-27 Bus source

0000 TOS	0110 3OR	1100 PC
0001 SOS	0111 4OR	1101 PSW
0010 3OS	1000 UDR0	1110 ZERO
0011 4OS	1001 UDR1	1111 none
0100 TOR	1010 UDR2	
0101 SOR	1011 UDR3	

20-23 Bus destination

0000 TOS	0110 3OR	1100 PC
0001 SOS	0111 4OR	1101 PSW
0010 3OS	1000 UDR0	1110 ZERO
0011 4OS	1001 UDR1	1111 none
0100 TOR	1010 UDR2	
0101 SOR	1011 UDR3	

16-19 Stack pointer control

0000 Push DS	0011 Pop RS	0110 Push DS, Pop RS
0001 Pop DS	0100 Pop DS & RS	0111 Pop DS, Push RS
0010 Push RS	0101 Push DS & RS	1000 nop

14 ALU result/FL register driven to Bbus

10-13 Condition select for loading FL register

0000 0	0110 0<	1100 <
0001 1	0111 0> =	1101 > =
0010 V	1000 Z	1110 C
0011 not(V)	1001 not(Z)	1111 not(C)
0100 >	1010 unsigned >	
0101 < =	1011 unsigned <	

8-9 Carry in select

00 0	10 FL register	11 not(FL register)
01 1		

7 Enable FL loading

0-6 ALU function (hexadecimal numbers)

15 A nand B	2F A xor B	4D B - A - not(CIN)
17 A or not(B)	41 not(A) + CIN	4E B - not(CIN)
1D not(A) or B	43 A + CIN	4F A + B + CIN
1F A or B	44 not(B) + CIN	55 A and B
20 0	45 not(A) + not(B) + CIN	57 not(A) and B
21 not(A)	46 not(B) - not(CIN)	5D A and not(B)
22 -1	47 A - B - not(CIN)	5F A nor B
23 A	49 not(A) - not(CIN)	6F A xnor B
24 not(B)	4B A - not(CIN)	
2C B	4C B + CIN	

Fig. 5.2 — FRISC 3 instruction formats. (c) ALU operations.

```
      3 3 2|2 2 2 2|2 2 2 2|1 1 1 1|1|1|1 1 1 1
(d)   1 0 9|8 7 6 5|4 3 2 1|0 9 8 7|6|5|4 3 2 1|0 9 8|7 6 5|4|3 2|1 0
      | type | r | source | dest | stacks |1|b| cond | cin |f| sh |r| st |f|-|
```

Bits   Function

29-31,15 Constant value of 011,1 specifies shift instruction

28   Subroutine return

24-27   Bus source

0000 TOS	0110 3OR	1100 PC
0001 SOS	0111 4OR	1101 PSW
0010 3OS	1000 UDR0	1110 ZERO
0011 4OS	1001 UDR1	1111 none
0100 TOR	1010 UDR2	
0101 SOR	1011 UDR3	

20-23   Bus destination

0000 TOS	0110 3OR	1100 PC
0001 SOS	0111 4OR	1101 PSW
0010 3OS	1000 UDR0	1110 ZERO
0011 4OS	1001 UDR1	1111 none
0100 TOR	1010 UDR2	
0101 SOR	1011 UDR3	

16-19   Stack pointer control

0000 Push DS	0011 Pop RS	0110 Push DS, Pop RS
0001 Pop DS	0100 Pop DS & RS	0111 Pop DS, Push RS
0010 Push RS	0101 Push DS & RS	1000 nop

14   ALU result driven to Bbus

0 ALU output   1 FL register

10-13   Condition select for loading FL register

0000 0	0110 0<	1100 <
0001 1	0111 0> =	1101 > =
0010 V	1000 Z	1110 C
0011 not(V)	1001 not(Z)	1111 not(C)
0100 >	1010 unsigned >	
0101 < =	1011 unsigned <	

8-9   Carry in select

00 0	10 FL register	11 not(FL register)
01 1		

7   Enable FL loading

5-6   Shift operation

00 Shift left   01 Shift right   11 nop

4   Right shift source

0 FL register   1 ALU condition code

2-3   Step operation

00 B + CIN	10 ?(A + B + CIN(FL))
01 B - A - CIN	11 ?(A + B + CIN(not(FL)))

1   Source of FL input

0 ALU condition code   1 Shift out bit

Fig. 5.2 — FRISC 3 instruction formats. (d) Shift operations.

format specify the ALU operation to be performed. The A side of the ALU is connected to the Tbus, while the B side is connected to the Bbus. Bit 7 enables loading the FL Register with the condition code selected by bits 10–13 of the instruction. These condition codes provide various combinations of a Zero bit, Negative bit, Carry out bit, and overflow bit, as well as constant 0 and 1. Bits 8–9 select the carry in to the ALU operation. Bit 14 selects whether the actual ALU result or the contents of the FL register is driven onto the Bbus. Bit 15 is a 0, indicating that the instruction is an ALU operation.

Bits 16–28 are identical to the memory access instruction format shown in Fig. 5.2(b). Bits 29–31 specify the ALU/shift operation instruction type.

Fig. 5.2(d) shows the shift instruction format. Bit 0 of this instruction format is unused. Bit 1 specifies whether the FL register input is taken from the condition codes selected by bits 10–13 or the shift-out bit of the selected shift register. Bits 2–3 select special step operations for performing multiplication and restoring division. Bit 4 selects whether the shift-right input bit comes from the FL register or the ALU condition code. Bits 5–6 specify either a left or a right shift operation. Bit 7 specifies whether the FL Register is to be loaded with the shift output bit or the condition code generated by bits 10–13 and bit 1. Bits 8–9 select the carry-in for the ALU operation, while bit 14 determines whether the ALU output or the FL register is driven to the Bbus. Bit 15 is a 1, indicating that the instruction is a shift operation.

Bits 16–28 are identical to the memory access instruction format shown in Fig. 5.2(b). Bits 29–31 specify the ALU/shift operation instruction type.

All instructions execute in one clock cycle, with the exception of the memory load and memory store instructions, which take two clock cycles. Each clock cycle is broken during execution into a source phase and a destination phase. During the source phase, the selected Bbus source and the Tbus value are read into the ALU input latches. During the destination phase, the Bbus destination is written. Each instruction is fetched in parallel with the execution of the previous instruction.

Subroutine calls are accomplished in a single clock cycle. Subroutine returns take no extra time to the extent that they can be combined with other instructions.

Most of the usual Forth primitives as well as manipulations of the top four stack elements on both the Data Stack and the Return Stack are supported by the FRISC 3 instruction set. Table 5.1 shows a representative sample of FRISC 3 instructions.

5.2.4 Architectural features

Like all the other machines designs discussed so far, the FRISC 3 has a separate memory address bus (the Abus) for fetching instructions in parallel with other operations. In addition, the FRISC 3 does not have a dedicated top-of-stack register for the Data Stack, but instead uses a dual-ported stack memory to allow arbitrary access to any of the top four stack elements. This provides a more general capability than a pure stack machine and can speed up some code sequences.

Table 5.1 — FRISC 3 instruction set summary

5.1(a) Forth primitives (see Appendix B for descriptions)

0	>R
0<	@
0=	AND
0>	BRANCH
0BRANCH	CALL
1	DROP
1+	DUP
1−	EXIT
2*	LITERAL
2+	NEGATE
2/	NOT
4+	OR
+	OVER
−1	R>
−	R@
<	S−>D
<>	U<
=	U>
>	XOR

5.1(b) Compound Forth primitives

The FRISC 3 is capable of a very large number of compound Forth primitives. Space precludes listing all of them, so we shall give some illustrative examples.

LIT + @	(address plus offset fetch)
LIT + !	(address plus offset store)
<variable> @	(fetch a variable)
<variable> !	(store a variable)
2 PICK	(copy the third element on the stack)
3 PICK	(copy the fourth element on the stack)

R> DROP	R@ <
SWAP DROP	OVER OVER +
LIT +	DROP LIT
OVER +	DUP LIT +
OVER −	DROP DUP
DUP +	DROP OVER
DUP AND	OVER @
DUP XOR	2 PICK @
DUP 1+	3 PICK @
OVER +	OVER !
2 PICK +	2 PICK !
3 PICK +	3 PICK !
R@ +	+ >R
R> +	DUP >R
DUP <	DUP R> DROP
DUP >	R> DROP DUP

The flexibility of the FRISC 3 also supports many operations not encompassed in the Forth language, such as stack manipulation words on the Return Stack (e.g. Return Stack **SWAP**).

The stack control logic is a means to prevent catastrophic stack overflow and underflow during program execution by 'dribbling' elements onto and off of the stack to keep at least 4 elements on the stack at all times without overflowing. This demand-fed approach to stack buffer management is discussed in greater detail in section 6.4.2.2. Each stack has 16 words used as a circular buffer. The stack controllers perform stack data movement to and from memory whenever there would be less than four or more than 12 elements in an on-chip stack. The movement is performed one element at a time, since the stack pointers can only be incremented or decremented once per instruction. Each stack element transfer to or from memory consumes two clock cycles. Chapter 6 discusses the cost of these extra cycles, which the FRISC 3 designers claim is typically below 2% of overall program execution time for their machine.

5.2.5   Implementation and featured application areas

The FRISC 3 is implemented on 2.0 micron CMOS technology with a silicon compiler using 35000 transistors. It is packaged in an 85-pin Pin Grid Array (PGA). The FRISC 3 runs at up to 10 MHz.

The FRISC 3 is designed for real-time control applications, especially in the area of spaceborne systems. It is designed to execute Forth efficiently, although it should be reasonably efficient at running C or other conventional languages. C support is enhanced by the capability of using one of the User Registers as a frame pointer and using the offset of the memory load and store instructions to do frame pointer plus offset addressing.

The information in this section is based on the description of the FRISC 3 in Hayes & Lee (1988). Information on previous versions of the FRISC architecture may be found in Fraeman *et al.* (1986), Hayes (1986), and Hayes *et al.* (1987).

5.3   ARCHITECTURE OF THE RTX 32P

5.3.1   Introduction

The Harris Semiconductor RTX 32P is a 32-bit member of the Real Time Express (RTX) processor family. The RTX 32P is a prototype machine that is the basis of Harris' commercial 32-bit stack machine design.

The RTX 32P is a CMOS chip implementation of the WISC Technologies CPU/32 (Koopman 1987c) which was originally built using discrete TTL components. The CPU/32 was in turn developed from the WISC CPU/16 described in Chapter 4. Because of this history, the RTX 32P is a micro-coded machine, with on-chip microcode RAM and on-chip stacks.

The RTX 32P is a 2-chip stack processor designed primarily for maximum flexibility as an architectural evaluation platform. It contains very large data and return stacks on-chip, as well as a large amount of on-chip microcode memory. This large amount of high speed RAM forced the design to use two chips, but this was consistent with the goal of producing a research and development vehicle. Real-time control is the primary application area for the RTX 32P.

The primary language for programming the RTX 32P is Forth. However, the RTX 32P's commercial successor will be enhanced for excellent support of more conventional languages such as C, Ada, Pascal; special purpose languages such as LISP and Prolog; and functional programming languages.

An important design philosophy of the RTX 32P is that as processor speeds increase, an ALU can be cycled twice for every off-chip memory access. Therefore the RTX 32P executes two microinstructions for each main memory access, including instruction fetches. Every instruction is two or more clock cycles in length, with a different microinstruction executed on each clock cycle. The reasons for adopting this strategy are discussed at greater length in section 9.4.

5.3.2   Block diagram
Fig. 5.3 is an architectural block diagram of the RTX 32P.

The Data Stack and Return Stack are implemented as identical hardware stacks consisting of a 9-bit up/down counter (the Stack Pointer) feeding an address to a 512-element by 32-bit-wide memory. The stack pointers are readable and writable by the system to provide an efficient way of accessing deeply buried stack elements.

The ALU section includes a standard multifunction ALU with a DHI register for holding intermediate results. By convention, the DHI register acts as a buffer for the top stack element. This means that the Data Stack Pointer actually addresses the element perceived by the programmer to be the second-from-top stack element. The result is that an operation on the top two stack elements, such as addition, can be performed in a single cycle, with the B side of the ALU reading the second stack element from the Data Stack and the A side of the ALU reading the top stack element from the Data Hi register.

The Data Latch on the B side of the ALU input is a normally transparent latch that can be used to retain data for one clock cycle. This speeds up swap operations between the DHI register and the Data Stack.

There are no condition codes visible to machine language programs. Add with carry and other multiple precision operations are supported by microcoded instructions that push the carry flag onto the data stack as a logical value (0 for carry clear, -1 for carry set).

The DLO register acts as a temporary holding register for intermediate results within a single instruction. Both the DHI and the DLO registers are shift registers, connected to allow 64-bit shifting for multiplication and division.

An off-chip Host Interface is used to connect to the personal computer host. Since all on-chip storage is RAM-based, an external host is required for initializing the CPU.

The RTX 32P has no program counter. Every instruction contains the address of the next instruction or refers to the address on the top of the return address stack. This design decision is in keeping with the observation that Forth programs contain a very high proportion of subroutine calls.

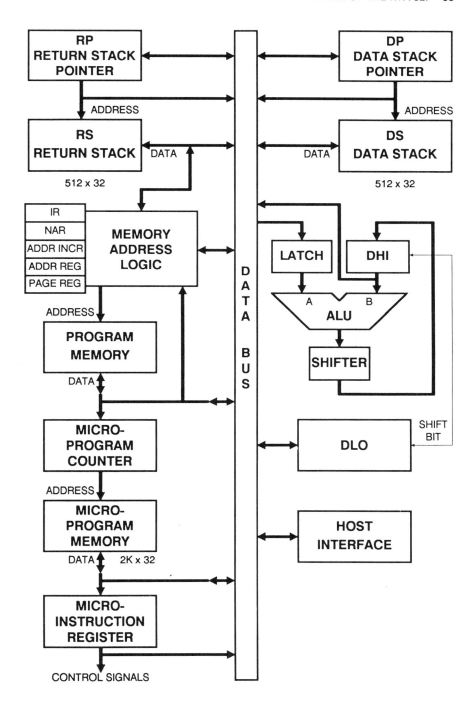

Fig. 5.3 — RTX 32P block diagram.

Section 6.3.3 discusses the affects of the RTX 32P's instruction format in greater detail.

Instead of a program counter, the block described as the Memory Address Logic contains a Next Address Register (NAR), which holds the pointer for fetching the next instruction. The Memory Address Logic uses the top element of the Return Stack to address memory for subroutine returns, while it uses the RAM address register (ADDR REG) for doing memory fetches and stores efficiently. The Memory Address Logic also contains an increment-by-4 circuit for generating return addresses for subroutine call operations. Since the Return Stack and Memory Address Logic can be isolated from the system Data Bus, subroutine calls, subroutine returns, and unconditional jumps can be performed in parallel with other operations. This results in these control transfer operations costing zero clock cycles in many cases.

Program memory is organized as up to 4G bytes of memory, addressable on byte boundaries. Instructions and 32-bit data items are required to be aligned on 32-bit memory boundaries, since data is accessed in 32-bit words from memory. The actual RTX 32P chips can address only 8M bytes because of a limited number of pins on the package.

Microprogram Memory is an on-chip read/write memory containing 2K elements by 30 bits. The memory is addressed as 256 pages of 8 words each. Each opcode in the machine is allocated its own page of 8 words. The Microprogram Counter supplies a 9-bit page address of which only the lowest 8 bits are used in this implementation. This scheme allows supplying 3 bits from the current microinstruction, the lowest bit of which is the result of a 1-in-8 conditional microbranch selection, as the address for the next microinstruction within the same microcode page. This allows conditional branching and looping during the execution of a single opcode.

Instruction decoding is accomplished simply by loading the 9-bit opcode into the Microprogram Counter and using that as the page address to Microprogram Memory. Since the Microprogram Counter is built with a counter circuit, operations can span more than one 8-microinstruction page if required.

The Microinstruction Register (MIR) holds the output of the Microprogram Memory. This allows the next microinstruction to be accessed from Microprogram Memory in parallel with execution of the current microinstruction. The MIR completely removes the Microprogram Memory access delay from the system's critical path. Its use also enforces a lower limit of two clock cycles on instructions. If an instruction could be accomplished in a single clock cycle, a second no-op microinstruction must be added to allow the next instruction to flow through the MIR fetching sequence properly.

The Host Interface allows the RTX 32P to operate in two possible modes: Master Mode and Slave Mode. In Slave Mode, the RTX 32P is controlled by the personal computer host to allow program loading, microprogram loading, and alteration of any register or memory location on the system for initialization or debugging. In Master Mode, the RTX 32P runs its program freely, while the host computer monitors a status register for a request for service. While the RTX 32P is in master mode the host computer may enter a dedicated service loop, or may perform other tasks such as prefetching the next block of a disk input stream or displaying an image, and only periodically poll the status register. The RTX 32P will wait for service from the host for as long as is necessary.

5.3.3 Instruction set summary

The RTX 32P has only one instruction format, shown in Fig. 5.4. Every instruction contains a 9-bit opcode which is used as the page number for addressing microcode. It also contains a 2-bit program flow control field that invokes either an unconditional branch, a subroutine call, or a subroutine exit. In the case of either a subroutine call or an unconditional branch, bits 2–22 are used to specify the high 21 bits of a 23-bit word-aligned target address. This design limits program sizes to 8M bytes unless the page register in the Memory Address Logic is used with special far jump and call instructions. Data fetches and stores see the memory as a contiguous 4G byte address space.

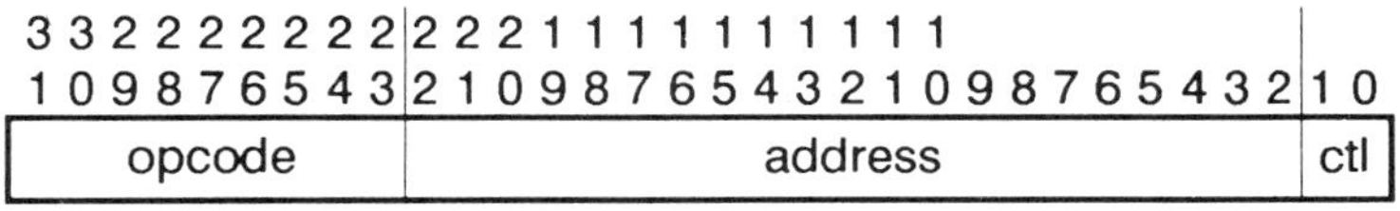

```
3 3 2 2 2 2 2 2 2|2 2 2 1 1 1 1 1 1 1 1 1 1
1 0 9 8 7 6 5 4 3|2 1 0 9 8 7 6 5 4 3 2 1 0 9 8 7 6 5 4 3 2|1 0
```

opcode	address	ctl

Bits   Function
23-31   Opcode
2-22   Address for jump or call (word aligned)
0-1   Program flow control
    00 Jump   10 subroutine call
    01 subroutine exit   11 unused

Fig. 5.4 — RTX 32P instruction format.

Wherever possible, the RTX 32P's compiler compacts an opcode followed by a subroutine call, return, or jump into a single instruction. In those cases where such compaction is not possible, a NOP opcode is compiled with a call, jump, or return, or a jump to next in-line instruction is compiled with an opcode. Tail-end recursion elimination is performed by compressing a subroutine call followed by a subroutine return into a simple jump to the beginning of the subroutine that was to be called, saving the cost of the return that would otherwise be executed in the calling routine.

Since the RTX 32P uses RAM for the microcode memory, the microcode may be completely changed by the user if desired. The standard software environment for the CPU/32 is a version of MVP-FORTH, a FORTH-79 dialect (Haydon 1983). Some of the Forth instructions included in the standard microcoded instruction set are shown in Table 5.2. One thing that

Table 5.2 — RTX 32P instruction set summary

5.2(a) Forth primitives (see Appendix B for descriptions)

!	DDROP
+	DDUP
+!	DNEGATE
−	DROP
0	DSWAP
0<	DUP
0=	I
0BRANCH	I'
1+	J
1−	LEAVE
2*	LIT
2/	NEGATE
<	NOP
PICK	NOT
ROLL	OR
=	OVER
>R	R>
?DUP	R@
@	ROT
ABS	S −> D
AND	SWAP
BRANCH	U*
D!	U/MOD
D+	XOR
D@	

5.2(b) Compound Forth primitives

\<variable\> @	(fetch a variable)
\<variable\> @ +	(fetch and add a variable)
\<variable\> !	(store a variable)
@+	DUP @
LIT +	
OVER +	
OVER −	
R>DROP	
R>SWAP >R	
SWAP !	
SWAP −	
SWAP DROP	

The RTX 32P instruction set may be extended by the user to incorporate any other stack manipulation primitives required for a particular application.

Table 5.2 — Continued.

5.2(c) Special words

Opcode	Data stack	Return stack
HALT	$\rightarrow$	$\rightarrow$
Returns control to host processor		
SYSCALL	N$\rightarrow$	$\rightarrow$
Requests I/O service number N from host		
DOVAR	$\rightarrow$ADDR	$\rightarrow$
Used to implement Forth variables		
DOCON	$\rightarrow$N	$\rightarrow$
Used to implement Forth constants		

5.2(d) Support words for high level operations

The following Forth operations have microcoded support words that do most of their work:

SP@	(fetch contents of data stack pointer)
SP!	(initialize data stack pointer)
RP@	(fetch contents of return stack pointer)
RP!	(initialize return stack pointer)
MATCH	(string compare primitive)
ABORT"	(error checking & reporting word)
+LOOP	(variable increment loop)
/LOOP	(variable unsigned increment loop)
CMOVE	(string move)
<CMOVE	(reverse order string move)
DO	(loop initialization)
ENCLOSE	(text parsing primitive)
LOOP	(increment by 1 loop)
FILL	(block memory initialization word)
TOGGLE	(bit mask/set primitive)

5.2(e) Extended math and floating point support words

Opcode	Data stack	Return stack
<UNORM>	EXP1 U2$\rightarrow$ EXP3 U4	$\rightarrow$
Floating point normalize of unsigned 32-bit mantissa		
ADC	N1 N2 CIN$\rightarrow$ N3 COUT	$\rightarrow$
Add with carry. CIN and COUT are logical flags on the stack.		
ASR	N1$\rightarrow$ N2	$\rightarrow$
Arithmetic shift right.		
BYTE-ROLL	N1$\rightarrow$ N2	$\rightarrow$
Rotate right by 8 bits.		
D+!	D ADDR$\rightarrow$	$\rightarrow$
Sum D into 32-bit number at ADDR.		
D>R	D$\rightarrow$	$\rightarrow$ D
Move D to return stack.		
DLSLN	D1 N2$\rightarrow$ D3	$\rightarrow$
Logical shift left of D1 by N2 bits.		

Table 5.2 — Continued.

Opcode	Data stack	Return stack
DLSR	D1→ D2	→
Logical shift right of D1 by 1 bit.		
DLSRN	D1 N2→ D3	→
Logical shift right of D1 by N2 bits.		
DR>	→ D	D →
Move D from return stack to data stack.		
DROT	D1 D2 D3→ D2 D3 D1	→
Perform double-precision ROT.		
LSLN	N1 N2→ N3	→
Logical shift left of N1 by N2 bits.		
LSR	N1→ N2	→
Logical shift right of N1 by 1 bit.		
LSRN	N1 N2→ N3	→
Logical shift right of N1 by N2 bits.		
Q+	Q1 Q2→ Q3	→
128-bit addition.		
QLSL	Q1→ Q2	→
Logical shift left of Q1 by 1 bit.		
RLC	N1 CIN→ N2 COUT	→
Rotate left through carry N1 by 1 bit. CIN is carry-in, COUT is carry-out.		
RRC	N1 CIN→ N2 COUT	→
Rotate right through carry N1 by 1 bit. CIN is carry-in, COUT is carry-out.		

Note: The RTX 32P uses RAM microcode memory, so the user may add or modify any instructions desired. The above list merely indicates the instructions supplied with the standard development software package.

is noticeable in this instruction set is the number and complexity of instructions supported.

Table 5.2(b) shows some common Forth word combinations that are available as single instructions. Table 5.2(c) shows some words that are used to support underlying Forth operations such as subroutine call and exit. Table 5.2(d) lists some high level Forth words that are directly supported by specialized microcode. Table 5.2(e) shows words that were added in microcode to support extended precision integer operations and 32-bit floating point calculations.

Since the instructions vary considerably in complexity, execution time of instructions ranges accordingly. Simple instructions that manipulate data on the stack such as + and **SWAP** take 2 microcycles (one memory cycle) each. Complex microinstructions such as **Q+** (128-bit addition) may take 10 or more microinstructions, but are still much faster than comparable high level code. If desired, microcoded loops can be written that can potentially last thousands of clock cycles to do things such as block memory moves.

As mentioned earlier, each instruction invokes a sequence of microinstructions on a Microprogram Memory page corresponding to the 9-bit opcode for the instruction. Fig. 5.5 shows the microinstruction format. The microcode used is horizontal, which means that there is only one format for microcode, and that the format is broken into separate fields to control different portions of the machine.

As with the WISC CPU/16, the simplicity of the stack machine approach and the RTX 32P hardware results in a simple microcode format, in this case only using 30 bits per microinstruction. The microcode format of the RTX 32P is similar to that of the CPU/16 discussed in the previous chapter.

Bits 0–3 of the microinstruction specify the source of the system Data Bus. Two of the bus sources are used as special control signals to configure the RTX 32P for one-clock-cycle-per-bit multiplication and nonrestoring division of 32/64-bit numbers.

Bits 8–9 specify the Data Bus destination. Two special cases for destinations exist: DLO may be independently specified as a bus destination using bits 22–23, and the DHI register is always loaded with the ALU output. Bits 8–9 and 10–11 specify Data Stack Pointer and Return Stack Pointer control, respectively. Bits 12–13 control a shifter on the output of the ALU. This shifter allows shifting left or right, as well as an 8-bit rotation function.

Bits 14–15 of the microinstruction are unused, and therefore not included in the Microcode RAM. Bits 16–20 control the function of the ALU. Bit 21 specifies a carry-in of 0 or 1. To synthesize multiple precision arithmetic, the microcode does a conditional microbranch based on the carry-out of the low half of the result, and then forces the next carry-in to 0 or 1 as appropriate. Bits 22–23 control the loading and shifting of the DLO register.

Bits 24–29 of the microinstruction are used to compute a 3-bit offset into the microprogram page for fetching the next microinstruction. Bits 24–26 select one of eight condition codes to form the lowest address bit, while bits 27–28 are used as constants to generate the two high order address bits. This allows jumping and 2-way conditional branching anywhere within the microprogram page on every clock cycle. Bit 29 can be used to increment the contents of the 9-bit Micro Program Counter to allow opcodes to use more than 8 Microcode Memory locations. Bit 30 initiates the instruction decoding sequence for the next instruction. This is required since instructions are a variable number of clock cycles long. Bit 31 controls the return address incrementer for use as a counter into memory for block data accesses.

One microinstruction is executed on every clock cycle, with two or more microinstructions executed for every machine macroinstruction.

5.3.4 Architectural features

The heritage of the WISC CPU/16 in the RTX 32P architecture is unmistakable. The most obvious area of improvement is the addition of more efficient Memory Address Logic and the isolation of the Return Address Stack from the Data Bus during subroutine call and return operations. These changes,

3	3	2	2	2	2	2	2	2	2	2	1	1	1	1	1	1	1	1	1	1											
1	0	9	8	7	6	5	4	3	2	1	0	9	8	7	6	5	4	3	2	1	0	9	8	7	6	5	4	3	2	1	0
i	d	m	nxt		cond		dlo	c		alu					---		s		rp		dp		dest				src			

Bits	Function

31 Increment return address register

30 Begin decoding next instruction

29 Increment MPC control

27-28 Next microaddress constant bits

24-26 Condition code select bits

000 0	011 Sign	110 Unused
001 Not(Carry-out)	100 DLO lowest bit	111 1
010 Not(Zero)	101 Unused	

22-23 DLO shift/destination control

00 Nop	10 Shift left	11 Load from bus
01 Shift right		

21 ALU carry-in/shift-in bit

16-20 ALU mode & function select

00000 A + not(CIN)	10001 A nor B	11010 B
00010 A-B-CIN	10011 0	11011 A and B
00110 A-B	10100 A nand B	11100 -1
01001 A + B + CIN	10101 Not(B)	11110 A or B
01100 A + A + CIN	10110 A xor B	11111 A
10000 Not(A)	11001 A xnor B	

14-15 Unused

12-13 ALU shifter control

00 Nop	10 Shift left 1 bit	11 Rotate right 8 bits
01 Shift right 1 bit		

10-11 RP count control

00 Nop	10 Increment RP	11 Decrement RP
01 Nop		

8-9 DP count control

00 Decrement DP	10 Nop	11 Nop
01 Increment DP		

4-7 Bus destination select

0000 None	0101 Addr Latch	1010 Return Addr Incr
0001 DP	0110 Status Reg	1011 RAM
0010 DS	0111 Flag Reg	1100 RAM-BYTE
0011 Unused	1000 RP	1101 Instruction Reg
0100 RAM Page Reg	1001 RS	1110 Microcode RAM

0-3 Bus source select

0000 Host	0101 Multiply-select	1010 Return Addr Incr
0001 DP	0110 Divide-select	1011 RAM
0010 DS	0111 FLAGS	1100 RAM-BYTE
0011 DLO	1000 RP	1101 Micro-PC
0100 DHI	1001 RS	1110 Microcode RAM

Fig. 5.5 — RTX 32P microinstruction format.

along with the RTX 32P's unique instruction format, allow subroutine calls, returns, and jumps to be processed 'for free' to the extent that they can be combined with opcodes.

The RTX 32P's clock runs at twice the speed that main memory can be accessed, thus giving two clock cycles per memory cycle, and a minimum of two clock cycles per instruction.

There are a number of uses for the RTX 32P's instruction format, many of which are not immediately obvious. One of them is for executing conditional branches. The RTX 32P does not have direct hardware support for conditional branches, since this would slow down the rest of the hardware too much on other instructions or require excessively fast program memory. Conditional branches are accomplished by using a special **0BRANCH** opcode combined with a subroutine call to the branch target. The subroutine call is processed by the hardware in parallel with the opcode's evaluation of whether the top stack element is zero (in which case the branch is taken). If the branch is to be taken, the Return Stack is popped, converting the subroutine call to just a jump, and execution continues. If the branch is not to be taken, the microcode pops the Return Stack and uses the value to fetch the branch fall-through instruction, in effect performing an immediate subroutine return. The cost for this conditional branch is 3 clock cycles to take a branch, 4 clock cycles to not take a branch. Remember that on this processor each memory cycle is 2 clock cycles.

Another interesting capability of the RTX 32P is quick access of any memory location as a variable. Even though the 0-operand instruction format would seem to require a second memory location to specify the variable address, the following operation can be used. A special opcode is compiled with a subroutine call, where the address of the 'subroutine' is actually the address of the variable desired to be fetched. The microcode then 'steals' the variable value as the instruction fetching logic reads it in, then forces a subroutine return before the value can be executed as an instruction.

The point of discussing these two methods is to illustrate that there are several significant capabilities of the hardware that are not immediately obvious to programmers who are used to more conventional machines. These capabilities are especially useful in programming data structure accesses (for example, expert system decision trees), and actually allow direct execution of data structures. This direct execution is accomplished by storing the data in a tagged format having a 9-bit tag (corresponding to special user-defined opcodes) and a 23-bit address that is a subroutine call or jump to the next data element in the structure, or a subroutine return for a nil pointer.

An important implementation feature of the RTX 32P is that all resources on the machine can be directly controlled by the host computer. This can be done because the host interface supports Microinstruction Register load and single-step clock features. With these features, any microinstruction desired can be executed by first loading values into any or all registers in the system, loading a microinstruction, cycling the clock, then reading data values back to examine the results. This design technique makes writing microcode extremely straightforward, eliminating the need for expensive external analysis hardware. It also makes testing and diagnostic programs very simple to write.

The RTX 32P supports interrupt handling, including interrupt on stack underflow and overflow for both the Data Stack and the Return Stack. The usual technique for handling these overflows and underflows is to page in or out half the on-chip stack contents to a holding area in program memory. This allows programs to use arbitrarily deep stacks. With a 512-element hardware stack buffer size, typical Forth programs never experience a stack overflow.

5.3.5   Implementation and featured application areas

The RTX 32P is implemented on 2.5 micron CMOS standard cell technology in a 2-chip set. The data path chip, which contains the ALU, data stack, and ALU bits of the microcode memory, is an 84-pin Leadless Chip Carrier (LCC). The control chip, which contains the rest of the system, is packaged in a 145-pin Pin Grid Array (PGA). The RTX 32P runs at 8 MHz.

The RTX 32P is designed for real-time control applications, especially in the area of embedded systems with low power and small size requirements. As was mentioned previously, the RTX 32P is a prototyping vehicle for a commercial processor which, as of this writing, is planned to be called the RTX 4000. This new processor will have several features that make it suitable for use in real-time control applications and personal computer coprocessor acceleration tasks including: a mixture of ROM and RAM microcode to shrink the system onto a single chip, stand-alone operation, on-chip hardware support for floating point math, a significantly faster clock speed, and on-chip support for dynamic program memory chips. Some versions of the chip may not have all these features. In addition, architectural enhancements will be made to support languages such as C, Ada, and LISP by allowing use of the address field in the instruction to specify fast-access 21-bit literals. This will allow crucial operations such as frame-pointer-plus-offset addressing to run at high speed.

The information in this section is based on the descriptions of the WISC CPU/32 in Koopman (1987c), and Koopman (1987d), and the introduction of the RTX 32P in Koopman (1989).

5.4   ARCHITECTURE OF THE SF1

5.4.1   Introduction

The Wright State University's SF1 (which stands for Stack Frame computer number 1) is an experimental multi-stack processor designed to efficiently execute high level languages, including both Forth and C. It is designed to have a large number of stacks, using five stacks in the implementation described here. While the SF1 has its roots in the Forth language, it crosses the boundary between ML0 and ML2 machines by allowing each instruction to address any of the elements of two stacks directly from the stack memory. It has an interesting mix of the features found on the FRISC 3 and the RTX 32P, as well as some unique innovations.

Wright State University has developed a series of stack-based computers starting with RUFOR (Grewe & Dixon 1984), which was purely a Forth-based processor built with bit-slice components. In 1985–1986, a computer architecture class built a discrete component prototype of a more genera-lized stack processor called the SF1. In 1986-1987, a VLSI class extended that architecture and made a multi-chip custom silicon implementation which was the VLSI version of the SF1. The following description is of this VLSI SF1 implementation.

The intended application area for the SF1 is real-time control using Forth, C, and other high level languages.

5.4.2   Block diagram
Fig. 5.6 is an architectural block diagram of the SF1.

The SF1 has two busses. The MBUS is multiplexed to transfer addresses to program memory and then instructions and data to or from program memory. The SBUS is used to transfer data between system resources. The two-bus design allows instructions to be fetched on the MBUS while data operations are taking place on the SBUS.

The ALU has an associated top-of-stack register (TOS) which receives the results of all ALU operations. The ALU input (ALUI) register acts as a holding buffer to contain the second operand for the ALU. ALUI may be loaded from either the SBUS for most operations, or the MBUS for memory fetches. Both the ALUI and the TOS may be routed to the MBUS or the SBUS. The TOS register by convention contains the top stack element of whatever stack is being used for a particular instruction, although it is up to the programmer to ensure it is managed properly.

There are eight different sources and destinations connected to the stack bus: S, F, R, L, G, C, I, and P:

    S — general-purpose stack for parameters
    L — loop counter stack
    G — global stack
    F — frame stack
    R — return address stack
    C — in-line constant value
    I — I/O address space
    P — Program counter

All eight are referred to as stacks in the machine's reference material, but in

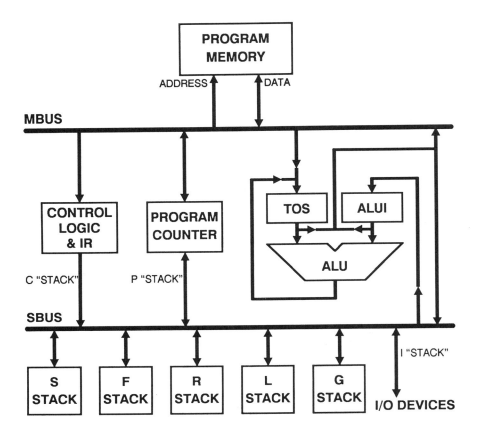

Fig. 5.6 — SF1 block diagram.

reality the C, I, and P resources are special nonstack structures. The stacks L, G, F, and R are for the most part interchangeable in practice, and may be used for any purpose. The S stack is somewhat specialized in that all subroutine return addresses are automatically pushed onto the S stack.

Any one of the top 8192 elements of these stacks may be specified as a bus source or destination. Whenever a stack is read, the top element may be either retained or popped. When a stack is popped, the top element is always shifted out of the stack memory, regardless of which element was actually read.

Similarly, when a stack is used as a bus destination, any one of the top 8192 elements of the stack may be written to, or the top stack element may be pushed with a value from the SBUS.

The C bus source is used to return a 13-bit signed constant from the address field of the instruction. P is used to load and store the program counter. I is used to address an I/O address space of 8K words.

The Program Counter (PC) is a counter that can be asserted on the

MBUS to provide addresses for instructions as well as loaded from the MBUS for jumps and subroutine calls. The PC can also be read and written on the SBUS to save and restore subroutine return addresses.

5.4.3 Instruction set summary

The SF1 has two instruction formats as shown in Fig. 5.7. The first instruction format is used for jumps and subroutine calls, the second for all other instructions.

Fig. 5.7(a) shows the jump/subroutine call instruction format. This instruction format is selected by a 0 in bit 0 of the instruction. Bit 1 of the instruction selects a jump if set to 1, or a subroutine call if set to 0. Bits 2–31 of the instruction select a word-aligned address as the jump/call target. This instruction format is quite similar to that of the RTX 32P shown in Fig. 5.4, but without the opcode in the highest order bits. Both jump and subroutine call instructions take one clock cycle.

Fig. 5.7(b) shows the operation instruction format, which is more like the FRISC 3 ALU instruction format shown in Fig. 5.2(c). Bit 0 is a constant 1 which selects this instruction format.

Bit 1 selects between a no-branch and a skip operation. If a skip operation is selected and the zero status flag is set, the next instruction in the instruction stream is fetched. This can be used to implement a conditional branch-on-zero instruction sequence.

Bits 2–7 select the ALU operations. A special ALU operation returns the status flags from the previous ALU instruction. These flags can be used as an offset into a multi-way jump table for branching on multiple condition codes. This conditional branching is slower than using a skip instruction, but is more flexible.

Before covering the operation of bits 8–28, we should describe the way the SBUS works during a clock cycle. The SBUS is used twice during each clock cycle. During the first half of the clock cycle, the SBUS is used to read one of 8 bus sources. The data read is always placed into the ALUI register. During the second half of the clock cycle, the ALU performs its operation on the new ALUI value and the old TOS value. Simultaneously, the old TOS value is written to one of 8 bus destinations. Bit 29 in the instruction format can override the selection of TOS as the value to be written by forcing ALUI (which was just loaded on the first half of the clock cycle) to be asserted on the SBUS during the second half of the clock cycle.

Bits 8–11 select the SBUS destination. This destination is written with the TOS value set by the previous instruction during the second half of the clock cycle. Bit 8 selects whether the destination stack is pushed or just written. Similarly, bits 12–15 select the SBUS source, which is read during the first half of the clock cycle. Bit 12 selects whether the source stack is popped.

Bits 16–28 provide an address that is used when reading and writing the stacks. This address allows reading or writing any one of the top 8K stack elements directly. Note that there is only one address in the instruction, so

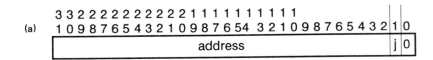

(a)

```
3 3 2 2 2 2 2 2 2 2 2 2 1 1 1 1 1 1 1 1 1 1
1 0 9 8 7 6 5 4 3 2 1 0 9 8 7 6 5 4  3 2 1 0 9 8 7 6 5 4 3 2 1 0
┌────────────────────────────────────────────────────────┬─┬─┐
│                         address                          │j│0│
└────────────────────────────────────────────────────────┴─┴─┘
```

Bits	Function
2-31	Target address
1	Branching mode select
	0 Subroutine call 1 Jump
0	Constant 0 specifies jump/call format

(b)

```
3 3 2 2 2 2 2 2 2 2 2 2 1 1 1 1 1 1 1 1 1 1
1 0 9 8 7 6 5 4 3 2 1 0 9 8 7 6 5 4 3 2 1 0 9 8 7 6 5 4 3 2 1 0
┌─┬─┬─┬──────────────┬─────┬─┬──────┬─┬──────┬─┬─┐
│e│r│a│   address    │ src │p│ dest │p│  alu │b│1│
└─┴─┴─┴──────────────┴─────┴─┴──────┴─┴──────┴─┴─┘
```

Bits	Function
31	Extended instruction select when 1
30	R/W for extended instructions (1 = read)
29	ALUI used instead of TOS when 1
16-28	Stack address (0 to 8191)
13-15	SBUS source select

000 S stack	100 G stack
001 F stack	101 Constant
010 R stack	110 I/O address space
011 L stack	111 Program counter

Bits	Function
12	SBUS selected source stack is popped when 1
9-11	SBUS destination select

000 S stack	100 G stack
001 F stack	101 none
010 R stack	110 I/O address space
011 L stack	111 Program counter

Bits	Function
8	SBUS selected destination stack is pushed when 1
2-7	ALU operation

000000 TOS + ALUI	100010 TOS shifted left
000010 TOS-ALUI	100000 TOS arithmetically shifted right
000100 ALUI-TOS	111000 ALUI
010010 TOS and ALUI	110100 ALUI shifted right
011110 TOS or ALUI	110010 ALUI shifted left
011100 TOS xor ALUI	110000 ALUI arithmetical shifted right
101000 TOS	
100100 TOS shifted right	000001 Read status flags

Bits	Function
1	Branching mode select
	0 No branch 1 Skip next word
0	Constant 1 specifies operation format

Fig. 5.7 — SF1 instruction formats. (a) Jump/Call. (b) Operation.

both the source and the destination stacks must use the same address on a given cycle.

Bit 29 is used to override the selection of TOS as the value to be written to the SBUS destination. When set, this bit uses the ALUI register instead of the TOS register. This allows direct data movement between any two SBUS resources by loading the value into the ALUI during the first half clock cycle, then storing that same value during the second half clock cycle.

Bits 30–31 are used to control memory accesses. Bit 31 selects an extended instruction cycle, which uses a second clock cycle to access RAM via the MBUS (the first clock cycle is used to fetch the next instruction). Bit 30 specifies a RAM read or write operation. The TOS register is read during the first clock cycle to provide an address, then read or written again during the second clock cycle to provide or receive the RAM data. Note that RAM reads and writes are performed on the second of two clock cycles, so bits 2–29 may be used to perform a normal instruction on the first of the two cycles. This first clock cycle is often used to reload the TOS register (which contained an address) with the value to be written into the RAM during the second clock cycle.

5.4.4 Architectural features

Once again, we see the importance of providing a dedicated path for instruction fetching in the form of the MBUS, with a second path for data manipulations in the form of the SBUS. As with the other stack machines, the SF1 is designed to support fast instruction execution and, in particular, quick subroutine calls.

The use of operands in the SF1 operation instruction format is novel. The use of a single top-of-stack register as one input for all ALU operations and the fact that only a single address field is provided makes the architecture feel like a 1-operand stack machine. However, the fact that both a source and a destination may be specified for each instruction makes the machine feel more like a 2-operand machine. Perhaps this instruction format is more properly called a 1-operand instruction, since only a single address is available while both a source and a destination may be selected.

The reason for having the top 8K elements of each stack directly addressable is to provide support for languages such as C which have the notion of a stack frame. In addition, one of the stacks can be used as a very large (8K word) register file by simply never pushing or popping that particular stack.

The reason for having several hardware stacks is to support fast context switching in real-time control applications. Although the implementation described only contains five hardware stacks, this number can be increased in other versions of the design. A simple way to allocate the stacks would be to dedicate one hardware stack to each of four high priority tasks, with the fifth stack saved and restored to and from program memory as required to process low priority tasks.

Subroutine returns are accomplished under program control by popping a stack and writing the top stack element into the PC. Because of a prefetch pipeline, the instruction following the subroutine return is also executed before the return takes effect.

32-bit literal values are obtained by using PC-relative addressing with a 13-bit offset to access a constant stored in the program space. This constant is typically placed after an unconditional branch, or after the subroutine return at the end of the procedure in which it is used.

5.4.5   Implementation and featured application areas

The SF1 is implemented on 3.0 micron CMOS MOSIS technology using a full-custom approach. Two custom chip designs are used. One chip contains the ALU and PC, while the other chip implements a 32-bit-wide stack. Control and instruction decoding is accomplished using programmable logic, but will eventually be incorporated onto custom VLSI as well.

The implementation of the stack chips is quite different than what has been seen on other stack machines. Since the stack must be designed for random access of elements, an obvious design method would be to incorporate an adder with a stack pointer into a standard memory. This method has the disadvantage that it is slow and difficult to expand to multi-chip stacks.

The approach taken in the SF1 is completely different. Each stack memory is actually a giant shift register that actually moves the stack elements between adjacent memory words when the stack is pushed or popped. Addressing the Nth word in the stack is done simply by addressing the Nth word in memory, since the top element on the stack is always kept shifted into the 0th memory address. One disadvantage of this approach is that shift register cells are larger than regular memory cells, so the largest stack chip made for the SF1 contains only 128 words by 32 bits of memory.

The SF1 is primarily a research platform, with an emphasis on real-time control with fast context switching (by dedicating a stack chip to each task) and support for high level languages.

The information in this section is based on the description of the SF1 given by Dixon (1987) and Longway (1988).

6

Understanding stack machines

In the preceding chapters, we have covered both an abstract description of a stack machine, and several examples of real stack machines that have been built. What we shall examine now is why they are designed the way they are, and why stack machines have certain inherent advantages over more conventional designs.

Three different approaches to computer design are used as reference points for this chapter. The first reference point is that of the Complex Instruction Set Computer (CISC), which is typified by Digital Equipment Corporation's VAX series and any of the microprocessors used in personal computers (e.g. 680x0, 80x86). The second reference point is the Reduced Instruction Set Computer (RISC) (Patterson 1985) as typified by the Berkeley RISC project (Sequin & Patterson 1982) and the Stanford MIPS project (Hennesy 1984). The third reference point is that of stack machines as described in the preceding chapters.

Section 6.1 discusses some of the history of the debates that have taken place over the years among advocates of register-based machines, stack-based machines, and storage-to-storage-based machines. A related topic is the more recent debates between proponents of high level language CISC architectures and RISC architectures.

Section 6.2 discusses the advantages of stack machines. Stack machines have smaller program sizes, lower hardware complexity, higher system performance, and better execution consistency than other processors in many application areas.

Section 6.3 presents the results of a study of instruction frequencies in Forth programs. Not surprisingly, subroutine calls and returns constitute a significant percentage of the instruction mix for Forth programs.

Section 6.4 examines the issue of stack management by using the results of a stack access simulation. The results indicate that fewer than 32 stack elements are needed for many application programs. This section also discusses four different methods of handling stack overflows: very large stacks, a demand-fed stack manager, a paging stack manager, and an associative cache memory.

Section 6.5 examines the cost of interrupts and multi-tasking on a stack-based machine. A simulation shows that context switching of the stack buffers is a minor cost in most environments. Furthermore, the cost of context switching with stack buffers may be further reduced by appropriately programmed interrupts, using lightweight tasks, and by partitioning the stack buffer into multiple small buffer areas.

6.1 AN HISTORICAL PERSPECTIVE

The debate between designers of machines with hardware supported stacks and other designers has a long history. This debate can be split into two major areas: the debate between register-based and non-register-based machine designers, and the debate between high level language machine designers and RISC designers. While we cannot hope to put forth definitive answers to the questions raised in these debates, the ideas presented in the references given are worthy of consideration by the interested reader.

6.1.1 Register vs. nonregister machines

The debate on whether to design a machine that makes registers explicitly available to the assembly language programmer dates back to design decisions made in the late 1950s. The existence of the stack-based KDF.9 computer (Haley 1962) is evidence that computer architects had begun thinking of alternatives to the standard register-based way of designing computers many years ago.

The debate on whether or not to use register-based machines involves a number of alternatives. These alternatives include: pure stack-based machines, single-operand stack-based machines (also called stack/accumulator machines), and storage-to-storage machines.

The pure stack machines, which fall into the SS0, MS0, SL0, and ML0 taxonomy categories, are exceedingly simple. An obvious argument in favor of stack-based machines is that expression evaluation requires the use of a stack-like structure. Register-based machines spend some of their time emulating a stack-based machine while evaluating expressions. However, pure stack machines may require more instructions than a stack/accumulator machine (SS1, MS1, SL1, ML1 taxonomy categories) since they cannot fetch a value and perform an arithmetic operation upon that value at the same time. The astute reader will notice that the 32-bit stack machines discussed in Chapter 5 use multiple-operation instructions such as "**<vari-able>** @ +" to compensate for this problem to a large degree.

Storage-to-storage machines, in which all instruction operands are in memory, are seen as being valuable in running high level languages such as C and Pascal. The reason given for this is that most assignment statements in these languages have only one or two variables on the right-hand side of the assignment operator. This means that most expressions can be handled with a single instruction. This eliminates instructions which otherwise would be required to shuffle data into and out of registers. The CRISP architecture (Ditzel *et al.* 1987a, 1987b) is an example of a sophisticated storage-to-storage processor.

Some of the most frequently cited references in this debate are a sequence of articles that appeared in *Computer Architecture News*: Keedy

(1978a), Keedy (1978b), Keedy (1979), Myers (1977), Schulthess & Mumprecht (1977), and Sites (1978). These articles do not address all the issues and are dated in some respects. Nonetheless, they form a good starting point for those who are interested in the historical roots of this ongoing debate.

6.1.2 High level language vs. RISC machines

A related debate is that between proponents of high level language machines and the RISC philosophy of machine design.

High level language machines may be thought of as one of the advanced evolutionary paths of the CISC philosophy. These machines have potentially very complex instructions that map directly onto the functions of one or more high level languages. In some cases, the output of the front end of a compiler is used to generate an intermediate level code that is executed directly by the machine, such as P-code for Pascal or M-code for Modula-2. The ultimate extension of this philosophy is probably the SYMBOL project (Ditzel & Kwinn 1980) which implemented all system functions in hardware, including program editing and compilation.

The RISC philosophy of high level language support is one of providing the simplest possible building blocks for the compiler to use in synthesizing high level language operations. This usually involves code sequences of loads, stores, and arithmetic operations to implement each high level language statement. RISC proponents claim that these collections of code sequences can be made to run faster on a RISC machine than equivalent complex instructions on a CISC machine.

The stack machine design philosophy falls somewhere in between the philosophies of high level language machine design and RISC design. Stack machines provide very simple primitives which may be executed in a single memory cycle, in the spirit of the RISC philosophy. However, efficient programs on stack machines make extensive use of application specific code that is accessed via cheap subroutine calls. This collection of subroutines may be thought of as a virtual instruction set that is tailored to the needs of high level language compilers, without requiring complicated hardware support.

A good sampling of references on the topic of high level language machines versus RISC machines is: Cragon (1980), Ditzel & Patterson (1980), Kavipurapu & Cragon (1980), Kavi et al. (1982), Patterson & Piepho (1982), and Wirth (1987).

6.2 ARCHITECTURAL DIFFERENCES FROM CONVENTIONAL MACHINES

The obvious difference between stack machines and conventional machines is the use of 0-operand stack addressing instead of register- or memory-based addressing schemes. This difference, when combined with support of quick subroutine calls, makes stack machines superior to conventional machines in the areas of program size, processor complexity, system complexity, processor performance, and consistency of program execution.

6.2.1 Program size

A popular saying is that 'memory is cheap'. Anyone who has watched the historically rapid growth in memory chip sizes knows the amount of memory available on a processor can be expected to increase dramatically with time.

The problem is that even as memory chip capacity increases, the size of problems that people are calling on computers to solve is growing at an even faster rate. This means that the size of programs and their data sets is growing even faster than available memory size. Further aggravating the situation is the widespread use of high level languages for all phases of programming. This results in bulkier programs, but of course improves programmer productivity.

Not surprisingly, this explosion in program complexity leads to a seeming contradiction, the saying that 'programs expand to fill all available memory, and then some'. The amount of program memory available for an application is fixed by the economics of the actual cost of the memory chips and printed circuit board space. It is also affected by mechanical limits such as power, cooling, or the number of expansion slots in the system (limits which also figure in the economic picture). Even with an unlimited budget, electrical loading considerations and the speed-of-light wiring delay limit bring an ultimate limit to the number of fast memory chips that may be used by a processor. Small program sizes reduce memory costs, component count, and power requirements, and can improve system speed by allowing the cost effective use of smaller, higher speed memory chips. Additional benefits include better performance in a virtual memory environment (Sweet & Sandman 1982, Moon 1985), and a requirement for less cache memory to achieve a given hit ratio. Some applications, notably embedded microprocessor applications, are very sensitive to the costs of printed circuit board space and memory chips, since these resources form a substantial proportion of all system costs (Ditzel *et al.* 1987b).

The traditional solution for a growing program size is to employ a hierarchy of memory devices with a series of capacity/cost/access-time tradeoffs. A hierarchy might consist of (from cheapest/biggest/slowest to most expensive/smallest/fastest): magnetic tape, optical disk, hard disk, dynamic memory, off-chip cache memory, and on-chip instruction buffer memory. So a more correct version of the saying that 'memory is cheap' might be that 'slow memory is cheap, but fast memory is very dear indeed'.

The memory problem comes down to one of supplying a sufficient quantity of memory fast enough to support the processor at a price that can be afforded. This is accomplished by fitting the most program possible into the fastest level of the memory hierarchy.

The usual way to manage the fastest level of the memory hierarchy is by using cache memories. Cache memories work on the principle that a small section of a program is likely to be used more than once within a short period of time. Thus, the first time a small group of instructions is referenced, it is copied from slow memory into the fast cache memory and saved for later use. This decreases the access delay on the second and subsequent accesses to program fragments. Since cache memory has a limited capacity, any instruction fetched into cache is eventually discarded when its slot must be used to hold a more recently fetched instruction. The problem with cache memory is that it must be big enough to hold enough program fragments long enough for the eventual reuse to occur.

A cache memory that is big enough to hold a certain number of instructions, called the 'working set', can significantly improve system performance. How does the size of a program affect this performance increase? If we assume a given number of high level language operations in the working set, consider the effect of increasing the compactness of the encoding of instructions. Intuitively, if a sequence of instructions to accomplish a high level language statement are more compact on machine A than machine B, then machine A needs a smaller number of bytes of cache to hold the instructions generated for the same source code as machine B. This means that machine A needs a smaller cache to achieve the same average memory response time performance.

By way of example, Davidson and Vaughan (1987) suggest that RISC computer programs can be up to 2.5 times bigger than CISC versions of the same programs (although other sources, especially RISC vendors, would place this number at perhaps 1.5 times bigger). They also suggest that the RISC computers need a cache size that is twice as large as a CISC cache to achieve the same performance. Furthermore, a RISC machine with twice the cache of a CISC machine will still generate twice the number of cache misses (since a constant miss ratio generates twice as many misses for twice as many cache accesses), resulting in a need for higher speed main memory devices as well for equal performance. This is corroborated by the rule of thumb that a RISC processor in the 10 MIPS (Million RISC Instructions Per Second) performance range needs 128K bytes of cache memory for satisfactory performance, while high end CISC processors typically need no more than 64K bytes.

Stack machines have much smaller programs than either RISC or CISC machines. Stack machine programs can be 2.5 to 8 times smaller than CISC code (Harris 1980, Ohran 1984, Schoellkopf 1980), although there are some limitations to this observation discussed later. This means that a RISC processor's cache memory may need to be bigger than a stack processor's entire program memory to achieve comparable memory response times! As anecdotal evidence of this effect, consider the following situation: while Unix/C programmers on RISC processors are unhappy with less than 8M to 16M bytes of memory, and want 128K bytes of cache, Forth programmers are still engaged in heated debate as to whether more than 64K bytes of program space is really needed on stack machines.

Small program size on stack machines not only decreases system costs by eliminating memory chips, but can actually improve system performance. This happens by increasing the chance that an instruction will be resident in high speed memory when needed, possibly by using the small program size as a justification for placing an entire program in fast memory.

How can it be that stack processors have such small memory requirements? There are two factors that account for the extremely small program sizes possible on stack machines. The more obvious factor, and the one usually cited in the literature, is that stack machines have small instruction formats. Conventional architectures must specify not only an operation on each instruction, but also operands and addressing modes. For example, a typical register-based machine instruction to add two numbers together might be: **ADD R1,R2**. This instruction must not only specify the **ADD** opcode, but also the fact that the addition is being done on two registers, and that the registers are **R1** and **R2**.

On the other hand, a stack-based instruction set need only specify an **ADD** opcode, since the operands have an implicit address of the current top of stack. The only time that an operand is present is when performing a load or store instruction, or pushing an immediate data value onto the stack. The WISC CPU/16 and Harris RTX 32P use 8- and 9-bit opcodes, respectively, yet have many more opcodes than are actually needed to run programs efficiently. Loosely encoded instructions found on the other processors discussed in this book, exemplified by the Novix NC4016, allow packing 2 or more operations into the same instruction to achieve little sacrifice in code density over a byte-oriented machine.

A less obvious, but actually more important, reason for stack machines having more compact code is that they efficiently support code with many frequently reused subroutines, often called threaded code (Bell 1973, Dewar 1975). While such code is possible on conventional machines, the execution speed penalty is severe. In fact, one of the most elementary compiler optimizations for both RISC and CISC machines is to compile procedure calls as in-line macros. This, added to most programmers' experience that too many procedure calls on a conventional machine will destroy program performance, leads to significantly larger programs on conventional machines.

On the other hand, stack-oriented machines are built to support procedure calls efficiently. Since all working parameters are always present on a stack, procedure call overhead is minimal, requiring no memory cycles for parameter passing. On most stack processors, procedure calls take one clock cycle, and procedure returns take zero clock cycles in the frequent case where they are combined with other operations.

There are several qualifications associated with the claim that stack machines have more compact code than other machines, especially since we are not presenting the results of a comprehensive study here. Program size measures depend largely on the language being used, the compiler, and programming style, as well as the instruction set of the processor being used. Also, the studies by Harris, Ohran, and Schoellkopf were mostly for stack machines that used variable length instructions, while machines described in this book use 16- or 32-bit fixed length instructions. Counterbalancing the fixed instruction length is the fact that processors running Forth can have smaller programs than other stack machines. The programs are smaller because they use frequent subroutine calls, allowing a high degree of code reuse within a single application program. And, as we shall see in a later section, the fixed instruction length for even 32-bit processors such as the RTX 32P does not cost as much program memory space as one might think.

6.2.2 Processor and system complexity

When speaking of the complexity of a computer, two levels are important: processor complexity, and system complexity. Processor complexity is the amount of logic (measured in chip area, number of transistors, etc.) in the actual core of the processor that does the computations. System complexity considers the processor embedded in a fully functional system which contains support circuitry, the memory hierarchy, and software.

CISC computers have become substantially more complex over the years. This complexity arises from the need to be very good at all their many functions simultaneously. A large degree of their complexity stems from an attempt to tightly encode a wide variety of instructions using a large number of instruction formats. Added complexity comes from their support of multiple programming and data models. Any machine that is reasonably efficient at processing COBOL packed decimal data types on a time sliced basis with running double precision floating point FORTRAN matrix operations and LISP expert systems is bound to be complex!

The complexity of CISC machines is partially the result of encoding instructions to keep programs relatively small. The goal is to reduce the semantic gap between high level languages and the machine to produce more efficient code. Unfortunately, this may lead a situation where almost all available chip area is used for the control and data paths (for instance the Motorola 680×0 and Intel 80×86 products). Additionally, an argument made by RISC proponents is that CISC designs may be paying a performance penalty as well as a size penalty.

The extremes to which some CISC processors take the complexity of the core processor may seem excessive, but they are driven by a common and well founded goal: establishment of a consistent and simple interface between hardware and software. The success that this approach can have is demonstrated by the IBM System/370 line of computers. This computer family encompasses a vast range of price and performance, from personal computer plug-in cards to supercomputers, all with the same assembly language instruction set.

The clean and consistent interface between hardware and software at the assembly language level means that compilers need not be excessively complex to produce reasonable code, and that they may be reused among many different machines of the same family. Another advantage of CISC processors is that, since instructions are very compact, they do not require a large cache memory for acceptable system performance. So, CISC machines have traded off increased processor complexity for reduced system complexity.

The concept behind RISC machines is to make the processor faster by reducing its complexity. To this end, RISC processors have fewer transistors in the actual processor control circuitry than CISC machines. This is accomplished by having simple instruction formats and instructions with low semantic content; they don't do much work, but don't take much time to do it. The instruction formats are usually chosen to correspond with requirements for running a particular programming language and task, typically integer arithmetic in the C programming language.

This reduced processor complexity is not without a substantial cost. Most RISC processors have a large bank of registers to allow quick reuse of frequently accessed data. These register banks must be dual-ported memory (allowing two simultaneous accesses at different addresses) to allow fetching both source operands on every cycle. Furthermore, because of the low semantic content of their instructions, RISC processors need much higher memory bandwidth to keep instructions flowing into the CPU. This means that substantial on-chip and system-wide resources must be devoted to cache memory to attain acceptable performance. Also, RISC processors characteristically have an internal instruction pipeline. This means that extra hardware or compiler techniques must be provided to manage the pipeline. Special attention and extra hardware resources must be used to ensure that the pipeline state is correctly saved and restored when interrupts are received.

Finally, different RISC implementation strategies make significant demands on compilers such as: scheduling pipeline usage to avoid hazards, filling branch delay slots, and managing allocation and spilling of the register banks. While the decreased complexity of the processor makes it easier to get bug-free hardware, even more complexity shows up in the compiler. This is bound to make compilers complex as well as expensive to develop and debug.

The reduced complexity of RISC processors comes, then, with an offsetting (perhaps even more severe) increase in system complexity.

Stack machines strive to achieve a balance between processor complexity and system complexity. Stack machine designs realize processor simplicity not by restricting the number of instructions, but rather by limiting the data upon which instructions may operate: all operations are on the top stack elements. In this sense, stack machines are *reduced operand set computers* as opposed to 'reduced instruction set computers'.

Limiting the operand selection instead of how much work the instruction may do has several advantages. Instructions may be very compact, since they need specify only the actual operation, not where the sources are to be obtained. The on-chip stack memory can be single ported, since only a single element needs to be pushed or popped from the stack per clock cycle (assuming the top two stack elements are held in registers). More importantly, since all operands are known in advance to be the top stack elements, no pipelining is needed to fetch operands. The operands are always immediately available in the top-of-stack registers. As an example of this, consider the T and N registers in the NC4016 design, and contrast these with the dozens or hundreds of randomly accessible registers found on a RISC machine.

Having implicit operand selection also simplifies instruction formats. Even RISC machines must have multiple instruction formats. Consider, though, that stack machines have few instruction formats, even to the extreme of having only one instruction format for the RTX 32P. Limiting the number of instruction formats simplifies instruction decoding logic, and speeds up system operation.

Stack machines are extraordinarily simple: 16-bit stack machines typically use only 20 to 35 thousand transistors for the processor core. In contrast, the Intel 80386 chip has 275 thousand transistors and the Motorola 68020 has 200 thousand transistors. Even taking into account that the 80386 and 68020 are 32-bit machines, the difference is significant.

Stack machine compilers are also simple, because instructions are very consistent in format and operand selection. In fact, most compilers for register machines go through a stack-like view of the source program for expression evaluation, then map that information onto a register set. Stack machine compilers have that much less work to do in mapping the stack-like version of the source code into assembly language. Forth compilers, in particular, are well known to be exceedingly simple and flexible.

Stack computer systems are also simple as a whole. Because stack programs are so small, exotic cache control schemes are not required for good performance. Typically the entire program can fit into cache-speed memory chips without the complexity of cache control circuitry.

In those cases where the program and/or data is too large to fit in affordable memory, a software-managed memory hierarchy can be used: frequently used subroutines and program segments can be placed in high speed memory, while infrequently used program segments are placed in slow memory. Inexpensive single-cycle calls to the frequent sections in the high speed memory make this technique very effective.

The Data Stack acts as a data cache for most purposes, such as in procedure parameter passing, and data elements can be moved in and out of high speed memory under software control as desired. While a traditional data cache, and to a lesser extent an instruction cache, might give some speed improvements, they are certainly not required, nor even desirable, for most small- to medium-sized applications.

Stack machines, therefore, achieve reduced processor complexity by limiting the operands available to the instruction. This does not force a reduction of the number of potential instructions available, nor does it cause an explosion in the amount of support hardware and software required to operate the processor. The result of this reduced complexity is that stack computers have more room left for program memory or other special-purpose hardware on-chip. An interesting implication is that, since stack programs are so small, program memory for many applications can be entirely on-chip. This on-chip memory is faster than off-chip cache memory would be, eliminating the need for complex cache control circuitry while sacrificing none of the speed.

6.2.3   Processor performance

Processor performance is a very tricky area to talk about. Untold energy has been spent debating which processor is better than another, often based on sketchy evidence of questionable benchmarks, heated by the flames of self interest and product loyalty (or purchase rationalization).

Some of the reasons that comparisons are so difficult stem from the question of application area. Benchmarks that measure performance at integer arithmetic are not adequate for floating point performance, business applications, or symbolic processing. About the best that one can hope for when using a benchmark is to claim that processor A is better than processor B when installed in the given hardware (with associated caches, memories, disks, clock speeds, etc.), using the given operating systems, using the given compilers, using the given source programming language, but only when running the benchmark that was measured. Clearly, measuring the performance of different machines is a difficult matter.

Measuring the performance of radically different architectures is even harder. At the core of this difficulty is quantifying how much work is done by a single instruction. Since the amount of work done by a polynomial evaluation instruction in a VAX is different than a register-to-register move in a RISC machine, the whole concept of 'Instructions Per Second' is tenuous at best (even when normalized to a standardized instruction measure, using those same benchmarks that we don't really trust). Adding to the problem is that different processors are built using different technology (bipolar, ECL, SOS, NMOS, and CMOS, with varying feature sizes) and different levels of design sophistication (expensive full-custom layout, standard cell automatic layout, and gate array layout). Yet, the very concept of comparing architectures requires deducting the effects of differences in implementation technologies. Furthermore, performance varies greatly with the characteristics of the software being executed. The problem is that in real life, the effectiveness of a particular computer is measured not only by processor speed, but also by the quality and performance of the system hardware, operating system, programming language, and compiler.

All these difficulties should lead the reader to the conclusion that the problem of finding exact performance measures is not going to be resolved here. Instead, we shall concentrate on a discussion of some reasons why stack machines can be made to go faster than other types of machines on an instruction-by-instruction basis, why stack machines have good system speed characteristics, and what kinds of programs stack machines are well suited to.

6.2.3.1   *Instruction execution rate*

The most sophisticated RISC processors boast that they have the highest possible instruction execution rate — one instruction per processor clock cycle. This is accomplished by pipelining instructions into some sequence of instruction address generation, instruction fetch, instruction decode, data fetch, instruction execute, and data store cycles as shown in Fig. 6.1(a). This breakdown of instruction execution accelerates overall instruction flow, but

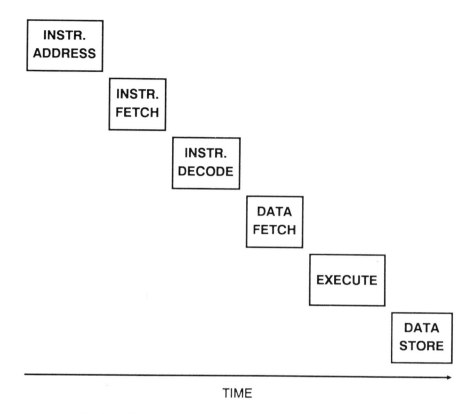

TIME

Fig. 6.1 — Instruction phase overlapping (a) Raw instruction phases.

introduces a number of problems. The most significant of these problems is management of data to avoid hazards caused by data dependencies. This problem comes about when one instruction depends upon the result of the previous instruction. This can create a problem, because the second instruction must wait for the first instruction to store its results before it can fetch its own operands. There are several hardware and software strategies to alleviate the impact of data dependencies, but none of them completely solves it.

Stack machines can execute programs as quickly as RISC machines, perhaps even faster, without the data dependency problem. It has been said that register machines are more efficient than stack machines because register machines can be pipelined for speed while stack machines cannot. This problem is caused by the fact that each instruction depends on the effect of the previous instruction on the stack. The whole point is, however, that stack machines *do not need* to be pipelined to get the same speed as RISC machines.

Consider how the RISC machine instruction pipeline can be modified when it is redesigned for a stack machine. Both machines need to fetch the

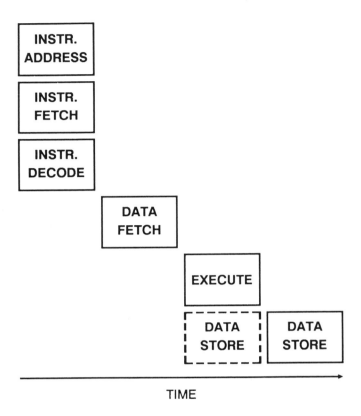

TIME

Fig. 6.1 — Instruction phase overlapping (b) Typical RISC machine.

instruction, and on both machines this can be done in parallel with processing previous instructions. For convenience, we shall lump this stage in with
instruction decoding. RISC and some stack machines need to decode the
instruction, although stack machines such as the RTX 32P do not need to
perform conditional operations to extract parameter fields from the instruction or chose which format to use, and are therefore simpler than RISC
machines.

In the next step of the pipeline, the major difference becomes apparent.
RISC machines must spend a pipeline stage accessing operands for the
instruction after (at least some of) the decoding is completed. A RISC
instruction specifies two or more registers as inputs to the ALU for the
operation. A stack machine does not need to fetch the data; this will be
waiting on top of the stack when needed. This means that as a minimum, the
stack machine can dispense with the operand fetch portion of the pipeline.
Actually, the stack access can also be made faster than the register access.
This is because a single-ported stack can be made smaller, and therefore
faster than a dual-ported register memory.

The instruction execute portion of both the RISC and the stack machine

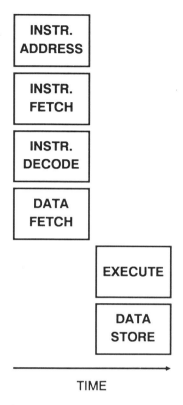

TIME

Fig. 6.1 — Instruction phase overlapping (c) Typical stack machine.

are judged to be about the same since the same sort of ALU can be used by both systems. But, even in this area, some stack machines can gain an advantage over RISC machines by precomputing ALU functions based on the top-of-stack elements before the instruction is even decoded, as is done on the M17 stack machine.

The operand storage phase takes another pipeline stage in some RISC designs, since the result must be written back into the register file. This write conflicts with reads that need to take place for new instructions beginning execution, causing delays or the need for a triple-ported register file. This can require holding the ALU output in a register, then using that register in the next clock cycle as a source for the register file write operation. Conversely, the stack machine simply deposits the ALU output result in the top-of-stack register and is done. An additional problem is that extra data forwarding logic must be provided in a RISC machine to prevent waiting for the result to be written back into the register file if the ALU output is needed as an input for the next instruction. A stack machine always has the ALU output available as one of the implied inputs to the ALU.

Fig. 6.1(b) shows that RISC machines need at least three pipeline stages and perhaps four to maintain the same throughput: instruction fetch, operand fetch, and instruction execute/operand store. Also, we have noted that there are several problems inherent with the RISC approach, such as data dependencies and resource contention, that are simply not present in the stack machine. Fig. 6.1(c) shows that stack machines need only a two-stage pipeline: instruction fetch and instruction execute.

What this all means is that there is no reason that stack machines should be any slower than RISC machines in executing instructions, and there is a good chance that stack machines can be made faster and simpler using the same fabrication technology.

6.2.3.2   *System Performance*

System performance is even more difficult to measure than raw processor performance. System performance includes not only how many instructions can be performed per second on straight-line code, but also speed in handling interrupts, context switches, and system performance degradation because of factors such as conditional branches and procedure calls. Approaches such as the Three-Dimensional Computer Performance technique (Rabbat *et al.* 1988) are better measures of system performance than the raw instruction execution rate.

RISC and CISC machines are usually constructed to execute straight-line code as the general case. Frequent procedure calls can seriously degrade the performance of these machines. The cost for procedure calls not only includes the cost of saving the program counter and fetching a different stream of instructions, but also the cost of saving and restoring registers, arranging parameters, and any pipeline breaking that may occur. The very existence of a structure called the Return Address Stack should imply how much importance stack machines place upon flow-of-control structures such as procedure calls. Since stack machines keep all working variables on a hardware stack, the setup time required for preparing parameters to pass to subroutines is very low, usually a single **DUP** or **OVER** instruction.

Conditional branches are a difficult thing for any processor to handle. The reason is that instruction prefetching schemes and pipelines depend upon uninterrupted program execution to keep busy, and conditional branches force a wait while the branch outcome is being resolved. The only other option is to forge ahead on one of the possible paths in the hope that there is nondestructive work to be done while waiting for the branch to take effect. RISC machines handle the conditional branch problem by using a 'branch delay slot' (McFarling & Hennesy 1986) and placing a nondestructive instruction or no-op, which is always executed, after the branch.

Stack machines handle branches in different manners, all of which result in a single-cycle branch without the need for a delay slot and the compiler complexity that it entails. The NC4016 and RTX 2000 handle the problem by specifying memory faster than the processor cycle. This means that there is time in the processor cycle to generate an address based on a conditional branch and still have the next instruction fetched by the end of the clock cycle. This approach works well, but runs into trouble as processor speed increases beyond affordable program memory speed.

The FRISC 3 generates the condition for a branch on one instruction, then accomplishes the branch with the next instruction. This is really a rather clever approach, since a comparison or other operation is needed before most branches on any machine. Instead of just doing the comparison operation (usually a subtraction), the FRISC 3 also specifies which condition code is of interest for the next branch. This moves much of the branching decision into the comparison instruction, and only requires the testing of a single bit when executing the succeeding conditional branch.

The RTX 32P uses its microcode to combine comparisons and branches into a two-instruction-cycle combination that takes the equivalent time as a comparison instruction followed by a condition branch. For example, the combination = **0BRANCH** can be combined into a single four-microcycle (two-instruction cycle) operation.

Interrupt handling is much simpler on stack machines than on either RISC or CISC machines. On CISC machines, complex instructions that take many cycles may be so long that they need to be interruptible. This can force a great amount of processing overhead and control logic to save and restore the state of the machine within the middle of an instruction. RISC machines are not too much better off, since they have a pipeline that needs to be saved and restored for each interrupt. They also have registers that need to be saved and restored in order to give the interrupt service routine resources with which to work. It is common to spend several microseconds responding to an interrupt on a RISC or CISC machine.

Stack machines, on the other hand, can typically handle interrupts within a few clock cycles. Interrupts are treated as hardware invoked subroutine calls. There is no pipeline to flush or save, so the only thing a stack processor needs to do to process an interrupt is to insert the interrupt response address as a subroutine call into the instruction stream, and push the interrupt mask register onto the stack while masking interrupts (to prevent an infinite recursion of interrupt service calls). Once the interrupt service routine is entered, no registers need be saved, since the new routine can simply push its data onto the top of the stack. As an example of how fast interrupt servicing can be on a stack processor, the RTX 2000 spends only 4 clock cycles (400 ns) between the time an interrupt request is asserted and the time the first instruction of the interrupt service routine is being executed.

Context switching is perceived as being slower for a stack machine than other machines. However, as experimental results presented later will show, this is not the case.

A final advantage of stack machines is that their simplicity leaves room for algorithm specific hardware on customized microcontroller implementations. For example, the Harris RTX 2000 has an on-chip hardware multiplier. Other examples of application specific hardware for semicustom components might be an FFT address generator, A/D or D/A converters, or communication ports. Features such as these can significantly reduce the parts count in a finished system and dramatically decrease program execution time.

6.2.3.3 *Which programs are most suitable?*

The type of programs which stack machines process very efficiently include: subroutine intensive programs, programs with a large number of control flow structures, programs that perform symbolic computation (which often involves intensive use of stack structures and recursion), programs that are designed to handle frequent interrupts, and programs designed for limited memory space.

6.2.4   Program execution consistency

Advanced RISC and CISC machines rely on many special techniques that give them statistically higher performance over long time periods without guaranteeing high performance during short time periods. System design techniques that have these characteristics include: instruction prefetch queues, complex pipelines, scoreboarding, cache memories, branch target buffers, and branch prediction buffers. The problem is that these techniques cannot guarantee increased instantaneous performance at any particular time. An unfortunate sequence of external events or internal data values may cause bursts of cache misses, queue flushes, and other delays. While high average performance is acceptable for some programs, predictably high instantaneous performance is important for many real-time applications.

Stack machines use none of these statistical speedup techniques to achieve good system performance. As a result of the simplicities of stack machine program execution, stack machines have a very consistent performance at every time scale. As we shall see in Chapter 8, this has a significant impact on real-time control applications programming.

6.3   A STUDY OF FORTH INSTRUCTION FREQUENCIES

Now that we have a conceptual understanding of how stack machines differ from other computers, let us look at some quantitative results that show how stack machines perform. Measurements of instruction frequencies and code sizes for stack-based and register-based machines abound (references include: Blake (1977), Cook & Donde (1982), Cook & Lee (1980), Cragon (1979), Haikala (1982), McDaniel (1982), Sweet & Sandman (1982), and Tanenbaum (1978)). Unfortunately, most of these measurements are for programs written in conventional languages, not in an inherently stack-based language such as Forth. Hayes *et al.* (1987) have previously published execution statistics for Forth programs, but we shall expand upon their findings.

The results in this chapter are all based on programs written in Forth, since these programs take the most advantage of the capabilities of a stack machine. The cautions about benchmarks are still applicable, so these results should be used as only rough approximations to 'truth' (whatever that is).

Six different benchmark programs are referred to in the following sections. Except as noted, all programs are written for a 16-bit Forth system. They are as follows:

Frac: a fractal landscape generation program that uses a random number generator. It is always seeded with the same initial value for consistency to generate a graphics image. (Koopman 1987e, Koopman 1987f)

Life: a simple implementation of Conway's game of Life on an 80-column by 25-row character display. Each program run computes ten generations of a screen full of gliders.

Math: a 32-bit floating point package written in high level Forth code with no machine-specific primitives for normalization, etc. Each program run generates a table of sine, cosine, and tangent values for integer degrees between 1 and 10. (Koopman 1985)

Compile: a script used to compile several Forth programs, measuring the execution of the Forth compiler itself.

Fib: computation of the 24th Fibonacci number using a recursive procedure (commonly called 'dumb' Fibonacci).

Hanoi: the Towers of Hanoi problem, written as a recursive procedure. Each program run computes the result for 12 disks.

Queens: the N Queens problem (derived from the 8 queens on a chess board puzzle) written as a recursive procedure. The program finds the first acceptable placement for N queens on an $N \times N$ board. Each program run computes the result for $N=12$ queens.

The three programs which represent the best mix of different application areas are Math, which uses intensive stack manipulation to manage 32-bit quantities (and a 48-bit temporary floating point format) on a 16-bit stack; Life, which does intensive management of an array of memory cells with much conditional branching; and Frac, which does graphics line drawing and rudimentary graphics projections.

The compilation benchmark is also useful in that it reflects the activities of a compiler which must do tokenizing of the input streams and identifier searches.

6.3.1   Dynamic instruction frequencies

Table 6.1 shows dynamic instruction execution frequencies for the most frequently executed primitives for Frac, Life, Math, and Compile. The dynamic frequency of an instruction is the number of times it is executed during a program run. Appendix C contains the unabridged version of the instruction frequencies given in Table 6.1. The AVE column shows the equally weighted average of the four benchmarks, which is a rough approximation of execution frequency for most Forth programs. The Forth words selected for inclusion in this table were either in the top ten of the Ave column, or in one of the top ten words for a particular program. For

Table 6.1 — Dynamic instruction execution frequencies for important Forth primitives

Names	Frac	Life	Math	Compile	Ave
	(%)	(%)	(%)	(%)	(%)
CALL	11.16	12.73	12.59	12.36	12.21
EXIT	11.07	12.72	12.55	10.60	11.74
VARIABLE	7.63	10.30	2.26	1.65	5.46
@	7.49	2.05	0.96	11.09	5.40
0BRANCH	3.39	6.38	3.23	6.11	4.78
LIT	3.94	5.22	4.92	4.09	4.54
+	3.41	10.45	0.60	2.26	4.18
SWAP	4.43	2.99	7.00	1.17	3.90
R>	2.05	0.00	11.28	2.23	3.89
>R	2.05	0.00	11.28	2.16	3.87
CONSTANT	3.92	3.50	2.78	4.50	3.68
DUP	4.08	0.45	1.88	5.78	3.05
ROT	4.05	0.00	4.61	0.48	2.29
USER	0.07	0.00	0.06	8.59	2.18
C@	0.00	7.52	0.01	0.36	1.97
I	0.58	6.66	0.01	0.23	1.87
=	0.33	4.48	0.01	1.87	1.67
AND	0.17	3.12	3.14	0.04	1.61
BRANCH	1.61	1.57	0.72	2.26	1.54
EXECUTE	0.14	0.00	0.02	2.45	0.65
Instructions:	2051600	1296143	6133519	447050	

example, **EXECUTE** has only a 0.65% AVE value, but has a 2.45% Compile value, which was tenth largest for the Compile measurements.

The first thing that is obvious about these numbers is that subroutine calls and exits dominate all other operations. This well known fact is why the Forth-derived stack processors place such a heavy emphasis on efficient subroutine calls and subroutine exits in combination with other instructions. The subroutine exit numbers are less than the subroutine call numbers because some Forth operations pop the return stack to climb up through two levels of subroutine calls. This performs a conditional premature exit of the calling routine.

The amount of time spent on stack manipulation primitives is also interesting. Of all the instructions in the sample, approximately 25% were spent manipulating the stacks. At first this seems rather high. However, since stack processors all have some capability for combining stack manipulations with other useful work (such as the combinations **OVER −**) this number is much higher than that seen in practice. Also, this 25% was skewed by up to 5% by the very high usage of >**R** and **R**> in the floating point math package to manipulate 32-bit quantities. This cost would not be present on a

32-bit processor or a 16-bit processor that used a fast access user memory space (such as the NC4016 and RTX 2000) to store intermediate results.

Also of interest is that the process of getting data onto the stack to be manipulated is very important (this process involves **VARIABLE, @, LIT, CONSTANT**, and **USER**). Fortunately, stack machines are able to combine these instructions with other operations as well.

As a final observation, many of the instructions shown in Appendix C have dynamic execution frequencies of less than 1%. However, these instructions should not immediately be dismissed as unimportant, because many of them can have long execution times if not supported by the hardware. It is not enough to just look at the execution frequency to determine the importance of an instruction.

6.3.2 Static instruction frequencies

Table 6.2 shows static instruction compilation frequencies for the most often compiled primitives for Frac, Life, and Math, and the most often compiled primitives used by the programs being compiled in the Compile benchmark (which includes Frac, Queens, Hanoi, and Fib.). The static frequency of an

Table 6.2 — Static instruction execution frequencies for important Forth primitives

Names	Frac	Life	Math	Compile	Ave
	(%)	(%)	(%)	(%)	(%)
CALL	16.82	31.44	37.61	17.62	25.87
LIT	11.35	7.22	11.02	8.03	9.41
EXIT	5.75	7.22	9.90	7.00	7.47
@	10.81	1.27	1.40	8.88	5.59
DUP	4.38	1.70	2.84	4.18	3.28
0BRANCH	3.01	2.55	3.67	3.16	3.10
PICK	6.29	0.00	1.04	4.53	2.97
+	3.28	2.97	0.76	4.61	2.90
SWAP	1.78	5.10	1.19	3.16	2.81
OVER	2.05	5.10	0.76	2.05	2.49
!	3.28	2.12	0.90	2.99	2.32
I	1.37	5.10	0.11	1.62	2.05
DROP	2.60	0.85	1.69	2.31	1.86
BRANCH	1.92	0.85	2.09	2.05	1.73
>R	0.55	0.00	4.11	0.77	1.36
R>	0.55	0.00	4.68	0.77	1.50
C@	0.00	3.40	0.61	0.34	1.09
=	0.14	2.76	0.29	0.26	0.86
Instructions:	731	471	2777	1171	

instruction is the number of times it appears in the source program. The AVE column shows the equally weighted average of the four benchmarks, which is a rough approximation of compilation frequency for most Forth programs. The Forth words selected for inclusion in this table were either in the top ten of the Ave column, or in one of the top ten words for a particular program.

In the static measurements, subroutine calls are very frequent, accounting for about one in four instructions compiled. Note that Frac is counted twice since it is included in Compile, so actually the subroutine call number is somewhat lower than it would otherwise be.

6.3.3 Instruction compression on the RTX 32P

With subroutine exits so common, it is no wonder that most of the stack machines have a mechanism for combining subroutine exits with other instructions. An important additional observation is that subroutine calls are more common than subroutine returns in the source code, and are even more attractive to combine with other operations.

The RTX 32P discussed in Chapter 5 is unique in that it has only a single instruction format that combines both an opcode and a subroutine call/ subroutine return/unconditional branch. While at first this may seem to be wasteful of memory, there are significant performance gains to be made, and the memory cost is relatively low. Unfortunately, this single instruction format is only useful for 32-bit processors, since 16-bit processors do not have enough bits in an instruction to combine both an opcode and a large address field.

Tables 6.3 and 6.4 are execution and compilation statistics gathered from versions of Frac, Life, and Math that were rewritten to take advantage of the capabilities of the 32-bit processor.

6.3.3.1 Execution speed gains

Table 6.3 has four profiles of dynamic program execution with different optimizations for the RTX 32P. Part (a) of the table shows the results of executing programs with no compression of opcodes and subroutines, and no peephole optimization of adjacent opcodes (opcode combination).

Part (b) of the table shows the effects of combining common opcode sequences (such as **SWAP DROP, OVER +,** <**variable**> @ and <**variable**> @+) into single instructions. The column marked OP-OP is the number of combinations of two opcodes treated as a single opcode in the OP, OP-CALL, OP-EXIT, and OP-CALL-EXIT measurements. The special cases of **LITERAL +, LITERAL AND,** etc. are all designated as LITERAL-OP. The special cases of <**variable**> @ and <**variable**>! are designated VARIABLE-OP. The special cases of <**variable**> @+ and <**variable**> @− are designated VARIABLE-OP-OP. All the literal and variable special cases require a full instruction to hold an opcode and address, so are not combinable with other instructions. For the example programs, peephole optimization of opcodes was able to achieve a 10% reduction in the number of instructions executed.

Table 6.3 — Dynamic instruction execution frequencies for RTX 32P instruction types

(a) Instruction compression OFF, Opcode combination OFF

	Frac	Life	Math	Ave
	(%)	(%)	(%)	(%)
OP	57.54	46.07	49.66	51
CALL	19.01	26.44	19.96	22
EXIT	10.80	12.53	16.25	13
OP+CALL	0.00	0.00	0.00	0
OP+EXIT	0.00	0.00	0.00	0
CALL+EXIT	0.00	0.00	0.00	0
OP+CALL+EXIT	0.00	0.00	0.00	0
COND	5.89	9.95	6.56	7
LIT	6.76	5.01	7.57	6
LIT-OP	0.00	0.00	0.00	0
VARIABLE-OP	0.00	0.00	0.00	0
VARIABLE-OP-OP	0.00	0.00	0.00	0
Instructions:	8381513	1262079	940448	
OP-OP	0.00	0.00	0.00	0

(b) Instruction compression OFF, Opcode combination ON

	Frac	Life	Math	Ave
	(%)	(%)	(%)	(%)
OP	50.92	42.22	45.94	46
CALL	17.81	28.31	21.42	23
EXIT	12.48	13.42	17.45	14
OP+CALL	0.00	0.00	0.00	0
OP+CALL	0.00	0.00	0.00	0
CALL+EXIT	0.00	0.00	0.00	0
OP+CALL+EXIT	0.00	0.00	0.00	0
COND	6.82	10.66	7.05	8
LIT	2.60	1.94	2.53	2
LIT-OP	5.21	3.43	5.59	5
VARIABLE-OP	2.67	0.00	0.01	1
VARIABLE-OP-OP	1.49	0.00	0.01	1
Instructions:	7250149	1178235	875882	
OP-OP	4.72	3.68	1.76	3

(c) Instruction compression ON, Opcode combination OFF

	Frac	Life	Math	Ave
	(%)	(%)	(%)	(%)
OP	48.84	31.26	40.81	40
CALL	8.46	22.20	15.53	15
EXIT	4.57	0.00	4.80	3

Table 6.3 — Continued.

	Frac	Life	Math	Ave
	(%)	(%)	(%)	(%)
OP+CALL	13.93	11.47	6.68	11
OP+EXIT	7.71	15.96	12.90	12
CALL+EXIT	0.80	0.00	2.04	12
OP+CALL+EXIT	0.15	0.00	0.03	0
COND	7.23	12.69	7.99	9
LIT	8.31	6.39	9.22	8
LIT-OP	0.00	0.00	0.00	0
VARIABLE-OP	0.00	0.00	0.00	0
VARIABLE-OP-OP	0.00	0.00	0.00	0
Instructions:	6827482	990313	772865	
OP-OP	0.00	0.00	0.00	0

(d) Instruction compression ON, OPcode combination ON

	Frac	Life	Math	Ave
	(%)	(%)	(%)	(%)
OP	39.05	24.91	39.19	34
CALL	6.75	24.27	15.94	16
EXIT	6.54	0.01	10.78	6
OP+CALL	12.71	12.53	6.87	11
OP+EXIT	6.78	17.44	7.40	11
CALL+EXIT	0.95	0.01	2.10	1
OP+CALL+EXIT	0.09	0.00	0.03	0
COND	7.84	13.86	8.21	10
LIT	3.00	2.52	2.95	3
LIT-OP	6.00	4.45	6.51	6
VARIABLE-OP	3.08	0.00	0.01	1
VARIABLE-OP-OP	1.72	0.00	0.01	1
Instructions:	6294109	906469	752257	
OP-OP	5.44	4.79	2.05	4

Part (c) of the table shows the effects of using instruction compression instead of opcode combination. This means that wherever possible, opcodes are combined with following subroutine calls and exits. Subroutine calls followed by exits are also combined into unconditional jumps to accomplish tail-end recursion elimination. The result is a total of 24% of all instructions can combine opcodes and subroutine calls/returns. This translates into about 40% of all subroutine calls in the original program being executed 'for free'. Almost all of the subroutine exits are executed 'for free', the exceptions being special instructions such as literals and return stack manipulations that cannot be combined with subroutine exits.

Part (d) of the table shows the effects of turning on both opcode combination and instruction compression. The resulting code takes 25% fewer instructions than the original programs. This performance speedup is possible at almost no software or processing hardware expense because of the inherent parallelism between subroutine calls and opcodes.

An interesting point is that the execution time for the Math benchmark reduced from 6.1 million instructions on the 16-bit system to only 940 thousand instructions on the RTX 32P, testimony to the need for a 32-bit processor when doing floating point calculations. The Life benchmark (which is mostly 8-bit data manipulation) remained almost the same between systems. The Frac benchmark apparently increased by a factor of four, but this was because of the fact that the 32-bit version used a higher graphics resolution, requiring 4 times the number of points to be computed, which takes approximately 4 times as many instructions.

6.3.3.2 Memory size cost

The performance speedup of combining opcodes with subroutine calls is worthwhile, especially since it takes essentially no extra hardware inside the processor. In fact, it actually simplifies the hardware by requiring only one instruction format. The question that must still be resolved is, what is the cost in memory space?

Fortunately, Forth programs have a static subroutine call frequency that is even higher than the dynamic frequency. This provides a ripe opportunity for opcode/subroutine call combinations. Table 6.4 shows the difference in static program size between raw programs with no compression and programs on which both instruction compression and opcode compression have been performed.

The RTX 32P uses 9-bit opcodes, 21-bit addresses, and 2-bit control fields. If we were to assume an optimally packed instruction format, we might design an instruction format that used 11 bits to specify an opcode with a single subroutine exit bit, and a 23-bit subroutine call/jump format. Also, let us be generous and assume that this instruction format would get all subroutine exits for free by combining them with opcodes or using a jump instead of call format. This supposes a machine with variable word width (11 or 23 bits), but let us not worry about that, since we are computing a theoretical minimum.

In the optimized form, the three programs together would consist of 1953 opcodes (at 11 bits each), 1389 subroutine calls (at 23 bits each), and 565 combination opcodes/address fields (at 34 bits each). This adds up to a total of 72 640 bits.

Now consider the actual program compiled using the optimizations on the RTX 32P. Considering that each instruction category uses a fixed 32-bit encoding with some potentially unused fields, the total is 3300 instructions at 32 bits, or 105 600 bits. The memory cost is then 32 960 bits, or 31% of memory 'wasted' over the theoretical minimum.

Of course, designing a machine to use 11-bit opcodes and 23-bit subroutine calls would be a neat trick. In a more practical vein, we should consider

Table 6.4 — Static instruction compilation frequencies for RTX 32P instruction types.

(a) Instruction compression OFF, Opcode combination OFF

	Frac	Life	Math	Ave
	(%)	(%)	(%)	(%)
OP	48.40	51.46	44.72	48
CALL	28.48	33.01	35.64	32
EXIT	5.12	6.41	7.55	6
OP+CALL	0.00	0.00	0.00	0
OP+EXIT	0.00	0.00	0.00	0
CALL+EXIT	0.00	0.00	0.00	0
OP+CALL+EXIT	0.00	0.00	0.00	0
COND	3.52	4.46	4.04	4
LIT	14.48	4.66	8.05	9
LIT-OP	0.00	0.00	0.00	0
VARIABLE-OP	0.00	0.00	0.00	0
VARIABLE-OP-OP	0.00	0.00	0.00	0
Instructions:	1250	515	2422	
OP-OP	0.00	0.00	0.00	0

(b) Instruction compression ON, Opcode combination ON

	Frac	Life	Math	Ave
	(%)	(%)	(%)	(%)
OP	33.71	35.78	37.05	36
CALL	17.33	21.94	27.03	22
EXIT	1.47	2.87	2.39	2
OP+CALL	11.65	21.15	10.54	14
OP+EXIT	3.78	4.70	1.73	3
CALL+EXIT	1.05	1.04	4.02	2
OP+CALL+EXIT	0.42	0.00	1.17	1
COND	4.62	6.00	4.98	5
LIT	16.17	4.18	8.61	10
LIT-OP	2.83	2.08	1.32	2
VARIABLE-OP	5.46	0.26	1.01	2
VARIABLE-OP-OP	1.47	0.00	0.15	1
Instructions:	952	383	1965	
OP-OP	2.73	5.22	1.98	3

that the number of 'empty' opcodes in the compressed version of the programs is 766 (at 9 bits each), and the number of 'empty' subroutine call fields is 917 (at 23 bits each). This is a total of 27 985 bits, only 27%, 'wasted' in exchange for 25% fewer instructions executed. So, we are getting a significant speedup at a relatively low cost over even a variable-length instruction format.

There is a slight problem with the measurements presented in this section in that they are for several relatively small programs. The programs do perform some fairly complex operations, so this observation is in part supportive evidence that stack machine programs are compact. The problem is that very large Forth programs are difficult to find. Nevertheless, the programs were chosen to represent a reasonable cross-section of commonly used Forth code and, in the author's considered opinion, the results are reasonably close to those that would be obtained by measuring a larger sample of programs.

Of course, one way to get much larger programs would be to use the output of a conventional language compiler, but that kind of code would probably have different characteristics, because programmers solve problems much differently in C or FORTRAN than they do in Forth. We shall revisit that thought in Chapter 7.

6.4   STACK MANAGEMENT ISSUES

Since stack machines depend on accessing a high speed stack memory on every instruction, the characteristics of use of the stack memory are of vital importance. In particular, as processors get faster, the question is: how much stack memory needs to be placed on-chip to obtain good performance? The answer to this question is crucial, since it affects the cost and performance of high-end stack processors that place stack memory on-chip.

An equally important question is how should the stacks be managed, especially in the realm of multi-tasking environments?

6.4.1   Estimating stack size: an experiment

The first question, the one of the size of the on-chip stack buffer, is best resolved by a simulation of various programs with different size stack buffers. This simulation measures the amount of traffic to and from memory generated by stack overflows and underflows. Overflows need to copy elements from the hardware stack buffer to a save area in memory. Underflows cause a copying of the elements back from memory to the stack buffer.

Table 6.5 and Fig. 6.2 show the results of a simulator that monitored the number of memory cycles spent on data stack buffer spilling and restoring for Life, Hanoi, Frac, Fib, Math, and Queens. While the 'toy' benchmarks Fib, Hanoi, and Queens are not representative of typical programs, all are deeply recursive and are representative of the worst one might expect of stack programs.

Table 6.5 — Memory cycles expended for Data Stack spills

	Frac	Life	Math	Fib	Hanoi	Queens
No. of instructions	2051600	1296143	6133519	880997	235665	140224
Max stack depth	44	6	23	25	52	29
No of stack operands	3670356	1791638	11786764	1483760	446642	257320
No. of stack spills For buffer size:						
0	3670356	1791638	11786764	1483760	446642	257320
2	838960	148448	3919622	370940	155656	41426
4	202214	4098	1313566	92732	69608	9216
8	39040	0	238020	13526	32752	512
12	10236	0	28300	1970	8184	196
16	3580	0	800	284	4088	64
20	1532	0	280	38	2040	22
24	636	0	0	2	1016	10
28	220	0	0	0	504	2
32	92	0	0	0	248	0
36	36	0	0	0	120	0
40	10	0	0	0	56	0
44	0	0	0	0	24	0
48	0	0	0	0	8	0
52	0	0	0	0	0	0

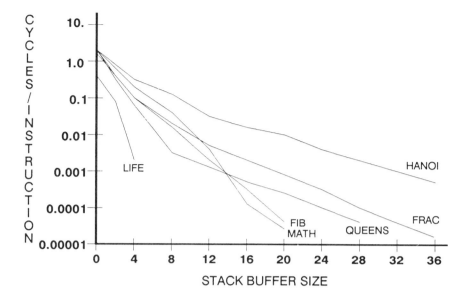

Fig. 6.2 — Data stack spilling.

The spilling algorithm that was used spilled exactly one element from the stack buffer each time a push operation was performed on a full stack, and read exactly one element into the stack buffer each time a read/pop operation was performed on an empty stack buffer. The simulation assumed that hardware automatically handled the spilling with a cost of one memory cycle per element read or written. The RTX 32P instruction set was used for this simulation, so each instruction was approximately twice as complex as would be seen in a hardwired processor such as the RTX 2000. The number of cycles measured were memory cycles, not microcycles. The purpose of the simulation was to show the best behavior that could be expected, which is certainly within a factor of three or four of the costs for most implementations.

Surprisingly, Frac behaves almost as badly as Hanoi when using the stack. This is because Frac pushes 6 elements onto the data stack at each step of a recursive subdivision algorithm for dividing a mesh of points. As is obvious, any recursive program has the potential to generate a large number of elements on the stack.

The good news about stack size is that stack overflow and underflow memory traffic tapers off at a steep exponential rate for all programs. At a stack buffer size of 24, even Hanoi generates a stack spill on fewer than 1% of instructions. As a practical matter, a stack size of 32 will eliminate stack buffer overflows for almost all programs.

Table 6.6 and Fig. 6.3 show simulator results for Return Stack spills and restores for the same programs. The results are similar, except that Math emerges as an unexpectedly heavy user of the Return Stack. This is because

Table 6.6 — Memory cycles expended for Return Stack spills

	Frac	Life	Math	Fib	Hanoi	Queens
No. of instructions	2051600	1296143	6133519	880997	235665	140224
Max stack depth	14	7	30	22	14	39
No of stack operands	725224	680676	3199170	185472	41056	53722
No. of stack spills for buffer size:						
0	725224	680676	3199170	185472	41056	53722
2	326778	135608	1235678	57312	12310	26070
4	179938	118	642798	21890	2048	13306
8	27932	0	273686	3192	128	1158
12	132	0	57262	464	8	572
16	0	0	13442	66	0	314
20	0	0	1062	8	0	154
24	0	0	382	0	0	62
28	0	0	42	0	0	32
32	0	0	0	0	0	16
36	0	0	0	0	0	8
40	0	0	0	0	0	0

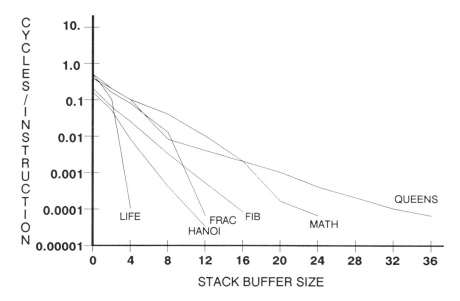

Fig. 6.3 — Return stack spilling.

the math package was written to be extremely modular and easy to port between systems, so it uses a large number of deeply nested subroutines. Also, Math uses the Return Stack for storing a large number of temporary variables to manipulate 48-bit data on a 16-bit processor.

6.4.2   Overflow handling
Now that we have examined how stack overflows and underflows occur in program execution, how should they be handled? Four possible ways of handling spills are: to ensure that they never happen, and treat them as catastrophic system failures; to use a demand-driven stack controller; to use a paging stack control mechanism; or to use a data cache memory. Each approach has its strengths and weaknesses.

6.4.2.1   A very large stack memory
The simplest way to solve the stack problem is simply to assume that stack overflows will never happen. While this may seem like a foolish strategy at first, it has some merit. The nicest result from using this strategy is that system performance is totally predictable (no stack spilling traffic to slow down the system) and that no stack management hardware is required.

This approach of using a very large stack memory to avoid overflows is the one taken by the MISC M17, which has a stack overflow only when program memory capacity is exceeded. The approach taken by the NC4016 is to use high speed off-chip stack memories that may be expanded to be several thousand elements deep. Both these processors have solved the stack overflow problem by simply designing it away. The price paid when using this approach is a tradeoff between off-chip memory size/speed and processor speed.

In the case where small on-chip stacks are used, the approach of treating overflows as a catastrophic system event when programs are being debugged can still be taken by simply declaring that the programmer has only X elements on the stacks to work with and is responsible for never overflowing this limit. This approach is very practical if only small, simple programs are being written and the value of X is greater than 16 or 32. The WISC CPU/16 uses this approach with a stack size of 256 elements to keep the hardware simple.

6.4.2.2 Demand-fed single-element stack manager

Given that stack overflows are allowed to occur on a regular basis, the most conceptually appealing way to deal with the problem is to use a demand-fed stack manager that moves single elements on and off the stack as required.

To implement this strategy, the stack buffer is set up as a circular buffer with a head and tail pointer. A pointer to memory is also needed to keep track of the top element of the memory-resident portion of the stack. Whenever a stack overflow is encountered, the bottom-most buffer-resident element is copied to memory, freeing a buffer location. Whenever an underflow is encountered, one element from memory is copied into the buffer. This technique has the appeal that the processor never moves a stack element to or from memory unless absolutely necessary, guaranteeing the minimum amount of stack traffic.

A possible embellishment of this scheme would be to have the stack manager always keep a few elements empty and at least several elements full on the stack. This management could be done using otherwise unused memory cycles, and would reduce the number of overflow and underflow pauses. Unfortunately, this embellishment is of little value on real stack machines, since they all strive to use program memory 100% of the time for fetching instructions and data, leaving no memory bandwidth left over for the stack manager to use.

The benefit to demand-fed stack management is that very good use is made of available stack buffer elements. Therefore, it is suitable for use in systems where chip space for stack buffers is at a premium. As an additional benefit, the stack underflows and overflows are spread throughout program execution at a maximum of two per instruction for the case of a data stack spill combined with a subroutine return underflow. The cost of this good performance is that reasonably complex control hardware and three counters for each stack are needed to implement the scheme.

The FRISC 3 stack management scheme is similar to the demand-fed strategy. The architects of this system have done considerable research in this area. A generalization of this algorithm, called the cutback-K algorithm, was proposed by Hasegawa & Shigei (1985). Stanley & Wedig (1987) have also discussed top-of-stack buffer management for RISC machines.

6.4.2.3   Paging stack manager

An alternative to the demand-fed strategy is to generate an interrupt on stack overflow and underflow, then use software to manage the stack spill. This approach uses less control hardware than the demand-fed method, but requires a stack buffer that is somewhat bigger to reduce the frequency of the interrupts.

The general strategy used in this scheme is to have limit registers pointing to locations near the top and bottom of the stack buffer space. When an instruction causes the stack pointer to be less than the underflow pointer, a half-buffer full of elements is copied from program memory. When an instruction exceeds the overflow pointer, a half-buffer full of elements is copied into program memory.

The paging scheme allows arbitrarily sized sections of a large stack memory to be used by different procedures on a time-sliced basis. Because of this, the stack buffer appears as a section of special memory, not as a circular buffer. Therefore, in practice, a stack overflow actually involves copying a half-buffer of elements to memory, then relocating the other half-buffer to place it at the start of the stack buffer area.

The cost of the paging management method is about twice that of the demand-fed method in terms of memory cycles spent shuffling elements. Also, the buffer size must be twice that of the demand-fed buffers to guarantee the same number of consecutive pushes and pops between overflows and underflows, although in practice that increase in size is seldom needed.

An interesting approach to using this method is to declare as a matter of programming style that stack overflows and underflows are unlikely and undesirable, since a buffer size of 32 essentially eliminates them anyway. Then the paging method provides an inexpensive hardware means for affording graceful degradation of a program that exceeds its buffer size. This way an ill behaved program will still function properly (although more slowly), while the operating system can generate a warning message identifying the culprit.

The RTX 2000 and the RTX 32P both use this paging method for stack management.

6.4.2.4   An associative cache

The method used by many conventional processors for managing the program stack is to use a conventional data cache memory, usually mapped into the program memory space. This method involves significant hardware complexity but does not provide any advantage over the previously mentioned methods for stack machines, since stack machines do not skip about much in accessing their stack elements. It does provide an advantage when variable length data structures such as strings and records are pushed onto a 'stack' as defined in a C or Ada programming environment.

Other publications of interest that discuss the stack management issue are: Blake (1977), Hennesy (1984), Prabhala & Sethi (1977), and Sites (1979).

6.5   INTERRUPTS AND MULTI-TASKING

There are three components to the performance of processing interrupts. The first component is the amount of time that elapses between the time that an interrupt request is received by the processor and the time that the processor takes action to begin processing the interrupt service routine. This delay is called interrupt latency.

The second component of interrupt service performance is interrupt processing time. This is the amount of time that the processor spends actually saving the machine state of the interrupted job and diverting execution to the interrupt service routine. Usually the amount of machine state saved is minimal, on the presumption that the interrupt service routine can minimize costs by saving only those additional registers that it plans to use. Sometimes, one sees the term 'interrupt latency' used to describe the sum of these first two components.

The third component of interrupt service performance is what we shall call state saving overhead. This is the amount of time taken to save machine registers that are not automatically saved by the interrupt processing logic, but which must be saved in order for the interrupt service routine to do its job. The state saving overhead can vary considerably, depending upon the complexity of the interrupt service routine. In the extreme case, state saving overhead can involve a complete context switch between multi-tasking jobs.

Of course, the costs of restoring all the machine state and returning to the interrupted routine are a consideration in determining overall system performance. We shall not consider them explicitly here, since they tend to be roughly equal to the state saving time (since everything that is saved must be restored), and are not as important in meeting a time-critical deadline for responding to an interrupt.

6.5.1   Interrupt response latency

CISC machines may have instructions which take a very long time to execute, degrading interrupt response latency performance. Stack machines, like RISC machines, can have a very quick interrupt response latency. This is because most stack machine instructions are only a single cycle long, so at worst only a few clock cycles elapse before an interrupt request is acknowledged and the interrupt is processed.

Once the interrupt is processed, however, the difference between RISC and stack machines becomes apparent. RISC machines must go through a tricky pipeline saving procedure upon recognizing an interrupt, as well as a pipeline restoring procedure when returning from the interrupt, in order to avoid losing information about partially processed instructions. Stack machines, on the other hand, have no instruction execution pipeline, so only the address of the next instruction to be executed needs to be saved. This means that stack machines can treat an interrupt as a hardware generated procedure call. Of course, since procedure calls are very fast, interrupt processing time is very low.

6.5.1.1 *Instruction restartability*
There is one possible problem with stack machine interrupt response latency. That is the issue of streamed instructions and microcoded loops.

Streamed instructions are used to repetitively execute an operation such as writing the top data stack element to memory. These instructions are implemented using an instruction repeat feature on the NC4016 and RTX 2000, an instruction buffer on the M17, and microcoded loops on the CPU/16 and RTX 32P. These primitives are very useful since they can be used to build efficient string manipulation primitives and stack underflow/overflow service routines. The problem is that, in most cases, these instructions are also noninterruptible.

One solution is to make these instructions interruptible with extra control hardware, which may increase processor complexity quite a bit. A potentially hard problem that nonstack processors have with this solution is the issue of saving intermediate results. With a stack processor this is not a problem, since intermediate results are already resident on a stack, which is the ideal mechanism for saving state during an interrupt.

Another approach that is used by stack processors is to use a software restriction on the size of the repeat count allowed to be used with streaming instructions. This means that if a block of 100 characters is to be moved in memory, the action may be accomplished by moving several groups of 8 characters at a time. This keeps interrupt latency reasonable without sacrificing much performance. As expected, there is a tradeoff between absolute machine efficiency (with long streamed instructions) and interrupt response latency.

In microcoded machines, the tradeoffs are much the same. However, there is a very simple microcode strategy to provide the best of both worlds which is designed into the RTX 32P commercial version. This strategy is having a condition code bit visible to the microcode indicating whether an interrupt is pending. At each iteration of a microcoded loop, the interrupt pending bit is tested, with no cost in execution time. If no interrupt is pending, another iteration is made through the loop. If an interrupt is pending, the address of the streamed instruction is pushed onto the return stack as the address to be executed upon return from the interrupt, and the interrupt is allowed to be processed. As long as the streamed instruction keeps all its state on the stack (which is simple with an operation such as a character block move), there is very little overhead associated with this method when processing an interrupt, and no overhead during normal program execution.

6.5.2   Lightweight interrupts

Let us examine three different degrees of state saving required by different interrupt categories: fast interrupts, lightweight threads for multi-tasking, and full context switching.

Fast interrupts are the kind most frequently seen at run time. These interrupts do things such as add a few milliseconds to the time-of-day counter, or copy a byte from an input port to a memory buffer. When conventional machines handle this kind of interrupt, they must usually save two or three registers in program memory to create working room in the register file. In stack machines, absolutely no state saving is required. The interrupt service routine can simply push its information on top of the stack without disturbing information from the program that was interrupted. So, for fast service interrupts, stack machines have zero state saving overhead.

Lightweight threads are tasks in a multi-tasking system which have a similar execution strategy as the interrupts just described. They can reap the benefits of multi-tasking without the cost of starting and stopping full-fledged processes. A stack machine can implement lightweight threads simply by requiring that each task run a short sequence of instructions when invoked, then relinquish control to the central task manager. This can be called nonpreemptive, or cooperative task management. If each task starts and stops its operation with no parameters on the stack, there is no overhead for context switches between tasks. The cost for this method of multi-tasking is essentially zero, since a task only relinquishes its control to the task manager at a logical breaking point in the program, where the stack probably would have been empty anyway.

From these two examples, we can see that interrupt processing and lightweight thread multi-tasking are very inexpensive on stack processors. The only issue that remains open is that of full-fledged, preemptive multi-tasking accomplished with context switching.

6.5.3   Context switches

Context switching overhead is usually said to be the reason why 'stack machines are no good at multi-tasking'. The argument behind such reasoning is usually based on having to save a tremendous amount of stack buffer space into program memory. This idea that stack machines are any worse at multi-tasking than other machines is patently false.

Context switching is a potentially expensive operation on any system. In RISC and CISC computers with cache memories, context switching can be more expensive than the manufacturers would have one believe, as a result of hidden performance degradations caused by increased cache misses after the context switch. To the extent that RISC machines use large register files, they face exactly the same problems that are faced by stack machines. An added disadvantage of RISC machines is that their random access to registers dictates saving all registers (or adding complicated hardware to detect which registers are in use), whereas a stack machine can readily save only the active area of the stack buffer.

6.5.3.1   A context switching experiment

Table 6.7 shows data gathered from a trace-driven simulation of the number of memory cycles spent saving and restoring data stack elements for Forth programs in a context switching environment. The programs simulated were Queen, Hanoi, and a Quick-sort program. Small values of N were used for Queen and Hanoi in order to keep the running time of the simulator reasonable. Both the effects of stack overflow and underflow as well as context switching were measured, since they interact heavily in such an environment.

Table 6.7(a) and Fig. 6.4 show the results for a page-managed stack. The notation 'xxx CLOCKS/SWITCH' indicates the number of clock cycles between context switches. At 100 clock cycles between context switches, the number of memory cycles expended on managing the stack decreases as the buffer size increases. This is because of the effects of a reduced spilling rate while the program accesses the stack. As the buffer size increases beyond 8 elements, however, the memory traffic increases since the increasingly large buffers are constantly copied in and out of memory on context switches.

Notice how the program behaves at 500 cycles between context switches. Even at this relatively high rate (which corresponds to 20 000 context switches per second for a 10 MHz processor — an excessively high rate in practice), the cost of context switching is only about 0.08 clocks per instruction for a stack buffer size greater than 12. Since in this experiment each instruction averaged 1.688 clocks without context switching overhead, this only amounts to a 4.7% overhead. At 10 000 cycles between context switch (1 millisecond between context switches), the overhead is less than 1%.

How is it possible to have such a low overhead? One reason is that the average stack depth is only 12.1 elements during the execution of these three heavily recursive programs. That means that, since there is never very much information on the stack, very little information needs to be saved on a context switch. In fact, compared to a 16-register CISC machine, the stack machine simulated in this experiment actually has *less* state to save on a context switch.

Table 6.7(b) and Fig. 6.5 show the results of the same simulation run using a demand-fed stack management algorithm. In these results, the rise on the 100-cycle-interval curve when more than 12 elements are in the stack buffer is almost nonexistent. This is because the stack was not refilled when restoring the machine state, but rather was allowed to refill during program execution in a demand-driven fashion. For reasonable context switching frequencies (less than 1000 per second), the demand-fed strategy is somewhat better than the paged strategy, but not by an overwhelming margin.

6.5.3.2   Multiple stack spaces for multi-tasking

There is an approach that can be used with stack machines which can eliminate even the modest costs associated with context switching that we have seen. Instead of using a single large stack for all programs, high-

Table 6.7 — Memory cycles expended for Data Stack spills for different buffer sizes and context swapping frequencies

Combination of Queens, Qsort, Hanoi
No. of Instructions = 36678
Average stack depth = 12.1
Maximum stack depth = 36

(a) Page-managed buffer management

Buffer size	Timer=100	Timer=500	Timer=1000	Timer=10000
2	17992	16334	16124	15916
4	12834	9924	9524	9214
8	8440	3950	3430	2910
12	10380	3944	3068	2314
16	11602	2642	1620	632
20	12886	3122	1846	626
24	13120	2876	1518	330
28	14488	3058	1584	242
32	15032	3072	1556	124
36	15458	3108	1568	82

(b) Demand-fed buffer management

Buffer size	Timer=100	Timer=500	Timer=1000	Timer=10000
2	26424	24992	24798	24626
4	11628	8912	8548	8282
8	7504	3378	2762	2314
12	6986	1930	1286	630
16	7022	1876	1144	322
20	7022	1852	1084	180
24	7022	1880	1066	124
28	7022	1820	1062	90
32	7022	1828	1060	80
36	7022	1822	1048	80

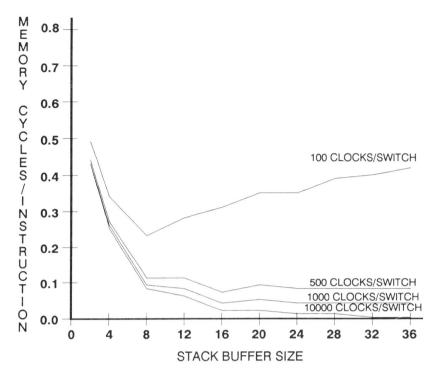

Fig. 6.4 — Overhead for a page managed stack.

priority/time-critical portions of a program can be assigned their own stack space. This means that each process uses a stack pointer and stack limit registers to carve out a piece of the stack for its use. Upon encountering a context switch, the process manager simply saves the current stack pointer for the process, since it already knows what the stack limits are. When the new stack pointer value and stack limit registers are loaded, the new process is ready to execute. No time at all is spent copying stack elements to and from memory.

The amount of stack memory needed by most programs is typically rather small. Furthermore, it can be guaranteed by design to be small in short, time-critical processes. So, even a modest stack buffer of 128 elements can be divided up among four processes with 32 elements each. If more than four processes are needed by the multi-tasking system, one of the buffers can be designated the low priority scratch buffer, which is to be shared using copy-in and copy-out among all the low priority tasks.

From this discussion we can see that the notion that stack processors have too large a state to save for effective multi-tasking is a myth. In fact, in many cases stack processors can be better at multi-tasking and interrupt processing than any other kind of computer.

Hayes and Fraeman (1988) have independently obtained results for

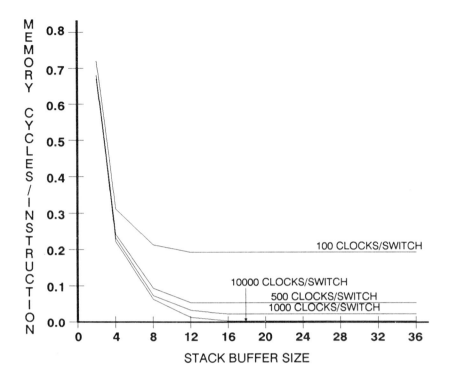

Fig. 6.5 — Overhead for a demand fed managed stack.

stack spilling and context switching costs on the FRISC 3 similar to the results reported in this chapter.

7

Software issues

Any computer system is worthless without software. Having hardware that effectively supports software requirements is of the utmost importance. Stack machines offer new tradeoffs and choices when considering software issues. Section 7.1 discusses the importance of fast subroutine calls, and how they can directly and indirectly affect not only program execution speed, but also software quality and programmer productivity.

Section 7.2 explains the choices and tradeoffs involved in choosing an appropriate language for programming stack machines, and how stack machines can support conventional languages efficiently.

Section 7.3 discusses the interfaces among all levels of a program written for a stack machine. The uniformity of software interface present in stack machines is not possible in register-based machines, and gives significant advantages.

7.1 THE IMPORTANCE OF FAST SUBROUTINE CALLS

'Programmers have learnt to avoid procedure calls and parameter passing for reasons of efficiency. These are, however, an important tool in the design of well organized programs and stack architectures carry the potential for very efficient invoking of procedures.' (Schulthess & Mumprecht 1977, p. 25)

The sentiment that expensive procedure calls lead to poorly structured programs by inhibiting programmers with efficiency considerations is echoed by software stylists as well as both RISC and CISC advocates (Atkinson & McCreight 1987, Ditzel & McLellan 1982, Parnas 1972, Sequin & Patterson 1982, Wilkes 1982). In fact, Lampson (1982) goes so far as to say that procedure calls should be made to run as fast as unconditional jumps.

7.1.1 The importance of small procedures

The use of a large number of small procedures when writing a program reduces the complexity of each piece that must be written, tested, debugged, and understood by the programmer. Lower software complexity implies lower development and maintenance costs, as well as better reliability. Why then, would programmers not make extensive use of small procedures?

Most application programs are written in general-purpose languages such as FORTRAN, COBOL, PL/1, Pascal, and C. The early high level programming languages such as FORTRAN were direct extensions of the philosophy of the machines they were run on: sequential von Neumann machines with registers. Consequently, these languages and their general usage have developed to emphasize long sequences of assignment statements with only occasional conditional branches and procedure calls.

In recent years, however, the complexion of software has begun to change. The currently accepted best practice in software design involves structured programming using modular designs. On a large scale, the use of modules is essential for partitioning tasks among members of programming teams. On a smaller scale, modules control complexity by limiting the amount of information that a programmer must deal with at any given time.

More advanced languages such as Modula-2 and Ada are designed specifically to promote modular design. The one hardware innovation that has resulted from the increasing popularity of modular, structured languages has been a register used as a stack pointer into main memory. With the exception of this stack pointer and a few complex instructions (which are not always usable by compilers), CISC hardware has not added much support for subroutine calls over the years. Because of this, the machine code output of optimizing compilers for modern languages still tends to look a lot like output from earlier, nonstructured languages.

Herein lies the problem. Conventional computers are still optimized for executing programs made up of streams of serial instructions. Execution traces for most programs show that procedure calls make up a rather small proportion of all instructions, which, of course, is partially attributable to the fact that programmers avoid using them. Conversely, modern programming practices stress the importance of nonsequential control flow and small procedures. The clash between these two realities leads to a suboptimal, and therefore costly, hardware/software environment on today's general-purpose computers.

This does not mean that programs have failed to become more organized and maintainable using structured languages, but rather that efficiency considerations and the use of hardware that encourages writing sequential programs has prevented modular languages from achieving all that they might. Although the current philosophy is to break programs up into very small procedures, most programs still contain fewer, larger, and more complicated procedures than they should.

7.1.2 The proper size for a procedure
How many functions should a typical procedure have? Miller gives evidence that the number seven, plus or minus two, applies to many aspects of thinking (Miller 1967). The way the human mind copes with complicated information is by chunking groups of similar objects into fewer, more abstract objects. In a computer program, this means that each procedure should contain approximately seven fundamental operations, such as assignment statements or other procedure calls, in order to be easily grasped. If a procedure contains more than seven distinct operations, it should be broken

apart by chunking related portions into subordinate procedures to reduce the complexity of each portion of the program. In another part of his book, Miller shows that the human mind can only grasp two or three levels of nesting of ideas within a single context. This strongly suggests that deeply nested loops and conditional structures should be arranged as nested procedure calls, not as convoluted, indented structures within a procedure.

7.1.3   Why programmers don't use small procedures
The only question now is, why don't most programmers follow these guidelines?

The most obvious reason that programmers avoid small, deeply nested procedures is the cost in speed of execution. Subroutine parameter setup and the actual procedure calling instructions can swamp the execution time of a program if used too frequently. All but the most sophisticated optimizing compiler cannot help if procedures are deeply nested, and even those optimizations are limited. As a result, efficient programs tend to have a relatively shallow depth of procedure nesting.

Another reason that procedures are not used more is that they are difficult to program. Often times the effort to write the pro-forma code required to define a procedure makes the definition of a small procedure too burdensome. When this awkwardness is added to the considerable documentation and project management obstacles associated with creating a new procedure in a big project (engendered by rules such as: each procedure must have a separate management control document), it is no wonder that average procedure sizes of one or two pages instead of one or two lines are considered appropriate.

There is an even deeper cause why procedures are difficult to create in modern programming languages, and why they are used less frequently than the reader of a book on structured programming might expect: conventional programming languages and the people who use them are steeped in the traditions of batch processing. Batch processing gives little reward in testability or convenience for working with small procedures. Truly interactive processing (which does not mean doing batch-oriented edit–compile–link–execute–crash–debug cycles from a terminal) is only available in a few environments, and is not taught in most undergraduate computer courses.

As a result of all these factors, today's programming languages provide only moderately useful capabilities for efficient modular programming. Today's hardware and programming environments unnecessarily restrict the usage of modularity, and therefore unnecessarily increase the cost of providing computer-based solutions to problems.

7.1.4   Architectural support for procedures
The problems that arise from poor performance on subroutine calls have been dealt with by computer architects in a variety of ways. RISC designers have taken two different approaches. The Stanford MIPS team uses compiler technology to expand procedures as in-line code wherever possible. The MIPS compiler then does very clever register allocation to avoid saving

and restoring registers for procedure calls. The statistics that support the choice for this strategy were taken from programs that follow the traditional software design methods, with fairly large and not deeply nested procedures. While the MIPS approach appears to work well on existing software, it may create the same stifling effect on better software development strategies that we saw in the CISC machines.

The second RISC approach, one originally advocated by the Berkeley RISC I team, uses register windows to form a register frame stack. A pointer into the register stack can be moved to push or pop a group of registers quickly, supporting quick subroutine calls. This approach has many of the same advantages as the stack machine approach. The detailed implementation questions, which in real life may determine the success or failure of a product, become ones of single vs. multiple stacks, fixed- vs. variable-sized register frames, spill management strategies, and overall machine complexity.

7.2 LANGUAGE CHOICE

The choice of which programming language to use to solve a particular problem should not be taken lightly. Sometimes the choice is dictated by external forces, such as when using Ada for a US Department of Defense contract. In other cases the language choice is constrained by the existence of a limited number of compilers. In general, though, there is considerable choice available in selecting the language for a new system design.

Software selection should not be considered as an isolated issue. The language used should reflect the entire system being developed, including the system operating environment, the suitability of the language to solve the problem at hand, development time and costs, the maintainability of the finished product, the strengths of the underlying processor at running various languages, and the previous programming experience of the programmers assigned to the project. Note that the experience of the programmers was not placed first on the list. A poor choice based on programmer bias for a familiar language can result in problems that more than offset any perceived gain in productivity.

7.2.1 Forth: strengths and weaknesses

Forth is the most obvious language to consider using on a stack machine. That is because the Forth language is based upon a set of primitives that execute on a virtual stack machine architecture. All the stack machines presented in this book support highly efficient implementations of Forth. All of these machines can use a Forth compiler to generate efficient machine code. The biggest advantage of using Forth then, is that the highest processing rate possible can be squeezed from the machine.

One of the characteristics of Forth is its very high use of subroutine calls. This promotes an unprecedented level of modularity, with approximately 10 instructions per procedure being the norm. Tied in with this high degree of modularity is the interactive development environment used by Forth compilers. In this environment, programs are designed from the top down, using stubs as appropriate. Then they are built from the bottom up, testing each and every short procedure interactively as it is written. On large projects, the top-down and bottom-up phases are repeated in cycles.

Since Forth is a stack-based, interactive language, no testing programs or 'scaffolding' need be written. Instead, the values to be passed to the procedure are pushed onto the stack from the keyboard, the procedure to be tested is executed, and the results are returned on the top of the stack. This interactive development of modular programs is widely claimed by experienced Forth programmers to result in a factor of 10 improvement in programmer productivity, with improved software quality and reduced maintenance costs. Part of this gain may come from the fact that Forth programs are usually quite small compared to equivalent programs in other languages, requiring less code to be written and debugged. A 32K byte Forth program, exclusive of symbol table information, is considered a monster, and may take several hundred thousand bytes of source code to generate.

One of the advantages of the Forth programming language is that it covers the full spectrum of language levels. Some languages, such as assembly language, allow dealing only at the hardware level. Other languages, such as FORTRAN, deal at an abstract level that has little to do with the underlying machine. Forth programs can span the full range of programming abstraction. At the lowest level, Forth allows direct access to hardware ports in the system for real-time I/O handling and interrupt servicing. At the highest level, the same Forth program can manage a sophisticated knowledge base.

The one facet of Forth that is most interesting (and baffling to many casual observers) is that it is an extensible language. As every procedure is added to the language, the apparent language available to the programmer grows. In this manner, Forth is much like LISP. There is no distinction made between core procedures in the language and extensions added by the programmer. This enables the language to be flexible to an extent beyond comprehension to people who have not extensively used the capability.

The extensibility of Forth does have mixed blessings. Forth tends to act as a programmer amplifier. Good programmers become exceptional when programming in Forth. Excellent programmers can become phenomenal. Mediocre programmers generate code that works, and bad programmers go back to programming in other languages. Forth also has a moderately difficult learning curve, since it is different enough from other programming languages that bad habits must be unlearned. New ways of conceptualizing solutions to problems must be acquired through practice. Once these new skills are acquired, though, it is a common experience to have Forth-based problem solving skills involving modularization and partitioning of programs actually improve a programmer's effectiveness in other languages as well.

Another problem with some Forth systems is that they do not include a rich enough set of programming tools to suit many programmers. Also, older Forth systems cooperate poorly with resident operating systems. These traits stem from Forth's history of use on very small machines with few hardware resources. In real-time control applications, these limitations are generally not much of a problem. Other applications need better support tools. Fortunately, the trend is for newer Forth systems to provide much better development environments and library support than in the past.

The result of all these effects is that Forth is best used on medium-sized programming projects involving no more than two or three programmers who have compatible programming styles. In any very large programming project, clashing styles and abilities tend to prevent the production of extremely high quality software. However, within these constraints, Forth programs are consistently delivered in a very short time with excellent results, often solving problems that could not be solved in any other language, or at least, not solved within budget and development time constraints.

7.2.2 C and other conventional languages

Of course, there will always be applications that are better done in conventional languages. Probably the most common reason for using a conventional language will be the existence of a large body of existing source code that must be ported onto a better processor.

To illustrate the tradeoffs involved, let us look at the problem of porting an application written in C onto a stack processor using a C compiler written for the stack machine. We shall skip over the problem of translating the program from the source C code into an intermediate form, since this is independent of the machine upon which the program is to run. The portion of the C compiler that is of interest is the so-called 'back end'. The back end is the portion of the compiler that takes a predigested intermediate form of a program and produces code for the target machine.

Actually, generation of stack-based code for expression evaluation is relatively straightforward. The topic of converting infix arithmetic expressions to stack-based (postfix/RPN) expressions is well researched (Bruno & Lassagne 1975, Couch & Hamm 1977, Randell & Russell 1964).

The problem in generating code for stack machines from C is that there are several assumptions about the operating environment deeply entrenched in the language. The most profound of these is that there must be a single program-memory-resident stack that contains both data and subroutine return information. This assumption cannot be violated without 'breaking' many C programs. As an example, consider the case of a pointer that references a local variable. That local variable *must* reside in the program memory space, or it cannot be properly referenced by the program.

To make matters worse, C programs typically push large volumes of data, including strings and data structures, onto the C stack. Then, C programs make arbitrary accesses within the area of the current stack frame (the portion of the stack containing variables belonging to the current procedure). These restrictions make it unfeasible to attempt to keep the C stack on a stack machine's Data Stack.

How then can a stack machine be made efficient at running C programs? The answer is that the stack machine must efficiently support frame-pointer-plus-offset addressing into program memory. The RTX 2000 can use its User Pointer to accomplish this efficiently. The FRISC 3 can use one of its user-defined registers and the load/store with offset instructions. The RTX 32P's commercial successor will have a frame pointer register and dedicated adder for computing memory addresses. In all cases, the access to local variables can be made in the same time as required for any other memory operation: two memory cycles — one for the instruction and one for the data. This is the best that can be hoped for in any processor that does not resort to expensive techniques such as separated data and instruction caches.

The other notion often found in C, and other high level languages, that does not map well onto stack machines is that of a 'register variable'. Since stack machines do not have a set of registers, this implies that compiler optimization opportunities may be missed by stack machines. This is only partially true. While it is true that stack machines are not well suited for juggling a large number of temporary values on the stacks, a small number of frequently accessed values can be kept on the stack for quick reference. For example, these values might include a loop counter kept on the return stack and two addresses for a string compare kept on the data stack. In this manner, most of the efficiency of the hardware can be captured for the majority of C programs.

There is one additional concept that can make most C programs as fast as Forth programs on stack machines. That is the concept of supporting Forth as the 'assembly language' of the processor. This approach is being vigorously pursued on by several stack machine vendors. Using this approach, existing C programs are transferred to the stack machine. Their execution characteristics are then profiled. This profiling information is used to identify the few critical loops within the program. These loops are then rewritten in Forth for better speed, perhaps augmented with application specific microcode in the case of the RTX 32P. Using this technique, C programs can attain virtually the same performance as all-Forth programs with very little effort.

When this good performance is added to the other stack machine qualities of low system complexity with high processing speed, C becomes a viable language in which to program stack machines.

7.2.3 Rule-based systems and functional programming

There is evidence that programming languages used to implement rule-based systems, such as those written in Prolog, LISP, and OPS-5 are very well suited to stack machines. One very exciting possibility is the marriage of real-time control applications with rule-based system knowledge bases. Preliminary research into this area has been encouraging. Much work has been done using Forth as an implementation vehicle. Areas explored include: LISP implementations (Hand 1987, Carr & Kessler 1987), an OPS-5 implementation (Dress 1986), a Prolog implementation (Odette 1987), neural network simulations (Dress 1987), and development environments for real-time expert systems (Matheus 1986, Park 1986). Most of these Forth implementations have subsequently been ported to stack machine hardware with excellent results. For example, the rule-based Expert-5 system described by Park (1986) runs 15 times faster on the WISC CPU/16 than on a standard IBM PC. A similar rule-based system (actually closer to Park's Expert-4, which is slower than Expert-5) runs approximately 740 times faster on the RTX 32P than on a standard 4.77 MHz 8088 PC. This speedup of nearly three orders of magnitude is astonishing to some, but merely reflects the suitability of using a stack machine, which is good at tree traversal, for solving problems that use decision trees.

The speedup observed for the rule-based system is actually based on a principle that applies to a wide variety of problem areas. Stack machines can treat a data structure as an executable program. Consider for a moment an example of a tree data structure, with pointers at the internal nodes and program action tokens at the leaves. The nodes of the trees that are pointers can just be the addresses of the children, which equates to subroutine calls in many stack processors. The leaves of the trees can be executable instructions, or subroutine calls to procedures that accomplish some task. A conventional processor would have to use an interpreter to traverse through the tree in search of the leaves. A stack processor can just directly execute the tree instead. Since stack machines execute subroutine calls very quickly, the results can be extremely efficient. The technique of directly executing tree-formatted data structures is responsible for the tremendous speed of the RTX 32P example cited in the previous paragraph.

Stack machines are well suited to LISP programming as well as to expert systems. This is because LISP and Forth are very similar languages in many respects. Both treat programs as lists of function calls to other lists. Both are extensible languages. Both use Polish notation for arithmetic operations. The major difference is that LISP involves dynamic storage allocation for its cells, while Forth uses a static storage allocation. Since there is no reason that a stack machine should be any worse at garbage collection than other machines, LISP should run efficiently on a stack machine.

Many of the same arguments about stack machines' suitability for LISP apply to Prolog. In a Prolog implementation for the RTX 32P, this author made an additional discovery about how to efficiently map Prolog onto stack machines. Prolog uses typed data that can be either an actual data element or a pointer to other data. A possible encoding for Prolog data elements is one that uses the highest 9 bits of a 32-bit word for a data type tag. The lowest 23 bits are then used as either a pointer to another node, a pointer to a 32-bit literal value, or a short literal value. Using this data format, data items are actually executable as instructions. Instructions for the RTX 32P can be constructed that allow traversing an arbitrarily long series of pointer dereferences at the rate of one dereference per memory cycle, simply by executing the data structure as a program. Nil pointer checking can be accomplished by defining the nil pointer value to be a subroutine call to an error trapping routine. These kinds of data handling efficiencies are simply not possible with other types of processors.

Functional programming languages offer the promise of a new way of solving problems using a different model of computation than that used by conventional computers (Backus 1978). A particular method of executing functional programs is the use of graph reduction. The same techniques of direct execution of the program graphs that were discussed for rule-based systems above are equally applicable to graph reduction. Thus, stack machines should be good at executing functional programming languages. Belinfante (1987) has published a Forth-based implementation of graph reduction. Koopman & Lee (1989) describe a threaded interpretive graph reduction engine.

From a theoretical point of view, efficient graph reduction machines such as the G-machine and Norma fall into the SL0 category of the taxonomy in Chapter 2. ML0 machines have a superset of the capabilities of SL0 machines, and should therefore be efficient at graph reduction as well. Initial investigations into this area by this author show that the RTX 32P, which is a very simple stack machine, can compete quite effectively with even very complex graph reduction machines such as Norma.

One of the side effects of using a functional programming language is that a high degree of parallelism is available during program execution. This raises the idea of a massively parallel computer made of stack processors that is programmed with a functional programming language.

7.3 UNIFORMITY OF SOFTWARE INTERFACES

A key conceptual feature of stack machines is their uniformity of interface between high level code and machine instructions. Both procedure calls and opcodes use the stack as a means of passing data. This consistent interface has several positive impacts on software development.

The source code for a program does not have to reflect in any manner which instructions are directly supported by the machine and which functions are implemented as procedures at the Forth language level. This capability suggests the use of a low level stack language, similar to Forth, that is the target of compilation for all languages. Given an assembler from this target language to the actual machine, the user is freed from worry about how particular functions are implemented. This means that various implementations of the same architecture can be made very compatible at the stack-based source code level without actually having to provide all instructions on low-cost implementations. If the same interface is used for conventional languages as well as Forth, then combinations of C code, Forth code, and code from other languages can be intermingled without problems.

In microcoded machines, such as the RTX 32P, this interface can be exploited one step further. Application specific microcode can be used to replace critical sequences of instructions in the application program, and common compiler generated code sequences transparently to the user. In fact, a common method of application code development on a microcoded stack machine is to first write the entire application in high level code, then go back to microcode the critical loops. The rewriting of subroutines from high level language to microcode is invisible to the rest of the program, except for the speed increase. This speed increase is a speedup factor of approximately two for many applications.

8

Applications

Stack machines, like most computers, are suitable for a wide variety of applications. Any system in which a high speed processor with low system complexity is needed is a good candidate for using a stack processor. Section 8.1 discusses one application area that has these requirements, and which is an ideal match for stack processors. That application area is real-time embedded control. Real-time control applications require small size, low weight, low cost, low power, and high reliability.

Section 8.2 examines the different capabilities and tradeoffs inherent in the choice between 16-bit and 32-bit hardware. The selection of the correctly sized processor is vital to the success of a design.

Section 8.3 discusses system implementation considerations. The choice between hardwired and microcoded systems involves tradeoffs among complexity, speed, and flexibility. The choice of integration level similarly affects system characteristics.

Section 8.4 lists eleven broad areas suitable for stack processors, with detailed lists of possible applications.

8.1 REAL-TIME EMBEDDED CONTROL

Real-time embedded control processors are computers that are built into pieces of (usually) complicated equipment such as cars, airplanes, computer peripherals, audio electronics, and military vehicles/weapons. The processor is embedded because it is built into a piece of equipment that is not itself considered a computer.

8.1.1 Requirements of real-time control

Often the fact that a computer is present in an embedded system is completely invisible to the user, such as in an automobile anti-skid braking system. Often times, a processor is used to replace expensive and bulky components of a system while providing increased functions and a lower cost. At other times, the fact a computer is present may be obvious, such as in an aircraft autopilot. In all cases, however, the computer is just a component of a larger system.

Most embedded systems place severe constraints on the processor in terms of requirements for size, weight, cost, power, reliability and operating environment. This is because the processor is just a component of a larger system, which has its own operating requirements and manufacturing constraints.

At the same time, however, the processor must deliver the maximum possible performance to respond to real-time events. Real-time events are typically external stimulae to the system which require a response within a matter of microseconds or milliseconds. For example, some high performance jet aircraft are inherently unstable, and depend on computer control systems to keep them flying. An airborne computer must be very light and small, and yet not make unreasonable demands for power and cooling. At the same time, it must not fall behind in its task of keeping the plane flying properly. When supersonic, the plane is moving at perhaps 1000 feet per second. At these speeds, a few milliseconds can make the difference between crashing or flying!

8.1.2   How stack machines meet these needs

The manufacturers of the stack machines described in Chapters 4 and 5 all have real-time control applications in mind as possible uses for their technology. What is it that makes stack machines so suitable for these applications?

Size and weight

We have seen that stack computers are very simple in terms of processor complexity. However, it is not the number of gates in the processor itself that determines overall system size and weight, but rather the overall system complexity. A processor that has a large number of pins takes up precious printed circuit board area. One that needs cache memory controller chips and large amounts of memory takes even more printed circuit board area. And systems that require a hard disk for virtual memory management because their software environment is huge are usually out of the question. The key to winning the size and weight issue is to keep component count small. Stack machines, with their low hardware system complexity and small program memory requirements, do that very well. Since stack machines are less complex than other machines, they are more reliable as well.

Power and cooling

The processor complexity can affect the power consumption of the system. The amount of power used by the processor is related to the number of transistors, and especially to the number of pins on the processor chip. Processors that rely on exotic process technology for speed are usually 'power hogs'. Processors that need huge numbers of power-consuming high speed memory devices likewise can break a power budget.

Stack computers tend to have low power requirements. The fabrication technology used can greatly affect power consumption, with newer CMOS chips often having minuscule power requirements compared to bipolar and NMOS designs. Of course, power consumption directly affects cooling requirements, since all power used by a computer is eventually given off as heat. The cooler operation of CMOS components can reduce the number of component failures, enhancing system reliability.

Operating environment

Embedded processing applications are notorious for extreme operating conditions, especially in automotive and military equipment. The processing system must deal with vibration, shock, extreme heat and cold, and perhaps radiation. In remotely installed applications, such as spacecraft and undersea applications, the system must be able to survive without field service technicians to make repairs. The general rule to avoiding problems caused by operating environments is to keep the component count and number of pins as low as possible. Stack machines, with their low system complexity and high levels of integration, do well at standing up to extreme operating environments.

Cost

The cost of the processor itself may be very important to low and medium performance systems. Since the cost of a chip is related to the number of transistors and to the number of pins on the chip, low complexity stack processors have an inherent cost advantage.

In high performance systems, the cost of the processor may be overwhelmed by the cost of the multi-layered printed circuit boards, support chips, and high speed memory chips. In these cases, the low system complexity of stack machines provides additional advantages.

Computing performance

Computing performance in a real-time embedded control environment is not simply an instructions-per-second rating. While raw computational performance is important, other factors which can make or break the system include interrupt response characteristics and context swapping overhead. An additional desirable characteristic is good performance in programs that are riddled with procedure calls as a means for reducing program memory size. Even if the cost of fast memory chips is no object, a lack of cubic inches and printed circuit board real estate may force the program into a small memory space. Previous discussions on the characteristics of stack machines show that they excel in these areas.

8.2   16-BIT VERSUS 32-BIT HARDWARE

A fundamental decision about which stack processor to select for a particular application is the size of the processor's data elements: 16 bits or 32 bits. The decision between 16- and 32-bit processors is driven by the factors of cost, size and performance.

8.2.1   16-bit hardware often best

16-bit stack processors in general have lower costs than 32-bit processors. Their internal data paths are narrower, so they use fewer transistors and cost less to manufacture. They only need 16-bit paths to external memory, so they have half as many memory bus data pins as 32-bit processors. System costs are also lower, since a minimum configuration 16-bit processor only needs to have half the number of memory chips as a 32-bit processor for a single bank of memory.

16-bit chips also have a reasonable amount of silicon area available for special features, such as hardware multipliers, on-chip program memory, and peripheral interfaces. The trend is for semicustom 16-bit stack processors such as the RTX 2000 to be complete systems-on-a-chip, including I/O peripherals and program memory for embedded applications.

16-bit processors should always be evaluated for an application, then rejected in favor of 32-bit processors only if there is a clear benefit for the change.

8.2.2   32-bit hardware sometimes required

Most traditional real-time control applications are well served by 16-bit processors. They offer high processing speed in a small system at minimum cost. Of course, part of the reason that traditional applications are well served by 16-bit processors is that capable 32-bit processors have not been widely available for very long. As the more capable 32-bit processors come into greater usage, new application areas will be discovered to put them to good use.

32-bit stack processors should be used instead of 16-bit processors only in cases where the application requires high efficiency at one or more of the following: 32-bit integer calculations, access to large amounts of memory, or floating point arithmetic.

32-bit integer calculations are obviously well suited to a 32-bit processor. Occasions where 32-bit integers are required include graphics and manipulation of large data structures. While a 16-bit processor can simulate 32-bit arithmetic using double-precision operands, 32-bit processors are much more efficient.

While 16-bit processors can use segment registers to access more than 64K elements of memory, this technique becomes awkward and slow if it must be used frequently. A program that must continually change the segment register to access data structures (especially single data structures that are bigger than 64K in size) can waste a considerable amount of time computing segment values. Even worse, since the addresses that must be manipulated when computing data record locations that are greater than 16 bits wide, address computations are also slower because of all the double-precision math involved. A 32-bit processor can offer a linear 32-bit address space with accompanying quick address calculations on a 32-bit data path.

Floating point calculations also require a 32-bit processor for good efficiency. 16-bit processors spend a significant amount of time manipulating stack elements when dealing with floating point numbers, whereas 32-bit processors are naturally suited to the size of the data elements. There are many instances in which scaled integer arithmetic is more appropriate than floating point numbers to increase speed on some processors. In these cases a 16-bit processor may suffice. However, floating point math must often be used to reduce the cost of programming a project, and to support code written in high level languages. Also, with the advent of very fast floating point processing hardware, the traditional speed advantage of integer operations over floating point operations is decreasing.

The disadvantages of 32-bit processors are cost and system complexity. 32-bit processor chips tend to cost more because they have more transistors and pins than do 16-bit chips. They also require 32-bit-wide program memory and a generally larger printed circuit board than 16-bit processors. There is less room on-chip for extra features such as hardware multipliers, but these items will appear as chip fabrication technology gets denser.

8.3   SYSTEM IMPLEMENTATION APPROACHES

Once a decision has been made between a 16-bit and 32-bit processor, there still remains the choice of selecting a manufacturer. Each of the seven stack machines covered in detail in this book has a different set of tradeoffs in the areas of system complexity, flexibility, and performance. These tradeoffs reflect their suitability for different applications. One of the tradeoffs is the decision between hardwired and microcoded control.

8.3.1   Hardwired systems vs. microcoded systems

The question of whether the control circuitry should be hardwired or microcoded is an old debate within all computing circles. The advantages of the hardwired approach are that it can be faster for executing those instructions that are directly supported by the system. The disadvantage is that hardwired machines tend to only support simple instructions, and must often execute many instructions to synthesize a complex operation.

Microcoded machines are more flexible than hardwired machines. This is because an arbitrarily long sequence of microcode may be executed to implement very complicated instructions. Each instruction may be thought of as a subroutine call to a microcoded procedure. In machines with microcode RAM, the instruction set may be enhanced with application specific instructions to provided significant speed increases for a particular program.

The hardwired stack machines all support some rather complex stack operations that are combinations of data stack manipulations, arithmetic operations, and subroutine exits. This is accomplished by manipulating different fields in the instruction format. To the degree that this is possible, the hardwired machine instruction formats are rather like microcode. In fact, Novix has called the NC4016 instructions a form of 'external microcode'.

In the microcoded stack machines, simple operations such as additions may often take longer than on a hardwired machine. Complicated opcodes, such as double-precision arithmetic operations, do not pack into a single instruction on the hardwired machines. For these complex instructions, the microcoded machines can run faster by providing special complex opcodes. In general, this increased flexibility can more than eliminate the raw speed gap between the two kinds of processors. The final conclusion as to which type of processor is faster for a particular application is in general not clear without evaluating both approaches. The important point is to perform a careful evaluation of the requirements of an application before selecting a stack processor.

8.3.2 Integration level and system cost/performance

In addition to exploring the implementation tradeoffs between hardwired control and microcoded control, the 16-bit stack processors discussed in Chapter 4 display the full range of integration level decisions. Integration level is the amount of system hardware that is placed onto the processor chip. The more system functions that are placed on the processor chip, the higher the integration level. Also at issue, however, are the cost/performance tradeoffs made in the design with respect to the minimum number and type of components necessary to run the system.

The WISC CPU/16 displays the lowest integration level of those processors examined. It uses off-the-shelf building blocks to create a processor with dozens of components. Of course, this design approach eliminates the need to repay the large initial chip layout investment required when producing a single-chip version.

The MISC M17 is a simple single-chip stack processor. Since it uses program memory for its stacks, only the processor chip and program memory are required for operation. The integration level is reasonably high, and the system complexity is low. The penalty paid for the simplicity of the design is that speed is somewhat slower than what is possible with separated stack memories.

The Novix NC4016 also is a single-chip processor, and has an integration level comparable to that of the M17. Not surprisingly, both processors are fabricated using gate arrays of roughly comparable sizes. The major distinction of the NC4016 is that it uses separate memory chips for both stacks. Separate stack memories provide faster potential processing rates for a given clock speed because of the increased memory bandwidth available, but at the cost of requiring more components at the system level.

The Harris RTX 2000 increases the level of system integration beyond the NC4016 by including on-chip stack memories. This actually reduces system complexity while providing potential speed increases, since on-chip memory can be faster than off-chip memory. The cost is more transistors on the chip. However, these extra transistors do not necessarily increase chip size by much. This is because the RTX 2000 uses a different design methodology called standard cell design that is well suited to providing on-chip memories. In fact, RTX 2000 customized systems can be designed that include program memory as well as stack memory on-chip, providing a single-chip stack computer system.

It is likely that most stack computers designed in the future will have differing tradeoffs in the areas of data path widths (16-bit and 32-bit widths for most processing, and perhaps 24-bit widths for signal processing and 36-bit widths for tagged data architectures), level of system integration, required off-chip support, and raw performance. These characteristics must all be taken into consideration when matching a processor selection to cost, performance, and other requirements in a target application.

8.4 EXAMPLE APPLICATION AREAS

Application areas for stack computers, like those for computers in general, are only limited by the imagination. Some of the applications that seem well suited for stack machines include:

Image processing
Object recognition, including optical character recognition, thumb print recognition and handwriting recognition as well as image enhancement require extremely powerful processors, but have wide application. Many commercially interesting applications require that the processor be small, inexpensive and portable.

Robotics controllers
Robot arms have 5 or 6 joints (degrees of freedom). A typical strategy is to have a microcontroller for each joint plus a more powerful processor for centralized control. With powerful microcontrollers, each joint can perform complex positional calculations in real time. In a mobile system, small size and low power consumption are vital.

Digital filters
Filters require high speed multiplications to keep up with high data flow rates. Stack processors have the room on-chip for hardware multipliers and algorithm specific hardware to quickly perform digital filter calculations.

Process control
More powerful processors can go beyond simple process control techniques to apply expert system technology to real-time process monitoring and control. Stack machines are particularly well suited for rule-based systems.

Computer graphics
While there are several special-purpose graphics accelerator chips on the market, these tend to concentrate on the primitives of drawing lines and moving blocks of bits. The exciting opportunity here is in the area of interpreting high level graphics command languages for both laser printers and device independent screen display languages. One of the predominant languages, Postscript, is similar to Forth.

Other computer peripherals
The low system cost of a stack machine makes it well suited for controlling computer peripherals such as disk drives and communication links.

Telecommunications
High speed controllers can provide the capability for data compression and therefore lower transmission costs for telefax and modem applications. They can also monitor the performance of transmission equipment.

Automotive control
The automotive market forces very severe restrictions on cost and environmental requirements. In this business a minute difference in cost per component can add up to large profits or losses. A high level of system integration is mandatory. Computers can improve car performance and safety even while reducing system cost in applications such as computerized ignition, braking, fuel distribution, anti-theft devices, collision alert systems, and dash display systems.

Consumer electronics
Consumer electronics are, if anything, more sensitive to pricing and system integration level than are automotive products. Anyone who has taken apart an inexpensive calculator or digital watch knows the miracles that can be accomplished with a few pieces of plastic and a single chip. Opportunities for the use of high speed, portable, inexpensive stack processors abound in music synthesis (such as MIDI compatible devices), compact laser disk sound and video playback devices, digital tape devices, slow scan television via telephone lines, interactive cable TV services, and video games.

Military and spaceborne control applications
While spaceborne applications may be used for commercial purposes, they have the same reliability and environmental requirements as many military applications. Stack processors are well suited to high speed control applications involving missiles and aircraft. In addition, there are applications in acoustic and electronic signal processing, image enhancement, communications, fire control, and battlefield management.

Parallel processing
Preliminary research shows that stack machines can execute functional programming languages very efficiently. Programs written in these languages have a great deal of inherent parallelism, which may be exploited by a multiprocessor stack machine system.

9

The future of stack computers

The stack machines reviewed in the earlier chapters represent the first generation of commercially available stack processors. As these machines come into wide use, the designs will be refined to meet market requirements and improve efficiency. The questions addressed in this chapter are: what kinds of refinements are we likely to see, and how will they affect stack machine architectures and applications?

It is too soon to answer all the questions about how stack machines will perform in many different circumstances. There are, however, a number of important topics upon which we can speculate. The opinions and reasoning presented herein may form the basis for further exploration of stack machine concepts. Ideas in this chapter should be taken as speculations, not as proven facts.

Section 9.1 discusses some areas that need to be examined when providing support for conventional programming languages on stack machines. As it turns out, existing stack machine designs handle most of the problems well already.

Section 9.2 discusses the issue of virtual memory and memory protection. Virtual memory support is not found on current stack machines because it is not needed for most of their application areas. Memory protection is also not supported, but will be needed for some applications in the future.

Section 9.3 examines the need for a third stack, and proposes that a memory-resident stack frame can meet the need for a third stack and conventional language support at the same time.

Section 9.4 discusses the impending limits of memory bandwidth, and the history behind the use of memory hierarchies in computers. Stack machines offer a solution to the memory bandwidth problem which is well suited to their important application areas.

Section 9.5 introduces two ideas for stack machine design that are intriguing, but not used in current designs. One idea involves the elimination of conditional branches by using conditional subroutine returns instead. The other idea involves using a stack to hold temporarily assembled programs.

Section 9.6 offers some speculation on the impact of stack machines on computing.

9.1   SUPPORT FOR CONVENTIONAL LANGUAGES

The initial market for stack machines is the real-time control area. The high level of system integration possible with stack machines may also lead to use as low cost, high performance coprocessor cards for personal computers and low-end workstations as well. These coprocessor cards may well be application specific for a certain class of problems, or even a single important software package. Both these environments will require running much application code in conventional programming languages.

Conventional languages can be implemented very easily on stack machines. The only problem is that pure stack machines probably cannot perform quite as well as register machines when running conventional programs written in the normal programming style. This problem is mostly one of a mismatch between stack machine capabilities and the requirements of conventional languages. Conventional programs tend to use few procedure calls and large numbers of local variables. Stack machines tend to be good at running programs with many small procedures and few local variables. In part, the difference is due to the programming styles encouraged by common practice and the structure of conventional programming languages. To some extent, the difference is that register machines are well suited to general-purpose data processing, whereas stack machines perform best in a real-time control environment. At any rate, performance of conventional languages on stack machines can be brought close to even the highest performance register machines for all applications by providing a modest level of hardware support. The idea, of course, is to approximately match register-based machines where they are best while not sacrificing the features that make stack machines better for other areas.

9.1.1   Stack frames

The issue, then, is to identify high level language structures that require additional hardware support. Strangely, the high level language run-time stack is the only major area in which pure stack machines fail to support conventional high level languages. This is because high level languages have the notion of 'activation records', which are 'frames' of elements pushed onto a software-managed stack in program memory upon every subroutine call. In the usual implementation, each stack frame is allocated only once as a large chunk of memory in the preamble to the subroutine being called. This frame contains the input parameters (which were actually allocated by the calling routine), the user declared local variables, and any compiler generated intermediate variables that might be necessary. During the course of the subroutine, arbitrary accesses are made within the stack frame without actually performing any pushes or pops.

The stack frame is used as a temporary memory allocation device for subroutine calling, not as a traditional pushdown stack for storing intermediate results between successive calculations. This means that it is incompatible with hardware stacks built into stack machines such as those we have been studying. An obvious approach to modify stack machines to meet this requirement is to build the primary stack so as to be allocated in large chunks with random access within a frame. This is precisely how the RISC machines with register windows (described as SL2 machines in Chapter 2) solve the problem. The reason why this does not make sense for stack machines is that all accesses to data pay the penalties associated with having operands in the instruction format.

An alternative approach is to build a secondary hardware stack for accessing local variables at a 'slow' speed, with primary data manipulations done on a LIFO hardware data stack. This lets us have the best of both worlds, but is not without cost. That secondary register frame stack will in general have to be 5 to 10 times as big as the data stack for good operating characteristics.

9.1.2 Aliasing of registers and memory

If this were the end of the tradeoff discussion, we might still be tempted to build a chip with on-chip frames. But, there is a deciding factor which tilts the balance in favor of placing the stack frames in program memory. That additional factor is that the semantics of conventional languages allow access to these local variables by memory address. The C language is notorious for this problem, which affects register machines and stack machines alike.

While the aliasing of registers to memory addresses can be handled with clever hardware or compilers, the costs in hardware and/or software complexity are not in keeping with the stack machine design philosophy of maximum performance with minimum complexity. Therefore, the best choice for a stack machine is to maintain the conventional language stack frames in program memory, with a Frame Pointer register available as a hardware pointer for stack frame accesses. If chip space is plentiful, a stack machine might provide on-chip RAM as part of the program memory space to speed up access to the stack frames.

It is indeed tempting to write complex compilers in an attempt to keep most local variables on the hardware stack while executing conventional languages. An experiment by this author with some stack machines has shown, however, that the difference between a C compiler that keeps all local variables on the hardware data stack and one that uses program memory with a frame pointer is small. In fact, if the machine has a hardware frame pointer, keeping the frames in program memory is actually somewhat faster.

Normally, one would think that keeping local variables on the hardware data stack would be faster than placing them in memory. The reason this is not so is because stack machines are relatively inefficient at accessing deeply buried elements, especially if they may have been spilled out of the stack buffer and into program memory. Much of the time in the all-on-hardware-stack approach is spent thrashing elements about on the stack. While access to memory-resident frame elements is somewhat slower than access to data on the hardware stack, in the end the savings on stack manipulations make up the difference.

9.1.3   A strategy for handling stack frames

A good compromise approach for handling frames is a mixture of the program-memory-resident and hardware-data-stack-resident methods. The details of the approach are as follows. All procedure calls place the parameters to be passed on the hardware stack. Since these parameters must be computed or moved from one stack frame location to another using the hardware data stack anyway, no time is lost doing this. The procedure call is then made. The called procedure then copies all but one or two of the parameters from the hardware stack into its newly allocated frame as local variables. The compiler must be sure that the parameters left on the data stack are not referenced by address. This can be accomplished with register variable declarations by the programmer, compiler analysis, or just playing it safe and copying all parameters to memory. Having only one or two parameters on the data stack minimizes stack spills and still provides good efficiency gains. When the procedure terminates, the returned value is placed on the hardware stack.

The compromise approach gives good efficiency by saving a large number of references to memory. It also provides an excellent interface between different languages, such as Forth and C. It is relatively easy to write compilers to handle this approach as well. Also, many stack machines now in existence have a hardware frame pointer, so can easily support this scheme.

9.1.4   Conventional language execution efficiency

From this discussion, we can see that stack machines can be reasonably efficient at supporting conventional programming languages with their stack frame approach. Of course, stack machines that use a hardware frame pointer into program memory cannot be expected to be as efficient as RISC machines, since they have massive on-chip register windows for direct frame support or exceedingly clever optimizing compilers that do sophisticated global register allocation.

To the extent that programs in conventional languages conform to the models used by high performance register machines, stack machines will seem to perform poorly. Aspects of conventional programs that cause this effect include: large segments of straight-line code, near-100% cache hit ratios, large numbers of local variables used across long procedures, and shallowly nested procedures that can be compiled as in-line code.

To the extent that programs use structures which run efficiently on stack machines, stack machines can approach or even exceed the performance of register-based machines. Code which is run well by stack machines contains: highly modular procedures with many levels of nesting and perhaps recursion; a relatively small number of frequently used subroutines and inner loops that may be placed in fast memory, and perhaps provided with microcode support; small numbers of local variables passed down through many layers of interface routines; and deeply nested subroutine calls. Also, programs that operate in environments with frequent interrupts and context switches can benefit from using stack machines.

   A practical method for using conventional languages on stack machines is to adopt the traditional approach of implementing the bulk of a program in a moderately efficient high level language. Then, the inner loops of the program are recoded in the assembly language of the machine. This affords very high performance with a modest amount of effort. In the case of a project where stack machines are needed for their excellent real-time processing characteristics, this approach can yield maximum processing speed for the programmer time invested.

   One should also keep in mind that there are reasons to select a computer other than raw processing speed for single programs. The reasons that might tilt the balance in favor of stack machines include: interrupt processing speed, task switching speed, low overall system complexity, and the need for application specific microcode and/or hardware support. In the final analysis, stack machines will probably not run many conventional language programs quite as quickly as register-based machines. But, other considerations will largely cancel out the drawbacks, especially for real-time control applications, making stack machines an excellent alternative.

9.2   VIRTUAL MEMORY AND MEMORY PROTECTION

The use of virtual memory and memory protection are concepts that have not yet been widely incorporated into existing stack machines. This is because most stack machine applications to date have been relatively small programs with tight constraints on hardware and software that did not require or leave room for these techniques.

9.2.1   Memory protection is sometimes important
Memory management can mean many things, but in this case we will focus only on memory management as it pertains to protection features. Protection is the one feature of memory management that is seen as most important by some real-time control users, especially the military. Protection is the capability for the hardware to prevent a program from accessing another program's memory except under very carefully controlled conditions. An unauthorized access to memory not owned by a particular program causes an interrupt. This interrupt causes the operating system to shut down or reset the offending task. This provides a security measure to prevent an ill-behaved program from demolishing other programs. The memory protection function is often performed by a separate chip that is managed by the operating system. There is nothing in stack machines that prevents this kind of chip from being used. An advantage of stack machines in this area is that they are small enough to allow the possibility of on-chip memory protection circuitry for increased system integration levels.

9.2.2   Virtual memory is not used in controllers
Likewise, there is no reason why stack machines cannot be provided with virtual memory capabilities. The one problem with virtual memory is the

effect of a virtual memory miss, which may require retrying an instruction. Since stack machines are in essence load/store machines, instruction restartability is no harder than on a RISC machine. In fact, since handling interrupts is quicker on a stack machine because of the lack of an instruction pipeline, stack machines should be better at handling virtual memory.

The reason why stack machines have not been designed with virtual memory is very simple. Most stack machines are targeted for real-time control applications. The performance variations and large hard disk hardware requirements associated with virtual memory are simply inappropriate in a real-time embedded control environment.

9.3   THE USE OF A THIRD STACK

An often proposed design alternative for stack machines is the use of a third hardware stack. The purposes given for adding a third hardware stack are usually for storage of loop counters and local variables.

Loop counters on the current stack machines are generally kept as the top element of the return address stack. This is because subroutines and loops are mutually well nested, and it is considered bad programming style for a subroutine to attempt to access the loop index of its parent procedure. So, while there is some conceptual merit to having loop indices in their own stack to avoid cluttering the return stack with nonaddress data, the performance and program effectiveness gains are not sufficient to justify the hardware expense.

Local variable storage is another issue. Even when using the Forth language, programmers have found that the concept of compiler-managed local variables can make some programs easier to create and maintain. In order to do this efficiently, the hardware needs access to a stack that is allocated in frames, with random access to locations within the frame. This is a requirement that is very like that for supporting conventional languages. So, in fact, the best solution is probably not to have a third hardware stack at all. Rather, stack machines should support a frame pointer into a software-managed program memory stack that is used both for conventional language support and for support for local variables in Forth.

9.4   THE LIMITS OF MEMORY BANDWIDTH

Perhaps the greatest challenge that has faced computer architects over the years is the problem of memory bandwidth. Memory bandwidth is the amount of information that can be transferred to and from memory per unit time. Put another way, memory bandwidth determines how often values can be accessed from memory.

The crux of the issue is that program memory usually is much bigger in terms of number of transistors or other devices than the processor. That means that the CPU can easily be made faster than the memory while keeping within budget. This comes from the general observation that faster components tend to be more expensive, consume more power, etc. for any given fabrication technology and geometry.

9.4.1   The history of memory bandwidth problems

The specter of memory bandwidth limitations has come and gone throughout computer design history. In the beginning, people were grateful that computers ran at all, so the speed of program memory and that of the processor were not a real issue. When electronic computers came along, much of the memory capacity of the computer was in fact magnetic tape used for data files, but it was better than nothing.

The magnetic core memories used in early large computers were very slow. This spawned very complex instruction sets that packed a lot of work into each instruction. It also made practical microcode, since a small amount of microcode memory could be made as fast as the CPU without breaking the budget, while the large amount of program memory could not. Once semiconductor memory was somewhat affordable, cache memories that captured small pieces of the program, especially loops, for reuse at execution time became popular. Cache memories became bigger and bigger, so that more and more of the programs resided in cache memory, which was fast enough to match the speed of the processor.

Then, microprocessors came into being. The early ones were slow enough that available program memory chips were sufficiently fast (and again, the issue was not how fast they ran as much as the wonder that they ran at all). The memory bandwidth problem was forestalled for a while. Microprocessor manufacturers followed in the footsteps of the big systems and used microcode with complex instruction sets.

Mainstream microprocessors developed quite a bit, then started needing 'wait states' when accessing memory. A wait state is a clock cycle wasted by a processor waiting for memory to respond when the processor is faster than its memory chips. One easy solution to this problem involves spending a lot of money to buy faster memory chips. The other easy solution is just to wait for the memory chip manufacturers to make faster memories at an affordable cost. Finally, the CISC microprocessors introduced cache memory and other techniques borrowed from large systems in an attempt to move more and more of the programs into fast memory.

RISC machines upset the applecart by claiming that processors with conventional microcode were bad. They, instead, use a very low level instruction set which can be best described as compiler-generated microcode that resides in program memory. This approach is claimed to give significant advantages, but at an admitted increase in memory bandwidth requirements. RISC machines depend heavily on cache memory for performance.

9.4.2   Current memory bandwidth concerns

With the latest generations of computers, there is a new problem. Cache memory chips will not be fast enough to keep up with processors of the future. This is not really because processor transistor switching speeds are increasing faster than memory chip speeds (they probably aren't). The problem is that the pins in and out of the processor and memory chips are beginning to dominate the timing picture.

The way that pins become the bottleneck is that transistors are getting smaller and faster as chips become denser. Unfortunately, pins that can be soldered and connected together haven't become much smaller except in very exotic packaging technologies. The number of electrons that must be pushed out on a pin and the wire connected to the pin becomes significant compared to the ability of the transistors to push electrons, so the pins become a bottleneck. This in turn means that any off-chip memory is slower by up to an order of magnitude than on-chip memory solely because of the delays introduced by going between chips.

Now we may have a situation where all off-chip memory is too slow to keep the processor busy. This creates a need for an additional layer of memory response speed: on-chip cache memory. Unfortunately, there is a fundamental problem with this approach compared to the previous memory approaches. Printed circuit boards may be made quite large without any problem. The yield of the circuit board varies linearly with the number of chips, and circuit boards are repairable if defects are discovered. Unfortunately, the yield of chips grows worse exponentially with area, and chips are not easily repairable.

Using separate cache memory chips, adding more chips to a printed circuit board can provide as much cache memory as was needed within reason. However, if a single-chip system does not have enough on-chip cache memory, increasing the chip size to provide more memory can make the processor unmanufacturable because of yield problems. The tremendous amounts of memory needed by high-speed processors, especially RISC machines, seem to indicate that the best we may hope for is a modest amount of high-speed cache memory on-chip, and a large amount of slow-speed off-chip cache memory. Now our program performance is at the mercy of the hit ratios for two different caches. Is this the best that we can hope for?

9.4.3   The stack machine solution
Stack machines provide a much different way to solve the problem. Conventional machines with their caches attempt to capture bits and pieces of programs as they are run. This is part of an attempt to reuse already fetched instructions as they are executed in loops or very frequently called procedures. Part of the problem that interferes with cache performance is that conventional programming languages and compilers produce rambling, sprawling code. Stack machines, on the other hand, encourage the writing of compact code with much reuse of procedures.

The impact of the way stack machine programs behave is that stack machines should not use dynamically allocated cache memory. They instead should use small, statically allocated or operating system managed program memory for high speed execution of selected subroutines. Frequently used subroutines may be placed in these portions of program memory, which can be used more freely by the compiler and the user with the knowledge that they will run quickly. Since stack machine code is very compact, a significant amount of a program can reside in high speed on-chip memory. This can further encourage the use of modular, reused procedures with the knowledge that they will actually help performance, instead of hurting it as is too often the case in other machines. Of course, since the on-chip program memory does not need complex and bulky control circuitry for management of cache, all the more room is available for extra program memory. On the 16-bit stack processors, it is quite reasonable for an entire real-time control program and the data memory for its local variables to reside entirely on-chip. With process technology at sub-micron levels, the same will begin to be true for 32-bit stack processors as well.

To consider how this different approach to memory hierarchies might work, consider a microcoded machine such as the RTX 32P. Large dynamic RAMs may be used to contain the bulk of a program and its data. Actually, this is really an extreme case, because programs for the RTX 32P seldom need more than the capacity of its static memory chips for programs, but let us assume that this is true anyway. The dynamic RAM form a storage element for the very highest levels of the program that are executed infrequently, and for data that is accessed sparsely or infrequently.

Next, static memory chips are added to the system. These are used for the medium-level layers of the program that are executed fairly frequently. Also, program data that will be manipulated frequently may be resident in this memory, or may be copied in from the dynamic memory for a period of time when it will be needed. In practice, there may be two levels of static memory chips: large, slow ones and small, fast ones, each with different power, cost, and printed circuit board space characteristics.

On-chip program memory can come next in the hierarchy. The inner loops of important procedures in the program can reside here for quick access by the processor. Several hundred bytes of program RAM can easily fit onto the processor chip for data and program. In the case of chips which run dedicated programs (which is often the case in the real-time embedded system environment), several thousand bytes of program ROM may reside on-chip. In practice, any language can use many common subroutines in ROM to assist the programmer and the compiler.

Finally, microcode memory resides on-chip for the actual control of the CPU. In the sense of the memory hierarchy, microcode memory may be thought of as just another level of program memory. It contains the most frequently executed actions for the processor, which correspond to supported machine instructions. Once again, a mixture of ROM and RAM is appropriate. And of course, the data stack acts as a fast access device for holding intermediate computation results.

What we have, then, is a layered hierarchy of memory sizes and speeds throughout the system. The concept of a hierarchy is not new. What is new is the thought that it need not be managed by hardware at run time. The compiler and programmer can easily manage it. The key is, since stack programs are very small, significant amounts of code can reside at each level of a statically allocate hierarchy. Since stack machines support very fast procedure calls, only the inner loops or small segments of code that are frequently executed need be stored in high-speed memory, not the entire bulk of user-defined procedures. This means that dynamic memory allocation is really not required.

9.5   TWO IDEAS FOR STACK MACHINE DESIGN

There are two interesting stack machine design details that are not in common usage, but which may prove useful in future designs.

9.5.1   Conditional subroutine returns

One of the design details is an observation by Doran (1972) that stack machines do not need conditional branches; they only need conditional subroutine return instructions. Consider an IF statement in a high level language. If we ignore the optional ELSE clause, an IF statement appears to be a piece of code with one entry point and two exit points. The entry point is the beginning of the statement, where the branch condition is evaluated. The first exit point is if the condition is false, in which case none of the rest of the statement is executed. The second exit point is the end of the statement, when all actions have been completed.

The usual way of implementing an IF statement is by using a conditional branch that is taken if the condition tested by the IF is false. Instead, consider a subroutine that contains the code for the entire IF statement. The entry point to the IF statement is a subroutine call into this special subroutine. The first exit point can be a conditional subroutine return instruction, that only returns if the condition clause of the IF statement is false. The second exit point can be an unconditional return.

What this scheme accomplishes is elimination of conditional branches with embedded addresses. All that is required is a conditional subroutine return statement. This technique is well suited to stack machines, because of the low cost of the initial subroutine call into the IF statement's subroutine and the low cost of the subroutine exits. It may lead to more efficient machines than those currently in use.

9.5.2   Use of the stack for holding code

Another interesting proposal for stack machine program execution was put forth by Tsukamoto (1977). He examined the conflicting virtues and pitfalls of self-modifying code. While self-modifying code can be very efficient, it is almost universally shunned by software professionals as being too risky. Self-modifying code corrupts the contents of a program, so that the programmer cannot count on an instruction generated by the compiler or assembler being correct during the full course of a program run.

Tsukamoto's idea allows the use of self-modifying code without the pitfalls. He simply suggests using the run-time stack to store modified program segments for execution. Code can be generated by the application program and executed at run-time, yet does not corrupt the program memory. When the code has been executed, it can be thrown away by simply popping the stack.

Neither of these techniques is in common use today, but either one or both of them may eventually find an important application.

9.6 THE IMPACT OF STACK MACHINES ON COMPUTING

We have seen that stack machines can be at least as fast as register-based machines in terms of raw instructions executed per second. They also display superior characteristics in real-time control applications. Still, they can fall short of register-based machines in environments that use many local variables in programs with little use of nested procedure calls. The question of whether RISC, CISC, or stack machines are best is not an appropriate query. All of these design techniques have their place among different applications. Stack machines do not seem to be best suited as primary CPUs for the workstation and minicomputer markets. For this reason, they may receive less attention than they perhaps deserve. But, in those areas where they are well suited, they are here to stay.

On second thought, we may speculate that the problem in supporting some sorts of computing tasks is not with the stack machines, but rather with current programming practices. Consider the kinds of programs that stack machines are well suited for: highly modular programs with many small, deeply nested procedures; programs that pass a small number of variables between procedures, hiding the details of their operation; programs that frequently reuse these small procedures to reduce program size and complexity; programs that are easily debugged because of small procedure size; and programs which present a uniform level of interface at all levels of module abstraction, from high level subroutines to instructions. All these characteristics seem desirable. Unfortunately, they are seldom practiced today. Perhaps the use of stack machines can help improve the situation.

It may be that deep-seated knowledge of the strong points of register-based machines has formed the characteristic conventional programming languages and hardware we use. Procedure calls are not used frequently because they are time consuming. Because procedures are somewhat long, language syntax has not been forced to make them extremely simple to define and use, so they require various amounts of specification code, parameter lists, typing information, and the like. Even project management styles can require separate paperwork and formal procedures each time a new subroutine is created. And, because using many small procedures has been made more difficult by small degrees, fewer procedures are used, fueling the cycle.

Stack machines present an opportunity to change this cycle. Procedures calls are extremely inexpensive. Languages such as Forth provide a minimum of overhead for defining new procedures, and actually provide an environment which encourages development and testing of modularized, easily tested code. What may be needed is a design of new programming languages that are well suited to high level language machines (Chen *et al.* 1980), and to stack machines in particular. What we may see happen are extensions and variations on traditional languages to incorporate control structures that better exploit stack machine hardware.

Register-based machines can offer performance rewards for poorly structured programs, often at the cost of harder maintenance, more difficult debugging, and increased program size. By rewarding programmers for writing well structured code, stack machines may encourage better programming practices. This in turn, may influence the evolution paths of conventional languages toward providing better means for creating, maintaining, and executing programs.

Appendix A
A survey of computers with hardware stack support

This appendix is a survey of the stack architectures included in Chapter 2. It includes most stack machines which have been presented in conferences and described in journals. Each machine has a summary of its taxonomy category, implementation technology, problem solving applications, and design history. Additionally, each entry has references and a summary description.

AADC

Taxonomy category: SL1
Implementation: 16-bit minicomputer
Applications: Direct APL execution, military environment
Who and when: Raytheon for the US Navy, 1971
References: Nissen, S. & Wallach, S. (1973)

The AADC (All Applications Digital Computer) was designed for direct execution of the APL language. The target application area was Naval platforms (especially Naval aircraft), so small size and weight were important. The APL language was chosen for efficient machine code and execution. In particular, APL was chosen for its conciseness, which was predicted to give smaller programs and therefore fewer page faults in a virtual memory environment. The AADC converted expressions from infix to Polish notation on-the-fly at execution time. Programs were interpreted at runtime by the program management unit and executed by an arithmetic processor. The execution unit used 1-operand stack notation.

AAMP

Taxonomy category: SS1
Implementation: 16-bit microcoded silicon-on-sapphire
Applications: Radiation hard for military use, multi-tasking
Who and when: Rockwell International, 1981
References: Best *et al.* (1982)

The AAMP (Advanced Architecture MicroProcessor) was designed for military and space use. A stack architecture was chosen for ease of compilation and good code density since it can use mostly 1-byte instructions. AAMP uses a single stack with a frame pointer for activation records as well as expression evaluation with a separate stack pointer. The expression evaluation area is just on top of the current frame. Many instructions are 1 byte long, with the possibility of using local variable addresses relative to the frame pointer for 1-operand addressing. Four top-of-stack registers are used for evaluation, with spillage into program memory.

ACTION PROCESSOR

Taxonomy category: MS0
Implementation: 16-bit microcoded bit-sliced
Applications: Direct execution of Forth
Who and when: Computer Tools, 1979
References: Rust (1981)

The ACTION Processor FORTHRIGHT is a microcoded Forth-language processor. Typical of Forth hardware implementations, it has a data stack used for expression evaluation and parameter passing as well as a return address stack used for subroutine return address storage. The top elements of both stacks are kept in registers in the bit slices. Stacks reside in program memory to reduce hardware costs.

AEROSPACE COMPUTER

Taxonomy category: SS0
Implementation: 64-bit processor
Applications: High reliability, multiprocessor spacecraft computer
Who and when: Intermetrics, 1973
References: Miller & Vandever (1973)

The Aerospace Computer used stack instructions to save program memory space, which has a major impact on reducing size, weight, power, and cost for spacecraft applications. Stack instructions were also chosen to direct support high order languages to enhance software reliability. The design draws heavily from the B6700 architecture. All computation was done in floating point in the ALU, with integers converted to floating point format as fetched from memory. When set, the highest bit of an operand on the stack indicated that the element was really a pointer to memory, which caused a transparent fetch.

ALCOR:

Taxonomy category: ML0
Implementation: Emulator on various early European computers

Applications: Conceptual machine emulated for transportable ALGOL
          programming
Who and when: ALCOR joint project, 1958–60
References: Samelson & Bauer (1962)

The ALCOR (**AL**gol **CO**nverte**R**) joint project was a very early conceptual design for the interpretation of ALGOL 60. The European group devised a high level language machine architecture which was emulated on various machines. The conceptual machine had two stacks which were used for expression parsing and evaluation. One stack held pending operations, while the other stack held intermediate results. Variables and return addresses were statically allocated in program memory.

AN ALGOL MACHINE

Taxonomy categcry: ML0
Implementation: Research prototype project
Applications: Direct execution of ALGOL
Who and when: Burroughs, 1961
References: Anderson (1961)

The exploration for a direct execution architecture was motivated by the observation that two-thirds of computer time was then spent doing compilation and debugging. The focus of the research was on making computers easier to use. The approach taken was to directly execute a high level language. The machine discussed used three hardware stacks to execute ALGOL constructs. Two stacks formed a value and operator stack pair for expression parsing and evaluation. The third stack held subroutine return address information.

AM29000

Taxonomy category: SL2
Implementation: 32-Bit microprocessor
Applications: General purpose RISC processor
Who and when: Advanced Micro Devices (AMD) 1987
References: Johnson (1987)

The AM29000 is a RISC processor. While its instructions are not stack-oriented, it provides considerable hardware support for stacks for parameter passing for high level languages. It has 192 registers, 64 of which are conventional registers, the other 128 of which are used as a stack cache. A stack frame pointer into the register file provides relative addressing of registers. If the stack cache overflows, it is spilled to program memory under software control. The chip has the capability of dividing the 256 register address space into 16 banks for multi-tasking. Each instruction may access registers either globally, or based on the register stack pointer.

APL LANGUAGE

Taxonomy category: MS0
Implementation: Microcoded emulation on IBM 360/25 with WCS
Applications: Direct execution of APL
Who and when: International Business Machines, 1973
References: Hassitt *et al.* (1973)

APL is an inherently interpreted language, so creating an APL direct execution machine is an attractive alternative to interpreters on conventional machines. This project used an IBM 360 Model 25 with writable control store to emulate an operational APL machine. The machine used two stacks resident in program memory: one for expression evaluation, the other for temporary allocation of variable space.

BUFFALO STACK MACHINE

Taxonomy category: SS1
Implementation: 32-bit microcoded emulation on a B1700
Applications: Block structured language execution
Who and when: State University of New York at Buffalo, 1972
References: Lutz (1973)

The BSM (Buffalo Stack Machine) was a microcoded emulation of a stack architecture that ran on a Burroughs B1700 system. The architecture was designed to support ALGOL-60-type languages. Variables were stored as tagged data in memory with 32 data bits and 4 tag bits. Interrupts were treated as hardware invoked procedure calls, thus saving state automatically on the stack. A sticky point with doing this was that interrupts on stack overflow/underflow had to be made before the stack is completely full/empty to prevent a system crash.

BURROUGHS MACHINES

Taxonomy category: SS0
Implementation: A family of minicomputers
Applications: General-purpose multi-user computing
Who and when: Burroughs Corporation: 1961–77 (and beyond)
References: Carlson (1963), Doran (1979), Earnest (1980), Organick (1973)

The Burroughs line of stack computers originated with the ALGOL-oriented B5000 machine in 1961. One of the motivations for this machine was the observation that conventional machines required compilers that were so complex that they were too expensive to run (in 1961).

The B5000 was a 0-operand pure stack machine that kept the stack elements in program memory. The top two stack elements of the B5000 were kept in special registers in the CPU. A special feature of these registers is that there were hardware status bits that allowed 0, 1, or 2 of the registers to contain valid data. This reduced the amount of memory bus traffic by eliminating redundant reads and writes to memory (for example, a POP followed by a PUSH would not cause the same value to be read in from memory, then written back out). The B7700 elaborated on this scheme by using a 32-register stack buffer.

The stacks on these machines were used both for expression evaluation and for stack frames for ALGOL procedure calls. Thus, return addresses were interleaved with parameters on the stack. One of the advantages to keeping the stacks resident in program memory was rapid response to interrupts and a low cost for task swapping. Stacks enabled the hardware to treat procedure calls, interrupts, and task calls in a uniform manner.

CALTECH CHIP

Taxonomy category: SS0
Implementation: 8-Bit microcoded VLSI chip
Applications: University VLSI design project
Who and when: California Institute of Technology, 1979
References: Efland & Mosteller (1979)

This stack machine was implemented as a student project for a VLSI design course. The objective was to design and lay out the simplest possible computer in a two-and-one-half-week period. To keep the design simple, the students chose a 0-operand stack machine. The stack on this machine was maintained in program memory with 2 registers containing the top two stack elements on-chip. The instruction set was patterned after the primitives needed by a student-written Pascal compiler.

CRISP

Taxonomy category: SL2
Implementation: 32-bit CMOS microprocessor
Applications: C language RISC machine
Who and when: AT&T Bell Laboratories, 1987
References: Ditzel *et al.* (1987a), Ditzel *et al.* (1987b), Ditzel & McLellan (1982), Ditzel & McLellan (1987)

The CRISP microprocessor is a RISC machine optimized for executing the C programming language. It is designed as a register-less machine, with all operands memory-resident. However, since the C language uses stacks to allocate storage for local parameters, most of the operand data references are to memory locations relative to a stack pointer register. To support these stack references, CRISP has a 32-element stack cache on-chip. Thus, when a memory-to-memory operation is performed on data near the top of the stack, the operands are fetched and stored using the on-chip cache. CRISP also supports branch folding, a technique where branches are executed in parallel with some instructions.

DRAGON

Taxonomy category: SL2
Implementation: 2-chip microprocessor
Applications: Experimental multiprocessor design
Who and when: Xerox Palo Alto Research Center, 1985
References: Atkinson & McCreight (1987)

The Dragon is an experimental design created with an emphasis on compact binary instruction encodings and fast procedure calls. Variable length instructions and the use of stack-register addressing keep instruction size small while allowing the use of 3-operand instructions. The Dragon has a 128-element execution unit register stack with variable size frames implemented by a pointer pair that define the upper and lower frame bounds.

EM-1

Taxonomy category: SS1
Implementation: Conceptual design
Applications: Structured programming
Who and when: Vrije University, The Netherlands, 1978
References: Tanenbaum (1978)

This often-cited paper gives a discussion of how structured programming techniques should impact machine design, then presents an example design, the Experimental Machine-1 (EM-1). The motivation behind the EM-1 is to provide an efficient environment for well-structured programs. To do this, it uses a single memory-resident stack in typical block-structured language style, and provides 1-operand addressing to access local variables on the stack frame for evaluation using the top of stack. The design skirts the issue of memory bus contention between stack items and instructions by presuming the existence of a stack cache independent of an instruction cache.

EULER

Taxonomy category: SS0
Implementation: Microcoded interpreter on IBM 360/30
Applications: Research into implementing direct high level interpreters in microcode
Who and when: IBM Systems Development Division, 1967
References: Weber (1967)

EULER is an extension of the ALGOL programming language. The EULER project discussed by this paper was an early attempt to implement a direct interpretation machine by adding special-purpose microprogramming to a standard IBM Model 360 computer. In operation, an EULER program was compiled to an intermediate byte-code format. Each byte-code invoked a routine resident in microprogram memory. This system may well have been the first 'p-coded' machine. The use of microcoded interpretation was justified for this project by the fact that EULER supports structures such as dynamic typing, dynamic storage allocation, and list processing that were poorly handled by available compilers. The EULER implementation used a single stack resident in program memory for dynamic data allocation and expression evaluation. Data operation instructions were 0-operand RPN byte codes.

FORTH ENGINE

Taxonomy category: ML0
Implementation: Discrete LS-TTL
Applications: Execution of Forth programming language
References: Winkel (1981)

The Forth Engine was a discrete TTL microcoded stack processor for the Forth language. In addition to a hardware stack for evaluation and subroutine parameter passing and the hardware stack for return address storage, this processor featured a 60-bit writable control store for microcode.

FORTRAN MACHINE

Taxonomy category: MS0
Implementation: Conceptual Design
Applications: Direct execution of the FORTRAN language
Who and when: University of Science and Technology of China, PRC, 1980
References: Chen *et al.* (1980)

This paper presents a conceptual design paper for a direct execution FORTRAN machine. The proposed machine would have several hardware stacks for return address, loop limit and branch address, and expression evaluation storage. While the implementation method was not specified, isolated memory space stacks would certainly be appropriate to reduce memory traffic. As with most other direct execution machines, stacks were mandatory to support program parsing.

FRISC 3

Taxonomy category: ML0
Implementation: 32-bit 2 micron silicon compiler CMOS microprocessor
Applications: General-purpose space-borne computing and control. Optimized for the Forth language
Who and when: Johns Hopkins University, 1986
References: Fraeman *et al.* (1986), Hayes (1986), Hayes & Lee (1988), Hayes *et al.* (1987), Williams *et al.* (1986)

The Johns Hopkins University/APL Forth processing chip is designed for spacecraft processing applications. The chip executes Forth primitives, and allows multiple operations to be compacted into microcode-like fields in the instruction. Although Forth is a 0-operand language, the chip allows selecting any of the top 4 stack elements to be used with the top stack element for an operation, thus making it a '$\frac{1}{2}$' operand machine. The on-chip data and return stacks are rather small: 16 elements each, forced mostly by technology constraints.

G-MACHINE

Taxonomy category: SL0
Implementation: 32-bit processor simulation
Applications: Graph Reduction
Who and when: Oregon Graduate Center, 1985
References: Kieburtz (1985)

The G-Machine was specially built to perform graph reduction in support of executing functional programming languages. It executed G-code, which was a zero-address machine language designed to manipulate its single stack. Program memory was highly structured to support the requirements of graph reduction. Each memory word included four fields used for reference counting and two 32-bit cells used for graph pointers.

GLOSS

Taxonomy category: SS0
Implementation: Conceptual design
Applications: Multiple communicating processors
Who and when: University of Washington, 1973
References: Herriot (1973)

The GLOSS conceptual design was an attempt to define a generic high level language machine for a variety of languages, including ALGOL 68, LISP 1.5, and SNOBOL 4. It was based on using a demand-driven data-flow system where sub-processes were invoked on multiple parallel processors in a manner similar to procedure calls. Each processor had a set of evaluation stacks resident in memory.

HITAC-10

Taxonomy category: SS0
Implementation: Add-on hardware to a minicomputer
Applications: Experimental minicomputer addition
Who and when: Keio University, Japan, 1974
References: Ohdate *et al.* (1975)

The stack hardware discussed in this paper was back-fitted onto an existing HITAC-10 minicomputer. In order to simplify the design and construction, the stack hardware was added as an I/O device on the system bus. The stack controller had four top-of-stack registers. All extra elements were stored in an area of memory using DMA. The controller had two stack limit pointers for memory bounds checking. The stack controller was used for subroutine parameter passing; no arithmetic could be performed on stack elements.

HP300 AND HP3000

Taxonomy category: SS1
Implementation: 16-bit minicomputer family
Applications: General-purpose multi-user computer
Who and when: Hewlett Packard, 1976–1980s
References: Bartlett (1973), Bergh & Mei (1979), Blake (1977)

The HP3000 family is a commercial line of minicomputers based on a 1-operand stack architecture. The origins of the family may be found in the HP300 computer, which could be considered a 3-address machine that had two top-of-stack registers buffering a program memory resident stack. Later, the HP3000 series used a stack/accumulator addressing mode, and included four top-of-stack registers. The stacks were featured in the architectures to ease implementation of reentrancy, recursion, code sharing, program protection, and dynamic storage allocation in a multi-user environment. The stack is used not only for expression evaluation, but also for parameter passing and subroutine return address storage.

HUT

Taxonomy category: MS0
Implementation: 16-bit AM2903 bit-sliced processor
Applications: Spacecraft experiment control. Optimized for the Forth language
Who and when: Johns Hopkins University, Applied Physics Laboratory, 1982
References: Ballard (1984)

The HUT processor was designed to control the Hopkins Ultraviolet Telescope (HUT) Space Shuttle experiment. At the time it was designed, no space-qualified microprocessors were powerful enough for the task, so a bit-sliced processor was custom designed for the job. The designers chose to implement a Forth language processor for simplicity of implementation, extensibility, and flexibility.

ICL2900:

Taxonomy category: SS1
Implementation: Family of minicomputers
Applications: General-purpose computing
Who and when: ICL, 1975
References: Keedy (1977)

The designers of the ICL family were concerned with protection and code sharing in a multiprogrammed environment, as well as efficient compilation and execution with compact object code. While often compared with the contemporary Burroughs machines, the ICL machines had several distinct characteristics. One of these was the use of a stack/accumulator 1-operand addressing scheme and several specialized registers. With this capability, a register or memory location could be used with the top stack element for operations.

INTEL 80x86

Taxonomy category: SS2 (when used in stack mode)
Implementation: Family of 16- and 32-bit microprocessors
Applications: General-purpose computing
Who and when: Intel Corporation, 1980s
References: Intel (1981)

The 80x86 processor family, which includes the 8088, 8086, 80186, 80286, and 80386, is a family of microprocessors with a general-purpose register architecture. Simple PUSH and POP instructions are supported to manipulate the stack. Many high level language compilers produce code that uses the BP (base pointer) register as a frame pointer to a combined return address and parameter passing stack. When used in this mode, the 80x86 family can be considered to be doing stack processing. In the context of stack computers, the 80x86 is simply included in this listing as a representative example of a conventional machine that can be used as an SS2 architecture.

INTERNAL MACHINE

Taxonomy category: MS0
Implementation: Conceptual design
Applications: Directly interpretable languages
Who and when: North Electric Co., 1973
References: Welin (1973)

The Internal Machine was a conceptual design for a machine that could efficiently execute directly interpretable languages. A stack instruction model was picked for generality. The design specifies two stacks: one for expression evaluation and parameter passing, and a second stack for subroutine return addresses.

IPL-VI

Taxonomy category: SS1
Implementation: Conceptual design for microcoded interpreter
Applications: General-purpose computing
Who and when: Rand Corporation, 1958
References: Shaw *et al.* (1959)

The Information Processing Languages (IPLs) were a series of conceptual language designs for implementing high level programs. IPL-VI was a language designed to be implemented as an interpreted language with microcode support. IPL-VI emphasized advanced (for 1959) computing structures for nonnumerical computing, especially list manipulation. A stack was used to pass parameters between subroutines. Since all memory in the IPL-VI design was formatted as list elements, the subroutine parameter LIFO consisted of a list of elements that pointed to the next element further down in the list. IPL-VI instructions used 1-operand addressing.

ITS (PASCAL)

Taxonomy category: SS0
Implementation: 16-bit microprocessor
Applications: Direct execution of Pascal P-code
Who and when: Nippon Electric Co., 1980
References: Tanabe & Yamamoto (1980)

The ITS processor was designed to execute UCSD Pascal P-code. The designers claimed a several-times speedup over fully compiled code on a contemporary microprocessor (presumably an 8086). The ITS had a 256-word stack on-chip, which was apparently only used for expression evaluation. The top two stack elements were kept in registers for speed.

KDF-9

Taxonomy category: ML0
Implementation: 48-bit mainframe
Applications: General-purpose computing using ALGOL
Who and when: English Electric, 1960
References: Allmark & Lucking (1962), Duncan (1977), Haley (1962)

The KDF-9 was perhaps the first true stack computer. It was inspired by the advent of ALGOL-60, and introduced many of the features found on modern stack computers. The KDF-9 had an expression evaluation stack which could be used for parameter passing, as well as a separate return address stack. Unfortunately, these stacks were limited by technology considerations to only 16 elements apiece (constructed from magnetic cores!). A problem with the design was that while 16 elements is quite sufficient for expression evaluation, the ALGOL compiler was constrained by the 16-element stack depth, causing slow compilation.

KOBE UNIVERSITY MACHINE

Taxonomy category: ML0
Implementation: 16-bit-wide AM2903 bit-slice with writable control store
Applications: Academic Research
Who and when: Kobe University, Kobe Japan, 1983

References: Kaneda *et al.* (1983), Wada *et al.* (1982a), Wada *et al.* (1982b)

This machine was designed to execute both Forth and Pascal efficiently using a stack architecture. Forth was executed by directly implementing Forth primitives in microcode. Pascal was executed by supporting a UCSD P-code emulator. This machine had separate data memory in addition to program memory.

LAX2

Taxonomy category: SS0
Implementation: Microcoded interpreter on Varian V73
Applications: Experimental
Who and when: Group for Datalogical Research & Royal Institute of Technology, Sweden, 1980
References: Bage & Thorelli (1980)

The LAX2 architecture was implemented as a partially microcoded interpreter with the goals of cost effective software production along with good memory and execution time economy for string manipulation and interactive applications. The architecture used tagged data types. Each process in the machine had a private memory area shared between the evaluation stack and a garbage-collected heap for temporary string storage.

LILITH

Taxonomy category: ML1/MS1
Implementation: 16-bit AM2901 bit-sliced processor
Applications: Direct execution of Modula-2 M-code and interactive user interfaces
Who and when: ETH (Swiss Federal Institute of Technology), 1979
References: Ohran (1984), Wirth (1979)

Lilith was a Modula-2 execution machine developed by Niklaus Wirth. The goals of the machine were to provide efficient support for the Modula-2 language as well as an effective user interface. A stack architecture was chosen for compact code. The Lilith had two stacks: a program memory resident stack for parameter passing, and a hardware expression evaluation stack. The instruction set was stack-based, with the ability to read an element from any location in the parameter stack and operate upon it with the top element of the evaluation stack.

LISP MACHINES

Taxonomy category: ML1
Implementation: Various machines. 1982 to present
Applications: List processing, artificial intelligence research
Who and when: Various companies (such as Symbolics)

References: Lim (1987), Moon (1985), Sansonnet *et al.* (1982)

LISP machine architecture is a whole topic in its own right; this is simply a summary of some of the common characteristics of LISP-specific processors. LISP machines tend to have multiple stacks and 1-address (relative to top of stack) instruction formats. Some machines have substantial hardware stacks (over 1K word) that can overflow into program memory. Procedure calls tend to be very important, because of the recursion commonly used in traversing lists. These machines typically store data elements in a garbage-collected program/data memory.

MCODE

Taxonomy category: SS1
Implementation: Unspecified
Applications: Execution of Modula-2 M-code (using StarMod language)
Who and when: University of Wisconsin–Madison, 1980
References: Cook, R. & Donde, N. (1982), Cook, R. & Lee, I. (1980)

The MCODE machine was designed to execute Modula-2 M-code, which was compiled from a language called StarMod, a Modula-2 derivative. MCODE was based on Tanenbaum's EM-1 design, but with several improvements to solve problems that arise in real computers. One improvement was the use of a set-mode instruction that changed the interpretation of the data types (integer, floating point, etc.) for all subsequent operations.

MESA

Taxonomy category: SS0
Implementation: Architectural family for workstations
Applications: Graphics-intensive workstations (Alto, Dorado machines)
Who and when: Xerox Office Products Division, 1979
References: Johnsson & Wick (1982), McDaniel (1982), Sweet & Sandman (1982)

Mesa was actually a modular high level language expanded to include an architecture for a family of processors. The goals of the architecture were efficient implementation, compact encoding, and technology independence. In order to accomplish these goals, the Mesa architecture specified a single stack for use in expression evaluation and parameter passing to procedures for the purpose of producing compact 0-operand stack instructions. While the stack implementation was not specified, Mesa follows the general pattern of machines with a small stack buffer and the bulk of the stack in program memory. An interesting instruction was the 'recover' operation, which captured a previously popped stack value that had not yet been overwritten by doing a stack push without writing a value.

MF1600

Taxonomy category: ML0
Implementation: TTL discrete components, 16-bit machine
Applications: General-purpose processing
Who and when: Xycom & Advance Processor Designs, 1987
References: Burnley & Harkaway, 1987

The Advanced Processor Design MF1600, which is the processor used on the Xycom XVME-616 product, is a high performance Forth machine design that makes use of fast TTL logic devices. It features a 16-bit data path and a microcode memory ROM that can be customized by the manufacturer for specific applications.

MICRO-3L

Taxonomy category: SL1
Implementation: Simulated machine
Applications: Functional Programs
Who and when: University of Utah, 1982
References: Castan & Organick (1982)

The μ-3L processor project used the 3L-model (Lisp Like Language model) for specifying a processor that is well suited to list processing. The project proposed creating a multiprocessor system to execute functional languages. Each μ-3L processor was to use a 256-element register file. 128 of the registers were intended to be used as a return address stack, with overflow handled by swapping into main memory. Data manipulations were performed using an Accumulator and an operand from the bottom 128 elements of the register file.

MICRODATA 32/S

Taxonomy category: SS0
Implementation: Microcode upgrade to a 16-bit register-oriented minicomputer.
Applications: Running a version of PL/I
Who and when: Microdata Corporation, 1973
References: Burns & Savitt (1973)

The Microdata 32/S was a version of the Microdata 3200 general-purpose minicomputer that had additional microcode to implement stack instructions. The 3200 system was a 16-bit minicomputer implemented in discrete TTL technology. The reason for adding the stack-based capabilities was that compilers of the time could not produce efficient code. Stack architectures made code generation easier. The reason good code generation is important is to remove the impetus for programming in assembly language. The main memory stack was used for expression evaluation and parameter passing, with up to four stack elements buffered in registers.

MISC M17

Taxonomy category: MS0
Implementation: 16-bit 2.0 Micron HCMOS gate array
Applications: Low cost real-time control
Who and when: Minimum Instruction Set Computer, Inc., 1988
References: MISC (1988)

The MISC M17 microprocessor is a low cost, embedded microcontroller. The M17 instruction set is based on Forth primitives. In contrast with most other Forth machines, the M17 reduces hardware costs at some compromise in performance by keeping its two stacks in program memory with a few top-of-stack buffer registers on-chip.

MOTOROLA 680x0

Taxonomy category: MS2 (when used in stack mode)
Implementation: Family of 32-bit microprocessors
Applications: General-purpose computing
Who and when: Motorola Corporation 1980s
References: Kane *et al.* (1981)

The 680x0 processor family, which includes the 68000, 68010, 68020, and 68030, is a family of microprocessors with a general-purpose register architecture. Registers are divided into two groups: address registers and data registers. The address registers support postincremented and predecremented addressing modes. This allows a programmer to use up to eight stacks, one stack per address register. By convention, the A7 register is used as the stack frame pointer for most languages. Of course, the 680x0 family is usually not used as a multiple-stack machine, but nonetheless this capability exists.

MU5

Taxonomy category: SS1
Implementation: Minicomputer
Applications: Research
Who and when: University of Manchester, 1971
References: Morris & Ibbett (1979)

The MU5 used a 1-operand instruction format with a single stack in program memory. Stack instructions were used because they led to easy code generation, compact programs, and easily pipelined hardware. An interesting twist is that there were five registers accessible to the programmer, all of which were simultaneously at the 'top-of-stack'. Pushing a value into any register pushed the previous register value onto the single stack. This arrangement is subtly different from having the top five stack elements accessible as registers.

NC4016

Taxonomy category: ML0
Implementation: 16-bit Gate Array processor
Applications: Real-time control, direct support for Forth programming language
Who and when: Novix, 1985
References: Golden *et al.* (1985), Jennings (1985), Miller (1987), Novix (1985)

The NC4000, later renamed the NC4016, was the first chip designed to execute Forth. Since it is on a gate array, the two hardware stack memories reside off-chip, connected to the processor by dedicated stack busses. The top two data stack elements are buffered on-chip, as is the top return stack element. The processor executes most Forth primitives including subroutine call in a single clock cycle, and allows multiple primitive operations to be compressed into a single instruction in some circumstances.

NORMA

Taxonomy category: SL0
Implementation: Experimental machine using MSI/LSI standard logic and gate arrays
Applications: Functional programming/graph reduction
Who and when: Burroughs Corporation Austin Research Center, 1986
References: Scheevel (1986)

The Normal Order Reduction MAchine (NORMA) is a research processor developed by Burroughs for high speed graph reduction operations in support of functional programming languages. Five specialized functional units that handle arithmetic, graph memory, garbage collection, graph processing, and external I/O are connected using a central bus. The graph processor maintains a single stack used during the depth-first traversal of the tree-structured program graphs.

OPA (PASCAL)

Taxonomy category: ML0
Implementation: Emulator running on Lilith computer
Applications: Support for Pascal and Modula-2 programs
Who and when: Federal Institute of Technology, Zurich, 1984
References: Schulthess (1984)

The Object Pascal Architecture (OPA) is a design for a machine that efficiently executes compiled Pascal code. The OPA contains three stacks: one for descriptors and expression evaluation, one for storing subroutine parameters, and one for return addresses. The OPA instruction set is billed as a 'reduced high level language' instruction set, since it supports Pascal constructs with a small number of opcodes.

PASCAL MACHINE

Taxonomy category: ML0
Implementation: Experimental processor
Applications: Direct execution of Tiny-Pascal source code
Who and when: University of Maryland, 1981
References: Lor & Chu (1981)

The Pascal interactive computer is an experimental system for direct execution of Pascal source code. Since the system includes a hardware compiler as well as execution unit, hardware stacks in the system abound. Some of the stacks are used to store return addresses, operator precedence, expression evaluation values, and subprogram nesting levels. Since expressions are evaluated as they are interpreted, the actions taken by the execution unit are the same as would be taken by a 0-operand stack architecture.

PDP-11

Taxonomy category: MS1 (when used in stack mode)
Implementation: Family of mini and microcomputers (also, later the VAX family)
Applications: General-purpose minicomputer
Who and when: Digital Equipment, 1970
References: Bell *et al.* (1970)

The DEC PDP-11 was an early general-purpose computer to integrate stack usage into a general-purpose register machine. While the machine is clearly register-oriented, it includes as a subset of its capabilities those of a one-address stack machine. By using register-indirect addressing with auto-postincrement and auto-predecrement, a general-purpose register can be used as a stack pointer for an evaluation stack. The PDP-11 also has a stack pointer for use with interrupts, traps, and subroutine calls. Later, the VAX line of computers introduced hardware support for single-stack dynamic frame allocation for block-oriented languages. Of course the PDP-11 is really a general-purpose register machine, but Bell *et al.'s* article describes how it can be used in an MS1 stack mode.

POMP PASCAL

Taxonomy category: SS1
Implementation: Bit-sliced processor (AMD 290x)
Applications: Research into emulating intermediate forms for block-structured languages
Who and when: Stanford University, 1980
References: Harris (1980)

The Pascal Oriented MicroProcessor (POMP) project used a bit-sliced processor to execute stack code. Stack code was chosen to reduce program size from 3 to 8 times smaller than traditional compiler outputs. In fact, the POMP code was claimed to be only 50% larger than Flynn's ideal DEL encoding, but is much easier to decode since it was encoded in byte-wide blocks. The stack machine could access up to 8 local variables for operations, making it a 1-operand machine.

PSP

Taxonomy category: ML2
Implementation: Architectural proposal
Applications: General-purpose computing
Who and when: University of Illinois, 1985
References: Eickemeyer & Patel (1985)

The Parallel Stack Processor (PSP) architecture is an attempt to preserve the function of a normal general-purpose register machine yet reap the benefits of having hardware stacks for saving registers on a subroutine call. To accomplish this, the machine hides a stack behind every register in the machine. Whenever a subroutine call is encountered, each register is pushed onto its own stack simultaneously, performing a single-cycle multiple-register save. Strictly speaking, this is more of a register machine that has hardware to save registers than a stack processor architecture, but the idea is intriguing for other stack applications.

PYRAMID 90X

Taxonomy category: SL2
Implementation: 32-bit minicomputer
Applications: General-purpose RISC processor
Who and when: Pyramid Technology, 1983
References: Ragan-Kelley & Clark (1983)

The Pyramid 90x was one of the first commercial processors to have many RISC attributes. The 90x uses a register stack that is organized as 16 nonoverlapped windows of 32 registers plus 16 global registers for a total of 528 registers. The registers are spilled to memory if subroutine nesting is more than 15 levels deep.

QFORTH

Taxonomy category: ML0
Implementation: Architectural study
Applications: Direct support for Forth programming language
Who and when: Queens College of CUNY, 1984
References: Vickery (1984)

The QFORTH architecture was built for multi-tasking single-user execution of the Forth programming language. The internal architecture included two source busses (from which could be read the top two elements of the data stack) and a single destination bus to write the top-of-stack back. The stack management unit internally buffered the top stack elements in high speed registers, and allowed for a single stack memory to be partitioned into several simultaneously used stacks.

REDUCTION LANGUAGE MACHINE

Taxonomy category: ML0
Implementation: Laboratory model
Applications: Execution of reduction language programs
Who and when: GMD Bonn, 1979
References: Kluge & Schlutter (1980)

Reduction languages use structures of the form: apply <function> to <argument>. These structures are well represented by subtrees with a function node having children that are its operands. Since the execution of a program involves evaluating these tree structures, three major stacks are central to the operation of the machine. One stack acts as a program source, another as a program sink, and the third as a temporary evaluation stack area. An interesting feature of the machine is that there is no program memory, and the operation of the machine does not involve any addresses as such. All programs are shuffled between the source and sink stack memories.

REKURSIV

Taxonomy category: ML0
Implementation: 1.5 Micron CMOS using 3 gate arrays
Applications: Object-oriented programming
Who and when: Linn Products, 1984–88
References: Pountain (1988)

Rekursiv is designed for fast execution of object-oriented programs. It supports a very high level instruction set that may be extended using a large amount of off-chip microcode, and has extensive support for memory management designed into the system. An evaluation stack is used for expression evaluation, while a control stack is used for microcode procedure return address storage.

RISC I

Taxonomy category: SL2
Implementation: 32-bit microprocessor
Applications: RISC processor for C and other high level languages
Who and when: University of California, Berkeley, 1981
References: Patterson & Piepho (1982), Patterson & Sequin (1982), Sequin
          & Patterson (1982), Tamir & Sequin (1983)

The RISC I was the first highly publicized RISC computer. It owes a substantial amount of its performance to the use of register windows. The 'gold' RISC I chip uses an overlapped register window scheme with 78 registers. At any given time, there are 32 addressable registers: 10 global registers, 6 registers shared with the calling subroutine, 10 private registers, and 6 registers used to pass parameters to subroutines at the next deeper nesting level. The registers are accessed using normal 2-operand register-to-register instructions. The RISC I allows accessing the contents of a register as a memory location by automatically mapping the memory access into the register space. This solves the up-level addressing problem that can occur in languages like Pascal.

ROCKWELL MICROCONTROLLERS

Taxonomy category: MS0
Implementation: Forth-in-ROM on 6502 and 68000 microcontrollers
Applications: Embedded controllers that run Forth programs
Who and when: Rockwell International, 1983
References: Dumse (1984)

While not strictly speaking hardware-supported stack machines, microcontrollers that have Forth burned into their ROM's are an interesting member of the stack-based computer family. The R65F11, based on the 6502 processor, and the F68K processor, based on the 68200 microcontroller of the 68000 processor family, are general-purpose microcontrollers that come with preprogrammed Forth primitives. These chips in effect emulate a two-stack Forth engine, using variables and program memory to provide the emulation. Other dedicated Forth microcontrollers have been made since (including the Zilog Super8 chip), but Rockwell was the first to do it.

RTX 2000

Taxonomy category: ML0
Implementation: 16-bit, 2 micron standard cell CMOS microprocessor
Applications: Semicustom design for application-specific designs. Optimized for Forth programming language
Who and when: Harris Semiconductor, 1987–89
References: Danile & Malinowski (1987), Harris Semiconductor (1988a), Harris Semiconductor (1988b), Jones et al. (1987)

The RTX (Real Time Express) is a macrocell in the Harris standard cell library. This allows the processor to be built as a stand-alone microprocessor, or as an integrated microprocessor with I/O devices, hardware multiplier and stack memory on-chip. The instruction set directly corresponds to FORTH programming language primitives. The design uses an unencoded instruction format that allows multiple operations to be compacted into each instruction. As with many Forth processors, the RTX 2000 supports single-cycle subroutine calls.

RTX 32P

Taxonomy category: ML0
Implementation: 32 bits, 2.5 micron CMOS
Applications: Stack-based processing for real-time control and expert systems
Who and when: Harris Semiconductor and WISC Technologies, 1987–89
References: Koopman (1987c), Koopman (1987d), Koopman (1989)

The Harris RTX 32P is a prototype 32-bit stack processor chip set. A unique feature of the RTX 32P is the combination of an opcode with a next-address field in every instruction. This allows zero-cost subroutine calls, returns, and unconditional branches by overlapping the next address computation with the opcode execution. The system can execute one opcode and a subroutine call each memory cycle.

RUFOR

Taxonomy category: ML0
Implementation: 16-bit AM2901 bit-slice microcoded processor
Applications: Research processor for Forth language
Who and when: Wright State University, 1984
References: Grewe & Dixon (1984)

The RUFOR system is a conventional bit-sliced approach to building a machine optimized for the Forth programming language. There are two hardware stacks, one for data and one for return addresses. The top entry of each stack is held in one of the 2901 internal registers, so that only a single input bus to the ALU and a single output bus back to the stacks are required.

SF1

Taxonomy category: ML2
Implementation: 3-Chip, 32-bit microprocessor using 3 micron CMOS
Applications: High level language support for real-time control
Who and when: Wright State University, 1987–88
References: Dixon (1987), Longway (1988)

The SF1 (which stands for Stack Frame computer number 1) is an experimental multi-stack processor designed to efficiently execute high level languages, including both Forth and C. The current implementation has five stacks, any two of which may be selected as the source and destination for an instruction. The SF1 allows arbitrary access to its stack elements by using a 13-bit address relative to the top stack element in the instruction format.

SOAR

Taxonomy category: SL2
Implementation: Microprocessor

Applications: Support for Smalltalk-80 language
Who and when: University of California, Berkeley, 1984
References: Bush *et al.* (1987)

The Smalltalk **On A R**ISC project (SOAR) modified the Berkeley RISC II architecture to adapt it to Smalltalk-80. Since Smalltalk-80 is a stack-oriented bytecode language, this is an exercise in mapping stack code onto a register-oriented RISC, which in turn has its registers arranged in an overlapped window register stack. The window size of the register stack was only 16 registers, half that of RISC II, since Smalltalk methods tend to be smaller than procedures in traditional programming languages.

SOCRATES

Taxonomy category: ML2
Implementation: Conceptual design
Applications: Use of bubble memories for main program storage
Who and when: University of Massachusetts/Amherst, 1975
References: Foster (1975)

SOCRATES (Stack-Oriented Computer for Research and Teaching) was a design that proposed using magnetic bubble memories as its main storage. At the time of the design, bubble memories were projected to cost 100 times less per bit than other memories. The only problem was that they could only be accessed sequentially. SOCRATES took advantage of this situation by proposing 64 addressable registers of 32 bits, with each register being the top element of a 32K word bubble memory configured as a LIFO stack.

SOVIET MACHINE

Taxonomy category: ML1
Implementation: Conceptual design
Applications: Execution of block-structured languages
Who and when: Academy of Sciences of the USSR, 1968
References: Myamlin & Smirnov (1969)

This paper presented a design for a stack computer for executing block-structured languages. The design had two stacks: one for holding arithmetic operations and one for holding operands. While not a directly interpreting machine, it was apparently intended to have source programs maintain an infix format with infix to postfix conversion done on-the-fly. Stacks could be addressed as part of program memory if desired, but were physically separate components.

SYMBOL

Taxonomy category: MS0
Implementation: Discrete TTL prototype machine

Applications: Research
Who and when: Iowa State University, 1971
References: Ditzel & Kwinn (1980), Hutchison & Ethington (1973)

The SYMBOL project constructed an operational computer using no software. The editor, debugger, and compiler were all implemented using random logic circuits. User programs were entered in source code, then compiled and executed using hardwired control circuits. The compilation unit transformed code into a stack-based intermediate form before execution. Several other stacks were used elsewhere as required by the compiler.

TRANSPUTER

Taxonomy category: SS0
Implementation: Family of 16- and 32-bit microprocessors
Applications: Parallel processing
Who and when: INMOS Limited, 1983
References: Whitby-Strevens (1985)

The Transputer is a single-chip microprocessor system designed for parallel processing. Since replicating a complete processor with memory and peripherals is very expensive, the Transputer attempts to squeeze an entire functional system onto a single chip to hold costs down for systems with large numbers of processors. This constraint places program memory space at a premium, so a stack-based instruction set was selected to reduce program size. The Transputer uses 3 registers to form an expression evaluation stack.

TM

Taxonomy category: ML0
Implementation: Simulated design
Applications: Research
Who and when: Carnegie Mellon University, 1980
References: Harbison (1982)

The Tree Machine (TM) architecture was an attempt to make compilers simpler by performing common compiler optimizations using a value cache. This cache would do common subexpression elimination and invariant code motion in hardware by caching results to recently computed expressions. A stack-based architecture was chosen because this allowed better operation with the value caching hardware and eliminated the compiler complexity associated with register allocation. The TM used two stacks: a data stack for expression evaluation, and a control stack for dependency information and return address storage.

TREE MACHINE

Taxonomy category: MS0
Implementation: Conceptual design

Applications: Executing block-structured languages
Who and when: Massey University, New Zealand, 1971
References: Doran (1972)

Doran's tree machine recognized that good programs have an inherent tree structure, and was tailored to execute these well-structured programs. The machine had three stacks resident in program memory: a control stack for return addresses, a value stack to store intermediate results for non-tree-leaf nodes, and a data stack for scratch storage allocation. An interesting feature of the machine was that conditional branches were not required. All conditional execution were accomplished with a conditional procedure return to the parent program node.

VAUGHAN & SMITH'S MACHINE

Taxonomy category: ML0
Implementation: Conceptual design
Applications: Support for Forth programming language
References: Vaughan & Smith (1984)

This paper discusses the design of a Forth-based computer. The architecture was chosen because Forth is good at representing the tree nature of structured programs. Forth's small subroutine size allows good code compaction through subroutine reuse. The proposed design featured two independent hardware stacks. The return stack had one top-of-stack register, while the data stack had two registers.

WD9000 P-ENGINE

Taxonomy category: SS0
Implementation: 5-chip LSI set
Applications: Direct execution of Pascal P-code
Who and when: Western Digital, 1979
References: O'Neill (1979)

The Western Digital Pascal micro-engine (the WD9000 chip set) was built to execute Pascal P-code. Since P-code presumes the existence of a single data stack, the WD9000 supported a single program memory resident stack for expression evaluation and parameter passing.

WISC CPU/16

Taxonomy category: ML0
Implementation: Discrete LS-TTL, 16-bit data paths
Applications: Stack-based processing
Who and when: WISC Technologies, 1986
References: Haydon & Koopman (1986), Koopman (1986), Koopman (1987b), Koopman & Haydon (1986)

The WISC CPU/16 is a user-microcodable processor with a Forth-language machine heritage. It has both a data stack and a return address stack. Additionally, it has a 2K word by 30-bit writable control store for user-defined microcode. The architecture is general, and allows supporting other languages besides Forth. An interactive single-step capability is intended for use in teaching microcode techniques to students.

WISC CPU/32

Taxonomy category: ML0
Implementation: 32 bits, discrete TTL
Applications: Stack-based processing for real-time control and expert systems
Who and when: WISC Technologies, 1986–87
References: Koopman (1987c), Koopman (1987d)

The WISC CPU/32 is the discrete TTL system upon which the Harris RTX 32P is based. The RTX 32P and CPU/32 are microcode and instruction set compatible.

OTHER REFERENCES

Bulman (1977)
A general tutorial on stack architectures with emphasis on the B5500 and HP3000 as example architectures. Also mentions the Data General Eclipse and PDP-11 as examples of conventional machines incorporating some stack concepts.

Carlson (1975)
A good survey of various high level language computer architectures, many of which are stack-oriented.

Doran (1975)
Reviews the use of stacks for expression evaluation, data tree traversal, and subroutine return address saving, concentrating on the Burroughs architectures.

McKeeman, W. (1975)
A comprehensive tutorial on the operation of stack-based computers and the role of stacks in general purpose computing.

Myers (1982)
While not specifically about stack machines, this text describes many of the architectural innovations that are pertinent to discussions on stack machines. Of particular interest is the discussion of semantic gap.

Siewiorek, Bell & Newell (1982)
This computer architecture text contains many chapters on stack machines.

Yamamoto, M. (1981)
Gives a large list of high level language machines developed in Japan, many of which are stack-oriented.

Appendix B
A glossary of Forth primitives

The Forth language is based on an extensible, interactive compiler that creates code for a virtual stack machine. The virtual machine has two stacks. The Data Stack is used for expression evaluation and subroutine parameter passing. The Return Stack is used for subroutine return address saving and for loop control variable storage. The source code for Forth directly reflects the underlying stack machine, and so uses Reverse Polish Notation (RPN) to perform all operations using.

Forth programs are built as a hierarchy of subroutines. Each subroutine is called a 'word' in Forth terminology. A program consists of a single Forth word which calls several other Forth words, and so on, forming a tree-structured program. At the lowest level, the leaves of the tree are invocations of Forth primitive words that manipulate the stacks and perform arithmetic.

Below is a glossary of the Forth primitive words found on stack machines discussed in this book. Most of these primitives are actually applicable to any program written in any language on a stack machine (for example, addition of the top two stack elements or swapping the order of the top two stack elements). Forth nomenclature is used in discussions to maintain consistency with an existing standard vocabulary for stack machine operation.

Each Forth word is followed by a 'stack picture' on the same line. This stack picture shows the input parameters and output parameters on the Forth Data Stack for the word being described. The values on the left of the '→' indicate the input parameters while those to the right of the '→' indicate output parameters. Each parameter list is ordered with the topmost stack element to the right. Notation in the stack lists is as follows: N1, N2, N3, etc. indicate single-precision integers. D1, D2, etc. indicate double-precision integers, which take up two elements on the data stack. ADDR indicates an address, which may be thought of as a pointer value. FLAG is an integer which is false if zero, true if non-zero. A more detailed glossary of Forth is Haydon's *All About Forth* (1983).

0   →   0
Push the integer 0 onto the stack.

0<   N1   →   FLAG
Return a true FLAG if N1 is negative.

0=   N1   →   FLAG
Return a true FLAG if N1 is zero.

0>   N1   →   FLAG
Return a true FLAG if N1 is greater than zero.

0BRANCH   N1   →
If N1 is false (value is 0) perform a branch to the address in the next program
cell, otherwise continue.

1+   N1   →   N2
Add one to N1, returning N2.

1−   N1   →   N2
Subtract one from N1, returning N2.

2+   N1   →   N2
Add two to N1, returning N2.

2*   N1   →   N2
Multiply N1 by two, returning N2.

2/   N1   →   N2
Divide N1 by two, returning N2.

4+   N1   →   N2
Add four to N1, returning N2.

<   N1 N2   →   FLAG
Return a true FLAG if N1 is less than N2.

<>   N1 N2   →   FLAG
Return a true FLAG if N1 is not equal to N2.

=   N1 N2   →   FLAG
Return a true FLAG if N1 equals N2.

>R   N1   →
Push N1 onto the return stack.

>   N1 N2   →   FLAG
Return a true FLAG if N1 is greater than N2.

!   N1 ADDR   →
Store N1 at location ADDR in program memory.

+   N1 N2   →   N3
Add N1 and N2, giving sum N3.

+!   N1 ADDR   →
Add N1 to the value pointed to by ADDR.

−   N1 N2   →   N3
Subtract N2 from N1, giving difference N3.

:   →
Define the start of a subroutine. The primitive [CALL] is compiled every
time this subroutine is reference by other definitions.

;   →
Perform a subroutine return and end the definition of a subroutine. The
primitive [EXIT] is compiled.

?DUP   N1   →   N1 N1 (if N1 non-zero)
                     N1   →   N1 (if N1 is zero)
Conditionally duplicate the input N1 if it is non-zero.

@   ADDR   →   N1
Fetch the value at location ADDR in program memory, returning N1.

ABS   N1   →   N2
Take the absolute value of N1 and return the result N2.

AND   N1 N2   →   N3
Perform a bitwise AND on N1 and N2, giving result N3.

BRANCH   →
Perform an unconditional branch to the compiled in-line address.

D!   D1 ADDR   →
Store the double-precision value D1 at the two memory words starting at
ADDR.

D+   D1 D2   →   D3
Return the double-precision sum of D1 and D2 as D3.

D@   ADDR   →   D1
Fetch the double precision value D1 from memory starting at address
ADDR.

DDROP   D1   →
Drop the double-precision integer D1.

DDUP   D1   →   D1 D1
Duplicate D1 on the stack.

DNEGATE   D1   →   D2
Return D2, which is the two's complement of D1.

DROP   N1   →
Drop N1 from the stack.

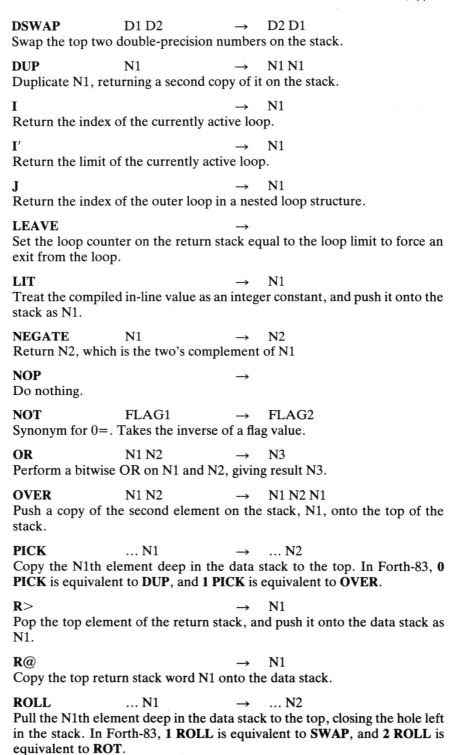

DSWAP   D1 D2   →   D2 D1
Swap the top two double-precision numbers on the stack.

DUP   N1   →   N1 N1
Duplicate N1, returning a second copy of it on the stack.

I   →   N1
Return the index of the currently active loop.

I′   →   N1
Return the limit of the currently active loop.

J   →   N1
Return the index of the outer loop in a nested loop structure.

LEAVE   →
Set the loop counter on the return stack equal to the loop limit to force an exit from the loop.

LIT   →   N1
Treat the compiled in-line value as an integer constant, and push it onto the stack as N1.

NEGATE   N1   →   N2
Return N2, which is the two's complement of N1

NOP   →
Do nothing.

NOT   FLAG1   →   FLAG2
Synonym for 0=. Takes the inverse of a flag value.

OR   N1 N2   →   N3
Perform a bitwise OR on N1 and N2, giving result N3.

OVER   N1 N2   →   N1 N2 N1
Push a copy of the second element on the stack, N1, onto the top of the stack.

PICK   ... N1   →   ... N2
Copy the N1th element deep in the data stack to the top. In Forth-83, **0 PICK** is equivalent to **DUP**, and **1 PICK** is equivalent to **OVER**.

R>   →   N1
Pop the top element of the return stack, and push it onto the data stack as N1.

R@   →   N1
Copy the top return stack word N1 onto the data stack.

ROLL   ... N1   →   ... N2
Pull the N1th element deep in the data stack to the top, closing the hole left in the stack. In Forth-83, **1 ROLL** is equivalent to **SWAP**, and **2 ROLL** is equivalent to **ROT**.

ROT   N1 N2 N3   →   N2 N3 N1
Pull the third element down in the stack onto the top of the stack.

S→D   N1   →   D2
Sign extend N1 to occupy two words, making it a double-precision integer
D2.

SWAP   N1 N2   →   N2 N1
Swap the order of the top two stack elements.

U<   U1 U2   →   FLAG
Return a true FLAG if U1 is less than U2 when compared as unsigned
integers.

U>   U1 U2   →   FLAG
Return a true FLAG if U1 is greater than U2 when compared as unsigned
integers.

U*   N1 N2   →   D3
Perform unsigned integer multiplication on N1 and N2, yielding the
unsigned double-precision result D3.

U/MOD   D1 N2   →   N3 N4
Perform unsigned integer division on D1 and N2, yielding the quotient N4
and the remainder N3.

XOR   N1 N2   →   N3
Perform a bitwise exclusive OR on N1 and N2, giving result N3.

Appendix C
Unabridged instruction frequencies

The following is an unabridged version of the dynamic instruction frequencies discussed in Chapter 6. The ten highest entries in each column are underlined.

Names	Frac	Life	Math	Compile	Ave
	(%)	(%)	(%)	(%)	(%)
!	1.89	0.00	0.71	0.98	0.90
*	0.00	0.00	0.02	0.05	0.02
+	3.41	10.45	0.60	2.26	4.18
+!	0.00	0.00	0.11	0.83	0.24
+−	0.34	0.00	0.00	0.02	0.09
−	0.97	1.24	0.08	1.94	1.06
/	0.07	0.00	0.00	0.05	0.03
0<	1.84	0.00	0.66	0.05	0.64
0=	0.00	0.00	0.77	0.00	0.19
0>	0.00	0.00	0.09	0.02	0.03
0BRANCH	3.39	6.38	3.23	6.11	4.78
1+	1.72	0.08	0.01	1.36	0.79
1−	0.41	0.00	0.54	0.01	0.24
2*	2.11	2.05	0.02	0.64	1.21
2+	0.49	0.00	0.19	0.66	0.34
2−	0.07	0.00	0.00	1.02	0.27
2/	0.92	0.00	0.00	0.01	0.23
<	0.11	0.08	0.01	1.087	0.32
<+LOOP>	0.00	0.00	0.00	0.00	0.00
</LOOP>	0.20	0.00	0.01	0.18	0.10
<<CMOVE>>	0.00	0.00	0.00	0.00	0.00
<CMOVE>	0.00	0.00	0.00	0.56	0.14
<DO>	0.23	0.00	0.09	0.02	0.09
<FILL>	0.00	0.00	0.00	0.00	0.00
<FIND>	0.00	0.00	0.00	0.84	0.21
<LOOP>	1.44	3.32	1.08	0.01	1.46
=	0.33	4.48	0.01	1.87	1.67
>	0.62	0.08	0.06	1.19	0.49
>R	2.05	0.00	11.28	2.16	3.87

?DUP	0.00	0.00	0.00	1.11	0.28
?STACK	0.00	0.00	0.00	0.49	0.12
@	7.49	21.05	0.96	11.09	5.40
ABS	0.51	0.00	0.01	0.01	0.13
ADC	0.00	0.00	2.53	0.00	0.63
AND	0.17	3.12	3.14	0.04	1.61
ASR	0.00	0.00	0.88	0.00	0.22
BRANCH	1.671	1.57	0.72	2.26	1.54
C!	0.07	0.36	0.03	0.87	0.33
C@	0.00	7.52	0.01	0.36	1.97
CALL	11.16	12.73	12.59	12.36	12.21
CONSTANT	3.92	3.50	2.78	4.50	3.68
CONVERT	0.00	0.00	0.00	0.04	0.01
D!	0.21	0.00	0.59	0.00	0.20
D+	1.15	0.00	0.54	0.00	0.42
D+−	0.07	0.00	0.03	0.02	0.03
D<	0.00	0.00	0.00	0.00	0.00
D@	0.21	0.00	0.62	0.00	0.21
DDROP	2.08	0.52	0.11	0.35	0.77
DDUP	1.86	0.00	1.16	0.84	0.97
DIGIT	0.00	0.00	0.00	0.00	0.00
DNEGATE	0.00	0.00	0.11	0.00	0.03
DOVER	0.00	0.00	0.91	0.00	0.23
DROP	3.08	0.16	0.68	1.04	1.24
DROT	0.00	0.00	0.17	0.00	0.04
DSWAP	0.00	0.00	0.92	0.00	0.23
DUP	4.08	0.45	1.88	5.78	3.05
ENCLOSE	0.00	0.00	0.00	0.58	0.15
EXECUTE	0.14	0.00	0.02	2.45	0.65
EXIT	11.07	12.72	12.55	10.60	11.74
I	0.58	6.66	0.01	0.23	1.87
I'	0.00	0.00	0.00	0.00	0.00
J	0.16	0.08	0.00	0.00	0.06
LEAVE	0.00	0.00	0.00	0.00	0.00
LIT	3.94	5.22	4.92	4.09	4.54
LSL	0.00	0.00	0.04	0.00	0.01
LSR	0.00	0.00	0.96	0.00	0.24
MAX	0.00	0.00	0.00	0.01	0.00
MIN	0.00	0.00	0.05	0.00	0.01
NEGATE	0.52	0.00	0.00	0.00	0.13
NOT	0.00	0.00	0.69	0.25	0.24
OR	0.00	0.08	1.41	0.64	0.53
OVER	1.23	1.75	1.24	0.89	1.28
PICK	1.92	0.00	0.53	0.09	0.64
R>	2.05	0.00	11.28	2.23	3.89
R@	0.14	0.00	0.02	0.71	0.22
RLC	0.00	0.00	0.01	0.00	0.00

ROLL	0.21	0.00	0.81	0.00	0.26
ROT	4.05	0.00	4.61	0.48	2.29
RP!	0.00	0.00	0.00	0.00	0.00
RP@	0.00	0.00	0.00	0.00	0.00
RRC	0.00	0.00	0.00	0.00	0.00
S−>D	0.07	0.00	0.00	0.01	0.02
SP@	0.00	0.00	0.00	0.05	0.01
SWAP	4.43	2.99	7.00	1.17	3.90
TOGGLE	0.00	0.06	0.00	0.08	0.04
TRAVERSE	0.00	0.00	0.00	0.05	0.01
U*	0.62	0.00	0.34	0.01	0.24
U/MOD	0.60	0.00	0.01	0.05	0.17
U<	0.00	0.00	0.00	0.00	0.00
USER	0.07	0.00	0.06	8.59	2.18
VARIABLE	7.63	10.30	2.26	1.65	5.46
XOR	0.29	0.00	0.24	0.01	0.14
Instructions:	2051600	1296143	6133519	447050	

The following is an unabridged verison of the static instruction frequencies discussed in Chapter 6. The ten highest entries in each column are underlined.

Names	Frac	Life	Math	Bench	Ave
	(%)	(%)	(%)	(%)	(%)
!	3.28	2.12	0.90	2.99	2.32
*	0.00	0.21	0.00	0.43	0.16
+	3.28	2.97	0.76	4.61	2.90
+!	0.00	0.00	0.18	0.17	0.09
+−	0.14	0.00	0.00	0.09	0.06
−	2.05	1.91	0.58	1.54	1.52
/	0.14	0.00	0.00	0.09	0.06
0<	0.96	0.00	0.65	0.68	0.57
0=	0.00	0.00	0.11	0.26	0.10
0>	0.00	0.00	0.47	0.00	0.12
0BRANCH	3.01	2.55	3.67	3.16	3.10
1+	0.41	0.64	0.72	0.51	0.57
1−	1.09	0.42	0.54	1.28	0.83
2*	1.92	2.12	0.14	1.79	1.49
2+	0.27	0.00	0.11	0.34	0.18
2−	0.27	0.00	0.00	0.34	0.15
2/	0.96	0.00	0.00	0.77	0.43
<	0.14	0.42	0.47	0.434	0.34
<+LOOP>	0.27	0.21	0.04	0.26	0.20
</LOOP>	0.27	0.00	0.00	0.17	0.11

<<CMOVE>>	0.00	0.00	0.00	0.00	0.00
<CMOVE>	0.00	0.00	0.00	0.00	0.00
<DO>	1.92	2.34	0.61	1.96	1.71
<FILL>	0.00	0.00	0.00	0.00	0.00
<FIND>	0.00	0.00	0.00	0.00	0.00
<LOOP>	1.37	2.12	0.58	1.54	1.40
=	0.14	2.76	0.29	0.26	0.86
>	1.23	0.21	0.32	1.11	0.72
>R	0.55	0.00	4.11	0.77	1.36
?DUP	0.00	0.00	0.04	0.00	0.01
?STACK	0.00	0.00	0.07	0.09	0.04
@	10.81	1.27	1.40	8.88	5.59
ABS	0.27	0.00	0.18	0.17	0.16
ADC	0.00	0.00	0.07	0.00	0.02
AND	0.27	1.06	0.54	0.43	0.58
ASR	0.00	0.00	0.11	0.00	0.03
BRANCH	1.92	0.85	2.09	2.05	1.73
C!	0.00	1.49	0.04	0.68	0.55
C@	0.00	3.40	0.61	0.34	1.09
CALL	16.82	31.44	37.61	17.62	25.87
CONSTANT	1.23	1.91	0.07	1.62	1.21
CONVERT	0.00	0.00	0.00	0.00	0.00
D!	0.41	0.00	0.18	0.17	0.19
D+	0.55	0.21	0.25	0.51	0.38
D+−	0.00	0.00	0.14	0.00	0.04
D<	0.00	0.00	0.14	0.00	0.04
D@	0.27	0.00	0.32	0.17	0.19
DDROP	2.60	0.42	0.79	1.88	1.42
DDUP	1.23	0.21	0.61	1.71	0.94
DIGIT	0.00	0.00	0.11	0.00	0.03
DNEGATE	0.00	0.00	0.18	0.00	0.05
DOVER	0.00	0.00	0.32	0.00	0.08
DROP	2.60	0.85	1.69	2.31	1.86
DROT	0.00	0.00	0.29	0.00	0.07
DSWAP	0.00	0.00	1.22	0.00	0.31
DUP	4.38	1.70	2.84	4.18	3.28
ENCLOSE	0.00	0.00	0.00	0.00	0.00
EXECUTE	0.00	0.00	0.07	0.00	0.02
EXIT	5.75	7.22	9.90	7.00	7.47
I	1.37	5.10	0.11	1.62	2.05
I'	0.00	0.00	0.07	0.00	0.02
J	0.27	1.91	0.07	0.26	0.63
LEAVE	0.00	0.00	0.00	0.09	0.02
LIT	11.35	7.22	11.02	8.03	9.41
LSL	0.00	0.00	0.04	0.00	0.01
LSR	0.00	0.00	0.07	0.00	0.02
MAX	0.00	0.00	0.11	0.09	0.05

MIN	0.00	0.00	0.04	0.17	0.05
NEGATE	0.14	0.00	0.04	0.26	0.11
NOT	0.00	0.00	0.47	0.26	0.18
OR	0.00	0.21	0.61	0.00	0.21
OVER	2.05	5.10	0.76	2.05	2.49
PICK	6.29	0.00	1.04	4.53	2.97
R>	0.55	0.00	4.68	0.77	1.50
R@	0.00	0.00	0.29	0.17	0.12
RLC	0.00	0.00	0.07	0.00	0.02
ROLL	0.14	0.00	0.32	0.09	0.14
ROT	1.50	0.00	0.58	1.37	0.86
RP!	0.00	0.00	0.00	0.00	0.00
RP@	0.00	0.00	0.00	0.00	0.00
RRC	0.00	0.00	0.07	0.00	0.02
S−>D	0.00	0.00	0.25	0.00	0.06
SP@	0.00	0.00	0.00	0.00	0.00
SWAP	1.78	5.10	1.19	3.16	2.18
TOGGLE	0.00	0.42	0.00	0.00	0.11
TRAVERSE	0.00	0.00	0.00	0.00	0.00
U*	0.41	0.00	0.14	0.26	0.20
U/MOD	0.14	0.00	0.00	0.09	0.06
U<	0.00	0.00	0.04	0.00	0.01
USER	0.00	0.00	0.00	0.00	0.00
VARIABLE	1.09	1.91	0.29	1.37	1.17
XOR	0.14	0.00	0.50	0.09	0.18
Instructions:	731	471	2777	1171	

Appendix D
Addresses for more information

These are addresses for contacting the makers of stack machines featured in this book. The addresses and telephone numbers are, of course, subject to change.

Harris RTX 2000 & RTX 32P
Harris Corporation
Semiconductor Products Division
PO Box 883
Melbourne, FL 32902-0883
USA
tel. (407) 729-4629

JHU/APL FRISC 3 (SC32)
The SC32 is now being developed and marketed by

Silicon Composers
210 California Avenue, Suite I
Palo Alto, CA 94306
USA
tel. (415) 322-8763

The FRISC 3 was originally developed by

Johns Hopkins University/Applied Physics Laboratory
Johns Hopkins Road
Laurel MD 20707
USA

MISC M17
Minimum Instruction Set Computer, Inc.
19704 East Loyola Circle
Aurora, CO 80013-3904
USA
tel. (303) 680-9749

Novix NC4016
Novix, Inc.
19925 Stevens Creek Blvd.
Suite 280
Cupertino, CA 95014
USA
tel. (408) 255-2750

WISC CPU/16
WISC Technologies, Inc.
19500 Skyline Dr.
Box 429, Star Rt. 2
La Honda, CA 94020
USA
tel. (415) 747-0760

For general information about the Forth language, contact
Forth Interest Group
PO Box 8231
San Jose, CA 95155
USA
tel. (408) 277-0668

The Forth Interest group sells books and software, publishes the magazine *Forth Dimensions*, and is a good source of information on Forth and stack machine manufacturers.

Institute for Applied Forth Research, Inc.
70 Elmwood Avenue
Rochester, NY 14611
USA
tel. (716) 253-0168

The Institute for Applied Forth Research hosts the Rochester Forth Conferences, publishes the referred *Journal of Forth Application and Research*, and publishes the *Bibliography of Forth References*. Many of the papers on stack machine implementation and their application appear in the Journal and the Proceedings of the Rochester Conferences.

References

Allmark, R. & Lucking, J. (1962) Design of an arithmetic unit incorporating a nesting store. In: *Information Processing 1962: Proc. of the IFIP Cong. 62, 27 August – 1 September 1962, Munich,* North-Holland, Amsterdam, 1963, pp. 694–698

Anderson, J. (1961) A computer for direct execution of algorithmic languages. In: *Proc. of the EJCC, 12–14 December 1961, Washington DC,* Vol. 20, Macmillan, New York, 1961, pp. 184–193

Atkinson, R. & McCreight, E. (1987) The Dragon processor. In: *Proc. of the Second Int. Conf. on Architectural Support for Programming Languages and Operating Systems (ASPLOS II), Palo Alto, CA, 5–8 October 1987,* pp. 65–69

Backus, J. (1978) Can programming be liberated from the von Neumann style? A functional style and its algebra of programs. *Comm. of the ACM,* August 1978, **21**(8) 613–641

Bage, G. & Thorelli, L. (1980) Partial evaluation of a high-level architecture. In: *Proc. of the Int. Workshop on High-Level Language Computer Architecture, Fort Lauderdale, FL, 26–28 May 1980,* pp. 44–51

Ballard, B. (1984) Forth direct execution processors in the Hopkins Ultraviolet Telescope. *J. Forth Application and Research,* **2**(1) 33–47

Bartlett, J. (1973) The HP 3000 computer system. In: *ACM–IEEE Symp. on High-Level-Language Computer Architecture, College Park, MD, 7–8 November 1973,* pp. 61–69

Belinfante, J. (1987) S/K/I: Combinators in Forth. *J. Forth Application and Research,* **4**(4) 555–580

Bell, G., Cady, R., McFarland, H., DeLaig, B., O'Laughlin, J., Noonan, R., & Wulf, W. (1970) A new architecture for minicomputers: the DEC PDP-11, *AFIPS Proc. SJCC,* 1970, pp. 657–675. Reprinted In: Siewiorek, D., Bell, C. G., & Newell, A. (1982) *Computer Structures: Principles and Examples,* McGraw-Hill, 1982, pp. 649–661

Bell, J. (1973) Threaded code. *Comm. of the ACM,* June 1973, **16**(6) 370–372

Bergh, A. & Mei, K. (1979) HP300 architecture. In: *Proc. of the nineteenth IEEE computer society Int. Conf. (Fall COMPCON 79), Washington DC, 4–7 September 1979,* pp. 62–66

Best, D., Kress, C., Mykris, N., Russell, J. & Smith, W. (1982) MOS/SOS Microprocessor. *IEEE Micro,* August 1982, **2**(3) 10–26

Blake, R. (1977) Exploring a stack architecture. *Computer,* May 1977, **10**(5) 18–28

Bruno, J. & Lassagne, T. (1975) The generation of optimal code for stack machines. *J. of the ACM,* July 1975, **22**(3) 382–396

Bulman, D. (1977) Stack computers: an introduction. *Computer,* May 1977, **10**(5) 18–28

Burnley, P. & Harkaway, R. (1987) A high performance VME processor card when 32–bit super–micros can't cut it. In: *Proc. of the 1987 Rochester Forth Conf., (J. Forth Application and Research,* **5**(1)) 101–107

Burns, R. & Savitt, D. (1973) Micro-programming, stack architecture ease minicomputer programmer's burden. *Electronics,* 15 February 1973, **46**(4) 95–101

Bush, W., Samples, A., Ungar, D., & Hilfinger, P. (1987) Compiling Smalltalk-80 to a RISC. In: *Proc. of the Second Int. Conf. on Architectural Support for Programming Languages and Operating Systems (ASPLOS II), Palo Alto CA, 5–8 October 1987,* pp. 112–116

Carlson, C. (1963) The mechanization of a push-down stack. In: *AFIPS Conf. Proc., 1963 FJCC,* Vol. 24, Spartan Books, Baltimore, pp. 243–250

Carlson, C. (1975) A survey of high-level language computer architecture. In: Chu, Y. (Ed.) *High-Level Language Computer Architecture,* Academic Press, New York, 1975 pp. 31–62

Carr, H. & Kessler, R. (1987) An emulator for Utah Common Lisp's abstract virtual machine. In: *Proc. of the 1987 Rochester Forth Conf., (J. Forth Application and Research* **5**(1)) 113–116

Castan, M. & Organick, E. (1982) μ3L: An HLL-RISC processor for execution of FP–language programs. In: *Conf. Proc.: The 9th Annual Symp. on Computer Architecture, 26–29 April 1982, Austin, TX,* pp. 239–247

Chen, Y., Chen, K., & Huang, K. (1980) Direct-execution high-level language FORTRAN computer. In: *Proc. of the Int. Workshop on High-Level Language Computer Architecture, Fort Lauderdale, FL, 26–28 May 1980,* pp. 9–16

Cook, R. & Donde, N. (1982) An experiment to improve operand addressing. In: *Proc. of the Symp. on Architectural Support for Programming Languages and Operating Systems (ASPLOS I), Palo Alto, CA, 1–3 March 1982,* pp. 87–91

Cook, R. & Lee, I. (1980) An extensible stack-oriented architecture for a high-level language machine. In: *Proc. of the Int. Workshop on High-Level Language Computer Architecture, Fort Lauderdale, FL, 26–28 May 1980,* pp. 231–237

Couch, J. & Hamm, T. (1977) Semantic structures for efficient code generation on a stack machine. *Computer,* May 1977, **10**(5) 42–48

Cragon, H. (1979) An evaluation of code space requirements and performance of various architectures. *Computer Architecture News*, February 1979, **7**(5) 5–21

Cragon, H. (1980) A case against high-level language computer architecture. In: *Proc. of the Int. Workshop on High-Level Language Computer Architecture, Fort Lauderdale, FL, 26–28 May 1980*, pp. 88–91

Danile, P. & Malinowski, C. (1987) Forth processor core for integrated 16-bit systems. *VLSI Systems Design*, June 1987, **8**(7) 98–104

Davidson, J. & Vaughan, R. (1987) The effect of instruction set complexity on program size and memory performance. In: *Proc. of the Second Int. Conf. on Architectural Support for Programming Languages and Operating Systems (ASPLOS II), Palo Alto, CA, 5–8 October 1987*, pp. 60–64

Dewar, R. (1975) Indirect threaded code. *Comm. of the ACM*, June 1975, **18**(6) 330–331

Ditzel, D. & Kwinn, W. (1980) Reflections on a high level language computer system, or, Parting thoughts on the SYMBOL project. In: *Proc. of the Int. Workshop on High-Level Language Computer Architecture, Fort Lauderdale, FL, 26–28 May 1980*, pp. 80–87

Ditzel, D. & McLellan, H. (1982) Register allocation for free: the C machine stack cache. In: *Proc. of the Symp. on Architectural Support for Programming Languages and Operating Systems (ASPLOS I), Palo Alto, CA, 1–3 March 1982*, pp. 48–56

Ditzel, D. & McLellan, H. (1987) Branch folding in the CRISP microprocessor: reducing branch delay to zero. In: *The 14th Annual Int. Symp. on Computer Architecture; Conf. Proc., 2–5 June 1987, Pittsburgh*, pp. 2–9

Ditzel, D., McLellan, H., & Berenbaum, A. (1987a) The hardware architecture of the CRISP microprocessor. In: *The 14th Annual Int. Symp. on Computer Architecture; Conf. Proc., 2–5 June 1987, Pittsburgh*, pp. 309–319

Ditzel, D., McLellan, H., & Berenbaum, A. (1987b) Design tradeoffs to support the C programming language in the CRISP microprocessor. In: *Proc. of the Second Int. Conf. on Architectural Support for Programming Languages and Operating Systems (ASPLOS II), Palo Alto, CA, 5–8 October 1987*, pp. 158–163

Ditzel, D. & Patterson, D. (1980) Retrospective on high-level language computer architecture. In: *Proc. of the 7th Int. Conf. on Computer Architecture*, 1980, pp. 97–104, Reprinted In: Fernandez, E. & Lang, T. (Eds.) *Tutorial: Software-Oriented Computer Architecture*, IEEE Computer Society Press, Washington DC, 1986, pp. 44–51.

Dixon, R. (1987) A stack-frame architecture language processor. In: *Proc. of the 1987 Rochester Forth Conf., (J. Forth Application and Research, 5(1))* 11–25

Doran, R. (1972) A computer organization with an explicitly tree-structured machine language. *The Australian Computer Journal,* February 1972, **4**(1) 21–30

Doran, R. (1975) Architecture of stack machines. In: Chu, Y. (Ed.) *High-Level Language Computer Architecture,* Academic Press, New York, pp. 63–108

Doran, R. (1979) *Computer Architecture: A Structured Approach* (APIC Studies in Data Processing No. 15), Academic Press, London.

Dress, W. (1986) REAL-OPS: a real-time engineering applications language for writing expert systems. In: *Proc. of the 1986 Rochester Forth Conf.,* (*J. Forth Application and Research,* **4** (2)) 113–124

Dress, W. (1987) High-performance neural networks. In: *Proc. of the 1987 Rochester Forth Conf.,* (*J. Forth Application and Research,* **5**(1)) 137–140

Dumse, R. (1984) The R65F11 and F68K single-chip Forth computers. *J. Forth Application and Research,* **2**(1) 11–21

Duncan, F. (1977) Stack machine development: Australia, Great Britain, and Europe. *Computer,* May 1977, **10**(5) 50–52

Earnest, E. (1980) Twenty years of Burroughs high-level language machines. In: *The Proc. of the Int. Workshop on High-Level Language Computer Architecture, 26–28 May 1980, Fort Lauderdale, FL,* pp. 64–71

Efland, G. & Mosteller, R. (1979) *Stack Data Engine; Description and Implementation,* Technical Report #3364, Computer Science Department, California Institute of Technology, Pasadena, CA, December 1979

Eickemeyer, R. & Patel, J. (1985) A parallel stack processor (PSP). In: *Proc.: IEEE Int. Conf. on Computer Design: VLSI in Computers (ICCD 85), 7–10 October 1985, Port Chester, NY,* pp. 473–476

Evey, R. (1963) Application of pushdown-store machines. In: *AFIPS Conf. Proc., 1963 FJCC,* Vol. 24, Spartan Books, Baltimore, MD, 1963, pp. 215–227

Foster, C. (1975) Socrates. In: *Conf. Proc.; The 2nd Annual Symp. on Computer Architecture, 20–22 January 1975,* pp. 165–169

Fraeman, M., Hayes, J., Williams, R., & Zaremba, T. (1986) A 32 bit processor architecture for direct execution of Forth. In: *1986 FORML Conf. Proc., 28–30 November 1986, Pacific Grove, CA,* pp. 197–210

Golden, J., Moore, C., & Brodie, L. (1985) Fast processor chip takes its instructions directly from Forth. *Electronic Design,* 21 March 1985, 127–138

Grewe R. & Dixon, R. (1984) A Forth machine for the S-100 system. *J. Forth Application and Research,* **2**(1) 23–32

Haikala, I. (1982) More design data for stack architectures. In: *Proc. of the ACM '82 Conf., Dallas, October 25–27 1982,* pp. 30–36

Haley, A. (1962) The KDF.9 computer system. In: *AFIPS Conf. Proc., Vol. 22: 1962 Fall Joint Computer Conf.,* Spartan Books, Washington DC, 1962, pp. 108–120

Hand, T. (1987) A Forth implementation of LISP. In: *Proc. of the 1987*

Rochester Forth Conf., (J. Forth Application and Research, **5**(1)) 141–144

Harbison, S. (1982) An architectural alternative to optimizing compilers. In: *Proc. of the Symp. on Architectural Support for Programming Languages and Operating Systems (ASPLOS I), Palo Alto, CA, 1–3 March 1982,* pp. 57–65

Harris, N. (1980) A directly executable language suitable for a bit slice microprocessor implementation. In: *Proc. of the Int. Workshop on High-Level Language Computer Architecture, Fort Lauderdale, FL, 26–28 May 1980,* pp. 40–43

Harris Semiconductor (1988a) *RTX 2000 Instruction Set,* Harris Corporation, Melbourne, FL

Harris Semiconductor (1988b) *RTX 2000 Real Time Express Microcontroller Data Sheet,* Harris Corporation, Melbourne, FL

Hasegawa, M. & Shigei, Y. (1985) High-speed top-of-stack scheme for VLSI processor: a management algorithm and its analysis. In: *The 12th Annual Int. Symp. on Computer Architecture, 17–19 June 1985, Boston,* pp. 48–54

Hassitt, A., Lageshulte, J., & Lyon, L. (1973) Implementation of a high level language machine. *Comm. of the ACM,* April 1973, **16**(4) 199–212.

Haydon, G. (1983) *All About Forth: An Annotated Glossary, 2nd Ed.,* Mountain View Press, Mountain View, CA

Haydon, G. & Koopman, P. (1986) MVP microcoded CPU/16: History. In: *Proc. of the 1986 Rochester Forth Conf. (J. Forth Application and Research,* **4**(2)) 273–276

Hayes, J. (1986) An interpreter and object code optimizer for a 32 bit Forth chip. In: *1986 FORML Conf. Proc., 28–30 November 1986, Pacific Grove CA* 211–221

Hayes, J. & Fraeman, M. (1988) Private communications, October 1988.

Hayes, J., Fraeman, M., Williams, R., & Zaremba, T. (1987) An architecture for the direct execution of the Forth programming language. In: *Proc. of the Second Int. Conf. on Architectural Support for Programming Languages and Operating Systems (ASPLOS II), Palo Alto, CA, 5–8 October 1987,* pp. 42–49

Hayes, J. & Lee, S. (1988) The Architecture of FRISC 3: a summary. In: *Proc. of the 1988 Rochester Forth Conf. 14–18 June 1987,* pp. 81–82.

Hennesy, J. (1984) VLSI Processor architecture. *IEEE Trans. Computers,* December 1984, **C-33**(12) 1221–1246. Reprinted In: Fernandez, E. & Lang, T. (Eds.) *Tutorial: Software-Oriented Computer Architecture,* IEEE Computer Society Press, Washington DC, 1986, pp. 90–115

Herriot, R. (1973) GLOSS: a high level machine. *ACM–IEEE Symp. on High-Level-Language Computer Architecture, 7–8 November 1973, College Park, MD,* pp. 81–90

Hutchison, P. & Ethington, K. (1973) Program execution in the Symbol 2R computer. *ACM–IEEE Symp. on High-Level-Language Computer Architecture, 7–8 November 1973, College Park, MD,* pp. 20–26

Intel (1981) *The iAPX 88 Book*. Intel Corporation, 1981

Jennings, E. (1985) The Novix NC4000 Project. *Computer Language,* October 1985, **2**(10) 37–46

Johnson, M. (1987) System considerations in the design of the AM29000. *IEEE Micro,* August 1987, **7**(4) 28–41

Johnsson, R. & Wick, J. (1982) An overview of the Mesa processor architecture. In: *Proc. of the Symp. on Architectural Support for Programming Languages and Operating Systems (ASPLOS I), Palo Alto, CA, 1–3 March 1982*, pp. 20–29

Jonak, J. (1986) Experience with a Forth-like language. *SIGPLAN Notices, February 1986,* **21**(2) 27–36

Jones, S. P. (1987) *The Implementation of Functional Programming Languages, Prentice–Hall,* New York

Jones, T., Malinowski, C., & Zepp, S. (1987) Standard-cell CPU toolkit crafts potent processors. *Electronic Design,* 14 May 1987, **35**(12) 93–101

Kane, G, Hawkins, D., & Leventhal, L. (1981) *68000 Assembly Language Programming,* Osborne/McGraw–Hill, Berkeley, CA

Kaneda, Y., Wada, K., & Maekawa, S. (1983) High-speed execution of Forth and Pascal programs on a high-level language machine. In: *Microcomputers: developments in industry, business and education, Ninth EUROMICRO Symp. on microprocessing and microprogramming, 13–16 September 1983, Madrid,* North-Holland, Amsterdam, 1983, pp. 259–266

Kavi, K., Belkhouche, B., Bullard, E., Delcamber, L., & Nemecek, S. (1982) HLL architectures: pitfalls and predilections. In: *Conf. Proc.: The 9th Annual Symp. on Computer Architecture, 26–29 April 1982, Austin, TX,* pp. 18–32

Kavipurapu, K. & Cragon, H. (1980) Quest for an 'ideal' machine language. In: *Proc. of the Int. Workshop on High-Level Language Computer Architecture, Fort Lauderdale, FL, 26–28 May 1980,* pp. 33–39

Keedy, J. (1977) An outline of the ICL 2900 series system architecture. *Australian Computer Journal,* July 1977, **9**(2) 53–62. Reprinted in: Siewiorek, D., Bell, C. G., & Newell, A., *Computer Structures: Principles and Examples,* McGraw-Hill, 1982, pp. 251–259

Keedy, J. (1978a) On the use of stacks in the evaluation of expressions. *Computer Architecture News,* February 1978, **6**(6) 22–28

Keedy, J. (1978b) On the evaluation of expressions using accumulators, stacks, and store-to-store instructions. *Computer Architecture News,* December 1978, **7**(4) 24–27

Keedy, J. (1979) More on the use of stacks in the evaluation of expressions. *Computer Architecture News,* 15 June 1979, **7**(8) 18–21

Kieburtz, R. (1985) The G-machine: a fast, graph-reduction evaluator. In: Jouannaud, J. (Ed.) *Functional Programming Languages and Computer Architecture, 16–19 September, Nancy, France,* pp. 400–413 (Goos, G. & Hartmanis, J. *Lecture Notes in Computer Science,* No. 201)

Kluge, W. & Schlutter, H. (1980) An architecture for direct execution of reduction languages. In: *Proc. of the Int. Workshop on High-Level Language Computer Architecture, Fort Lauderdale, FL, 26–28 May 1980*, pp. 174–180

Kogge, P. (1982) An architectural trail to threaded-code systems. *Computer*, March 1982, **15**(3) 22–32

Koopman, P. (1985) *Forth Floating Point: MVP-FORTH Series Vol. 3 (revised)*, Mountain View Press, Mountain View, CA

Koopman, P. (1986) CPU/16 Technical Reference Manual. WISC Technologies, Inc., La Honda, CA.

Koopman, P. (1987a) Microcoded versus hard-wired control. *Byte*, January 1987, **12**(1) 235–242

Koopman, P. (1987b) The WISC concept. *Byte*, April 1987, **12**(4) 187–194

Koopman, P. (1987c) Writable instruction set, stack oriented computers: the WISC concept. In: *Proc. of the 1987 Rochester Forth Conf.*, (*J. Forth Application and Research*, **5**(1)) 49–71

Koopman, P. (1987d) CPU/32 Technical Reference Manual. WISC Technologies, Inc., La Honda, CA.

Koopman, P. (1987e) Bresenham line drawing. *Forth Dimensions*, March/April 1987, **8**(6) 12–16. Reprinted In: *Dr. Dobb's Toolbook of Forth*, Vol. 2, M&T Books, Redwood City, CA, 1987, pp. 347–356

Koopman, P. (1987f) Fractal Landscapes. *Forth Dimensions*, March/April 1987, **9**(1) 12–16. Reprinted In: *Dr. Dobb's Toolbook of Forth*, Vol. 2, M&T Books, Redwood City, CA, 1987, pp. 357–365

Koopman, P. (1989) Introduction of the RTX 32P. *J. Forth Application and Research*, **5**(2), forthcoming

Koopman, P., & Haydon, G. (1986) MVP microcoded CPU/16: architecture. In: *Proc. of the 1986 Rochester Forth Conf.*, (*J. Forth Application and Research* **4**(2)) pp. 277–280

Koopman, P., & Lee, P. (1989) A fresh look at combinator graph reduction. In: *1989 Conference on Programming Language Design and Implementation*, June.

Lampson, B. (1982) Fast procedure calls. In: *Proc. of the Symp. on Architectural Support for Programming Languages and Operating Systems (ASPLOS I), Palo Alto, CA, 1–3 March 1982*, pp. 66–76

Lim, R. (1987) LISP machine architecture issues. In: *Digest of Papers, Thirty-second IEEE Computer Society Int. Conf. (Spring COMPCON 87), San Francisco, 23–27 February 1987*, pp. 116–119

Lipovski, G. (1975) On a stack organization for microcomputers. In: Hartenstein, R. & Zaks, R. (Eds.) *Workshop on the Micro-architecture of Computer Systems, 23–25 June 1975, Nice*, North-Holland, Amsterdam, 1975, pp. 137–147

Longway, C. (1988) *Instruction Sequencing and Decoding in the SF1*, Master of Science thesis, Wright State University

Lor, K. & Chu, Y. (1981) *Design of a PASCAL Interactive Direct-Execution Computer, Technical Report TR–1088*, Department of

Computer Science, University of Maryland, College Park, MD, August 1981

Lutz, M. (1973) The design and implementation of a small scale stack processor system. In: *AFIPS Conf. Proc., Vol. 42: 1973 National Computer Conf. and Exposition, 4–8 June 1973*, AFIPS Press, Montvale, NJ, pp. 545–553

Matheus, C. (1986) The Internals of FORPS: a Forth-based production system. *J. Forth Application and Research*, **4**(1) 7–27

McDaniel, G. (1982) An analysis of a Mesa instruction set using dynamic instruction frequencies. In: *Proc. of the Symp. on Architectural Support for Programming Languages and Operating Systems (ASPLOS I), Palo Alto, CA, 1–3 March 1982*, pp. 167–176

McFarling, S. & Hennesy, J. (1986) Reducing the cost of branches. In: *The 13th Annual Int. Symp. on Computer Architecture; Conf. Proc., 2–5 June 1986, Tokyo*, pp. 396–403

McKeeman, W. (1975) Stack computers. In: Stone, H. (Ed.) *Introduction to Computer Architecture*, Science Research Associates, Chicago, 1975, pp. 281–317

Miller, D. (1987) Stack machines and compiler design. *Byte*, April 1987, **12**(4) 177–185

Miller, G. (1967) *Psychology of Communication: Seven Essays*, Basic Books, New York

Miller, J. & Vandever, W. (1973) Instruction architecture of an aerospace multiprocessor. In: *ACM-IEEE Symp. on High-Level-Language Computer Architecture, 7–8 November 1973, College Park, MD*, pp. 52–60

MISC (1988) *MISC M17 Technical Reference Manual*, MISC Inc., 1988

Moon, D. (1985) Architecture of the Symbolics 3600. In: *The 12th Annual Int. Symp. on Computer Architecture, 17–19 June 1985, Boston*, pp. 76–83

Moore, C. (1980) The evolution of Forth, an unusual language. *Byte*, August 1980, **5**(8), 76–92.

Morris, D. & Ibbett, R. (1979) *The MU5 Computer System*, Springer-Verlag, New York

Myamlin, A. & Smirnov, V. (1969) Computer with stack memory. In: Morell, A. (Ed.) *Information Processing 68: Proc. of IFIP Cong. 1968, 5–10 August 1968, Edinburgh*, Vol. 2, North-Holland, Amsterdam, 1969, pp. 818–823

Myers, G. (1977) The case against stack-oriented instruction sets. *Computer Architecture News*, August 1977, **6**(3) 7–10

Myers, G. (1982) *Advances in Computer Architecture*, John Wiley & Sons, New York, 1982

Nissen, S. & Wallach, S. (1973) The all applications digital computer. In: *ACM–IEEE Symp. on High-Level-Language Computer Architecture, 7–8 November 1973, College Park, MD*, pp. 43–51

Novix (1985) *Programmers' Introduction to the NC4016 Microprocessor*, Novix Inc., Cupertino, CA

Odette, L. (1987) Compiling Prolog to Forth. *J. Forth Application and Research*, **4**(4) 487–533

Ohdate, S., Yamashita, K. & Hishinuma, C. (1975) Push-down stack architecture to a minicomputer interface. In: *Information Processing in Japan*, Vol. 15, Information Processing Society of Japan, Tokyo, 1975

Ohran, R. (1984) Lilith and Modula-2. *Byte*, August 1984, **9**(8) 181–192

O'Neill, E. (1979) Pascal microengine. In: *Proc. of the nineteenth IEEE computer society Int. Conf. (Fall COMPCON 79), Washington DC, 4–7 September 1979*, pp. 112–113

Organick, E. (1973) *Computer System Organization: The B5700/B6700 Series*, Academic Press, New York, 1973

Park, J. (1986) Toward the development of a real-time expert system. In: *Proc. of the 1986 Rochester Forth Conf., (J. Forth Application and Research.* **4**(2)) 133–154

Parnas, D. (1972) On the criteria to be used in decomposing systems into modules. *Comm. of the ACM*, December 1972, **15**(12) 1053–1058

Patterson, D. (1985) Reduced instruction set computers. *Comm. of the ACM*, January 1985, **28**(1) 8–21. Reprinted In: Fernandez, E. & Lang, T. (Eds.) *Tutorial: Software-Oriented Computer Architecture*, IEEE Computer Society Press, Washington DC, 1986, pp. 76–89

Patterson, D. & Piepho, S. (1982) RISC assessment: a high-level language experiment. In: *Conf. Proc.: The 9th Annual Symp. on Computer Architecture, 26–29 April 1982, Austin TX*, pp. 3–8

Patterson, D. & Sequin, C. (1982) A VLSI RISC. *Proc. of the Eighth Int. Symp. on Computer Architecture, May 1981*, pp. 443–457. Reprinted In: Milutinovic, V. (Ed.) *Tutorial on Advanced Microprocessors and High-Level Language Computer Architecture*, IEEE Computer Society, Washington DC, 1986, pp. 145–157

Pountain, D. (1988) Rekursiv: an object-oriented CPU. *Byte*, November 1988, **13**(12) 341–349

Prabhala, B. & Sethi, R. (1977) A comparison of instruction sets for stack machines. In: *Conf. Record of the Ninth Annual ACM Symp. on Theory of Computing, Boulder, CO, 2–4 May 1977*, pp. 132–142

Rabbat, G., Furht, B., & Kibler, R. (1988) Three-dimensional computer performance. *Computer*, July 1988, **21**(7) 59–60

Ragan-Kelley, R. & Clark, R. (1983) Applying RISC theory to a large computer. *Computer Design*, November 1983. Reprinted In: Milutinovic, V. (Ed.) *Tutorial on Advanced Microprocessors and High-Level Language Computer Architecture*, IEEE Computer Society, Washington DC, 1986, pp. 297–301

Randell, B. & Russell, L. (1964) *ALGOL 60 Implementation: the translation and use of ALGOL 60 programs on a computer (APIC Studies in Data Processing No. 5)*, Academic Press, London, 1964, pp. 22–33

Rust, T. (1981) ACTION processor FORTHRIGHT. In: *Proc. of the 1981 Rochester Forth Standards Conf.*, Institute for Applied Forth Research, Rochester, NY, 1981, pp. 309–315

Samelson, K. & Bauer, F. (1962) The ALCOR project. In: *Symbolic languages in data processing: Proc. of the Symp. organized and edited by the Int. Computation Center, Rome, 26–31 March 1962*, Gordon and Breach, New York, pp. 207–217

Sansonnet, J., Castan, M, Percebois, C., Botella, D., & Perez, J. (1982) Direct execution of LISP on a list-directed architecture. In: *Proc. of the Symp. on Architectural Support for Programming Languages and Operating Systems (ASPLOS I), Palo Alto, CA, 1–3 March 1982*, pp. 132–139

Scheevel, M. (1986) NORMA: a graph reduction processor. In: *Proc. of the 1986 ACM Conf. on LISP and Functional Programming*, pp. 212–218

Schoellkopf, J. (1980) PASC-HLL: a high-level-language computer architecture for Pascal. In: *Proc. of the Int. Workshop on High-Level Language Computer Architecture, Fort Lauderdale, FL, 26–28 May 1980*, pp. 222–225

Schulthess, P. (1984) A reduced high-level-language instruction set. *IEEE Micro*, June 1984, **4**(3) 55–67

Schulthess, P. & Mumprecht, E. (1977) Reply to the case against stack-oriented instruction sets. *Computer Architecture News*, December 1977, **6**(5) 24–26

Sequin, C. & Patterson, D. (1982) Design and implementation of RISC I. In: Randell, B. & Treleaven, P. (Eds.) *VLSI Architecture: Advanced Course on VLSI Architecture, 19–30 July 1982, Bristol, England*, Prentice-Hall, 1983, pp. 276–298

Shaw, J., Newell, A., Simon, H., & Ellis, T. (1959) A command structure for complex information processing. In: *Proc. of the Western Joint Computer Conf., 6–8 May 1958, Los Angeles CA*, American Institute of Electrical Engineers, 1959, pp. 119–128

Siewiorek, D., Bell, C. G., & Newell, A. (1982) *Computer Structures: Principles and Examples*, McGraw-Hill, 1982

Sites, R. (1978) A combined register-stack architecture. *Computer Architecture News,* April 1978, **6**(8) 19

Sites, R. (1979) How to use 1000 registers. In: Seitz, C. (Ed.) *Proc. of the Caltech Conf. on Very Large Scale Integration, 22–24 January 1979*, pp. 527–532

Stanley, T. & Wedig, R. (1987) A performance analysis of automatically managed top of stack buffers. In: *The 14th Annual Int. Symp. on Computer Architecture; Conf. Proc., 2–5 June 1987, Pittsburgh*, pp. 272–281

Stephens, C. & Watson, W. (1985) *Preliminary Report on the Novix 4000*, Computer Solutions Ltd., Chertsey, Surrey, England.

Sweet, R. & Sandman, J. (1982) Empirical Analysis of the Mesa instruction set. In: *Proc. of the Symp. on Architectural Support for Programming Languages and Operating Systems (ASPLOS I), Palo Alto, CA, 1–3 March 1982*, pp. 158–166

Tamir, Y. & Sequin, C. (1983) Strategies for managing the register file in RISC. *IEEE Trans. Computers*, November 1983, **C-32**(11) 977–989. Reprinted In: Milutinovic, V. (Ed.) *Tutorial on Advanced Microprocessors and High-Level Language Computer Architecture*, IEEE Computer Society, Washington DC, 1986, pp. 167–179

Tanabe, K. & Yamamoto, M. (1980) Single chip Pascal processor: ITS architecture and performance evaluation. In: *Proc. of the twenty-first IEEE computer society Int. Conf. (Fall COMPCON 80), Washington DC, 23–25 September 1980*, pp. 395–399

Tanenbaum, A. (1978) Implications of structured programming for machine architecture. *Comm. of the ACM*, March 1978, **21**(3) 237–246

Tsukamoto, M. (1977) Program stacking technique. In: *Information Processing in Japan*, Vol. 17, Information Processing Society of Japan, Tokyo, 1977, pp. 114–120

Vaughan, J. & Smith, R. (1984) The design of a Forth computer. *J. Forth Application and Research*, **2**(1) 49–64

Vickery, C. (1984) QFORTH: a multitasking Forth language processor. *J. Forth Application and Research*, **2**(1) 65–75

Wada, K., Kaneda, Y., & Maekawa, S. (1982a) Software and system evaluation of a Forth machine system. *Systems, Computers, Controls*, 1982, **13**(2) 19–28

Wada, K., Kaneda, Y., & Maekawa, S. (1982b) System design and hardware structure of a Forth machine system. *Systems, Computers, Controls*, 1982, **13**(2) 11–18

Weber, H. (1967) A microprogrammed implementation of EULER on IBM System/360 Model 30. *Comm. of the ACM*, September 1967, **10**(9) 549–558

Welin, A. (1973) The internal machine. In: *ACM-IEEE Symp. on High-Level-Language Computer Architecture, 7–8 November 1973, College Park, MD*, pp. 101–108.

Wilkes, M. (1982) Keynote Address: the processor instruction set. *15th Workshop on Microprogramming*, p. 3–5

Whitby-Strevens, C. (1985) The Transputer. In: *The 12th Annual Int. Symp. on Computer Architecture, 17–19 June 1985, Boston*, pp. 292–300

Williams, R., Fraeman, M., Hayes, J., & Zaremba, T. (1986) The development of a VLSI Forth microprocessor. In: *1986 FORML Conf. Proc., 28–30 November 1986, Pacific Grove, CA*, pp. 189–196

Winkel, D. (1981) The Forth engine. *Forth Dimensions*, September/ October 1981, **3**(3) 78–79

Wirth, N. (1968) Stack vs. Multiregister computers. *SIGPLAN Notices*, March 1968, **3**(3) 13–19

Wirth, N. (1979) A personal computer based on a high-level language. In: Tobias, J. (Ed.), *Language Design and Programming Methodology. Proc. of a Symp. Held in Sydney, Australia, 10–11 September 1979*, pp. 191–193. Reprinted in: Goos, G. & Hartmanis, J. (Ed.) (1980) Lecture notes in computer science, Springer-Verlag, Berlin

Wirth, N. (1987) Hardware architectures for programming languages and programming languages for hardware architectures. In: *Proc. of the Second Int. Conf. on Architectural Support for Programming Languages and Operating Systems (ASPLOS II), Palo Alto, CA, 5–8 October 1987,* pp. 2–7

Yamamoto, M. (1981) A survey of high-level language machines in Japan. *Computer,* July 1981, **14**(7) 68–78

Index

DATE D